W9-CHS-361

JEFFERSON COUNTY LIBRARY
620 Cedar Avenue
Port Hadlock, WA 98339
(360) 385-6544 www.jclibrary.info

2-20
DATE DUE

MAR 2 2

Dare I Call It
Murder?

A Memoir of Violent Loss

Larry M. Edwards

Wigeon
Publishing
San Diego

Copyright © 2013 by Larry M. Edwards

All rights reserved. No part of this book may be reproduced or transmitted in any form or by any means, electronic or mechanical, including photocopying, recording, or by any information storage and retrieval system, without permission in writing from the publisher.

Wigeon Publishing
San Diego, California
www.WigeonPublishing.com

First Edition: July 9, 2013

ISBN-10: 0985972823

ISBN-13: 978-0-9859728-2-0

Cover by Tim Brittain
Cover photo by Larry Edwards

Library of Congress Control Number: 2013931818

Printed in the United States of America

For my parents, Loren and Joanne "Jody" Edwards.

Praise for the Book

. . . chilling . . . palpable . . . powerful . . .
—Kirkus Reviews

Dare I Call It Murder? *is a top-notch true-crime book. But as a memoir, it's a gut-wrenching look into Larry Edwards' hell on earth after his parents' deaths at sea. . . . You won't be able to put down this tautly written and emotional look at the fatal splintering of a family and the search for truth by a survivor.*

—Cathy Lubenski, author
Trashy Chic, Snarky Park

This is a powerfully written and personalized odyssey of the violent deaths of both of his parents and the disintegration of the family in the aftermath of traumatic grief. Suspected homicide is always tragic for a family, but this book is a lucid testament to the destructive power on the survival of the family when one family member is suspected of murdering another family member. We are swept up by the author's frustrated quest for justice and psychological coherence.

—Dr. Edward K. Rynearson
Medical Director, Separation and Loss Services
Program, Virginia Mason Medical Center

It's the kind of book you can't put down. You will live this story.
—Connie Saindon, MA, MFT,
author, *The Journey: Ten Steps to
Learning to Live With Violent Death*

Also by LARRY M. EDWARDS
Official Netscape Internet Business Starter Kit
Food & Provisions of the Mountain Man

Author's Note

Surviving a violent loss is a journey—a journey of emotional trauma, anger, grief, denial, and depression. A journey no one wants to take.

When you have lost a loved one to violent death, however, you have no choice. It comes uninvited and unanticipated. You are blindsided. You are driving through an intersection of life when a contemptuous scofflaw plows into you.

Your life is never the same.

There is no going back.

The journey begins.

This book recounts my journey. A journey I wouldn't wish on anyone. But if my telling this story proves helpful to others, then it takes on greater meaning. It expands the value of the work and lifts it to a higher plane.

To that end, my intent is that this book serves a broader purpose than simply laying out the untold story of my parents' deaths and refuting the errors in previously published material. I want to see this book generate greater awareness of and conversations about violent loss and its impact on the survivors and their families.

Our society has an unmet need: professionally trained therapists who understand the distinction between natural death and violent/criminal death. Survivors of violent loss and criminal death often suffer from intense anger, severe depression, and post-traumatic stress disorder (PTSD). Therapists trained in the fundamentals of dealing with this type of loss are better able to help the survivors through what's become known as *complicated bereavement* to develop the resilience they need to lead more productive, happier lives.

I also believe that survivors of violent loss will benefit from this book through knowing they are not alone, that there are others who have endured the traumatic grief, anger, and sense of injustice that accompany such a loss—that there are others who understand that survivors are not "crazy," but that this is the "new normal." Together, we comfort one another and strengthen our innate resilience to persevere and find joy in our lives.

Perhaps even more important, I believe members of the extended family, as well as friends and associates of those who have suffered such a loss, will benefit from knowing that while survivors of violent loss might put on a polite or even smiling public face, grief and anger may be gnawing away at their guts.

A percentage of the proceeds from the sale of this book will be donated to the Survivors of Violent Loss Program or other organizations serving a similar purpose.

The information presented in this work is factual. It is based not only on my memories, but also on journals and records I kept over the years, as well as correspondence, published news accounts, legal documents, meetings with French and American law-enforcement officers, and the Federal Bureau of Investigation's prosecutorial report on the murder investigation of the deaths of Loren and Joanne Edwards. Any errors or misstatements are unintentional.

The conversations and correspondence portrayed in this work are condensed for brevity and clarity while maintaining the essence and factual nature of their original content. The names of some individuals mentioned in this work have been changed and are denoted by an asterisk (*) following the first reference.

Larry M. Edwards
San Diego, California

Principal individuals in the narrative

Larry M. Edwards—the author; age at time of parents' deaths, 28

Loren I. Edwards—"Dad," the author's father; age at time of death, 50

Joanne H. "Jody" Edwards—"Mom," the author's stepmother; age at time of death, 43

Gary L. Edwards—the author's brother; age at time of parents' deaths, 27

Aileen* [Edwards]—oldest of the author's three sisters (stepsister, adopted by author's father); age at time of parents' deaths, 23

Bobbie [Edwards]—second oldest of the author's three sisters (stepsister, adopted by author's father); age at time of parents' deaths, 22

Kerry Edwards—youngest of the author's three sisters (half-sister); age at time of parents' deaths, 20

Ira Edwards—Loren Edwards' father

Ruby Edwards—Loren Edwards' mother

Vernon Howatson—Joanne Edwards' father

Hazel Howatson—Joanne Edwards' mother

Vivian Edwards Parks—Loren Edwards' older sister

Linda Parks Caruso—Vivian's second daughter; the author's cousin

Verney Howatson Dickson—Joanne Edwards' younger sister

Phyllis Schmidt Howard—"Birth Woman," the author's biological mother

Jane Funk Thompson—Phyllis's mother

Ruth*—Aileen's daughter, the author's niece; age at the last time she saw her grandparents, 3½

Lori Huey Oskam—family friend; age at time of the Edwardses' deaths, 21

Chris Peters—Australian; helped sail Spellbound from Rangiroa to Tahiti; assisted Larry in translating French to English

Connie Saindon—founder of Survivors of Violent Loss Program

Revelation

"A half-dozen French and American doctors have examined the X-rays," the FBI agent said. "They all came to the same conclusion—she did not have an accident."

A lump filled my throat and I struggled to breathe.

Foreword

How do folks survive when a loved one is murdered or has died in a violent way? It's a question that I as a therapist grapple with every day, not only because I am a survivor—my seventeen-year-old sister was murdered in a small New England town "where bad things didn't happen"—but because in my line of work I routinely counsel survivors of violent loss. One of these survivors is Larry Edwards, who has shared his story with us all.

Compelling, intriguing, informative—those are the words I use to describe this book. A book that is as hard to put down as it is to read. Is this a memoir, a true-crime book, a case study for mental health clinicians, a lesson book for the criminal justice system and upcoming attorneys, or a good read for the public? All of the above.

The public's affinity for murder stories is enormous, as shown by a recent Internet search returning 309 million hits for the topic. The number of books, movies, and TV shows that deal with murder further illustrates a very human fascination with this morbid subject. Larry's book has that, but it goes beyond being a mere account of his parents' deaths. It delves firsthand into the emotional toll that violent death and injustice exact from those who experience it.

What compels an individual to take the life of another? Eric Hickey, editor of the *Encyclopedia of Murder and Violent Crime*, lists a number of motives, including abandonment/rejection, hate/resentment, power/control, and rivalry/jealousy. The loss of human life by violence inflicts enormous grief and anger upon its survivors and is highly detrimental to the social order of communities. The comprehensive effect of such a loss is larger than is frequently known or written about. There can be seven to ten people seriously impacted by each loss. The estimated 15,240 murders in the United States in 2009 had the potential for significantly affecting 152,400 survivors.

Many in the population at large do not understand that death by violence is the kind of loss that one does not "get over"; it does not go away with time. At any given moment, the number of people suffering from the trauma of murder in the United States alone is likely to number in the millions. This, in turn, has an impact on all of those around them—family, friends, and colleagues.

Each story of violent loss has its incredible "you won't believe it" aspect, and Larry's work has the potential to inspire many of these stories to be told. More of these stories need to be written by those who have lived through it and know the details, rather than leaving it to murder-mystery authors writing fictional accounts. It's through such stories that survivors of violent loss learn that they are not alone.

A little-known fact about violent death is that family members and close friends—the "survivors"—are at increased risk for being clinically traumatized: Depression, post-traumatic stress, substance abuse, and other health issues are complications in the aftermath of violent death. These symptoms are normal reactions to abnormal events and do not fit a traditional grief process where monthly drop-in groups are sufficient.

This book illustrates that precept. In it, Larry portrays his personal struggle in a forthright way that will resonate with many survivors, particularly when, following the deaths, he writes: . . . *immersed in the criminal investigation, I didn't grieve.*

Each family member has his or her unique way of living with what has happened. They know too that remembering loved ones is a double-edged sword, as recalling memories also triggers recollections of how those loved ones died. Researchers have found that these survivors, who suffer from what is known as *traumatic bereavement* or *complicated grief,* benefit from counseling by therapists with specific training in this field.

In 1998, I formed the Survivors of Violent Loss Program to replicate the work of Dr. Ted Rynearson, the internationally renowned psychiatrist from Seattle who developed the "restorative retelling" model following the death of his wife. The approach used by the Survivors program is based on Dr. Rynearson's findings and includes the application of restorative retelling for treating violent death bereavement and post-traumatic stress disorder (PTSD). Through the program, participants increase their innate resiliencies, learn to cope with their loss in a constructive manner, and enhance post-traumatic growth.

Early referral and intervention has been shown to significantly reduce the distress of unnatural death. In Larry's case, however, he did not seek professional counseling until thirty years after his parents' deaths, when he enrolled in the Survivors program. His story offers insight into the aftermath of violent loss, not just from a clinical perspective, but from a very human perspective.

When a loved one dies, family members are exposed to grotesque, gruesome details, real and imagined. What has happened is incomprehensible. It is especially difficult for all when it is unsolved or the solution is unsatisfactory.

Working with hundreds of family members over the past two decades, I have found that the quest for justice, for comprehending what happened, becomes a compulsive inquiry, taking over the rudder of life for the person possessed by it. In cold cases, this becomes even more true. For survivors, it seems like no one cares, so they must find the truth on their own. Larry is the person in his family who could not let what happened lie. When the criminal justice system failed him and his family, someone had to investigate it.

No one expects to lose a loved one to violence, and when it happens, families become detectives in pursuit of this answer. A pursuit that often becomes a lifelong quest. However, the family is the least inclined to name one of its own, while for law enforcement everyone is a suspect. Larry battles this conflicting view throughout his book: *What if I'm wrong? What if, as preposterous as it seems, my brother is telling the truth, or at least some semblance of the truth?*

As a therapist and a Violent Death Bereavement Specialist, I know the impact on "living victims of murder" and other violent deaths, those who have become members of a club they never wanted to join. However, details from the inside looking out, details that give therapists a glimpse into a much larger and more complex phenomenon than is generally known about such cases, are rare. Larry offers us that rare glimpse.

This real event changed Larry's life forever, in positive as well as negative ways. Survivors have both the wounds and the resiliencies of their loss. Larry did many things that caused him to be swallowed up by the story while developing into a lone but careful investigator. He engaged in self-destructive habits that prolonged the grief as well as activities that helped him manage the intensity of the emotions he continues to live with.

You, the reader, are now invited to join Larry in his investigation as he endeavors to unravel the mystery of how, and why, his parents died. Were his parents murdered? More is revealed in each chapter as he lays out the contradictory testimony and family conflicts while you travel with him on this dark yet enlightening literary voyage to the truth.

This story is an intriguing and continuously unfolding puzzle that spans several decades and involves foreign and domestic law enforcement as well as a divided family. While it is an account of one man's search for justice and peace, it will hold interest and value for many, whether they are fans of memoirs, true crime, or whodunits, or they are therapists or clinicians, or simply another human being trying to make sense of this sometimes incomprehensible world we live in.

It's the kind of book you can't put down. You will live this story.

How do folks survive when a loved one is murdered or dies in a violent way? This story offers one perspective.

—Connie Saindon, MA

Connie Saindon is a licensed marriage and family therapist, the author of *The Journey: Ten Steps to Learning to Live With Violent Death*, and the founder of the Survivors of Violent Loss Program in San Diego, California.

Sprang: That time of year when flowers go bloom—and doors boom.

1

July 2010

The DayMinder sits splayed on my desk, the date mocking me.

The telephone dares me to pick up the handset and punch the requisite keys—keys whose numbers have faded from wear, in part from the hundreds of times I've called before.

But this day I can't call, not even on her birthday. My sister Aileen* and I no longer communicate—not by phone, not by email, not by old-fashioned, handwritten letter. The pain lies fresh in my gut, a festering wound that recalls her betrayal.

I snort at the irony.

The unresolved murder investigation into our parents' deaths should have kept us united, strengthening our bonds. Three decades earlier, while our family crumbled around us, Aileen and I became the closest of friends. Only a year ago, I visited her in Seattle. We stayed up late drinking gin, lamenting over the justice our parents had been denied. We promised to see each other again soon. Meanwhile we'd continue our frequent exchange of emails and periodic phone calls, keeping intact what remained of our tattered family.

Now, even we no longer speak to each other. I imagine Dad, in need of a shave and wearing a varnish-streaked T-shirt, shaking his head and saying, "You have to learn to get along."

Another snort.

Dad's naïveté underlay it all. As a carpenter, he built sturdy homes. As a parent, well, things hadn't gone according to the blueprint. Not for him. Not for Mom.

I close the DayMinder with an angry flip of the cover and stomp to the kitchen to make coffee. While the water heats, I stand at the window, peering into the yard.

"You OK?" asks Janis, my wife. She pecks my cheek.

I circle my arms about her, nestling my face into the crook of her neck. "Yeah," I say, but it holds no conviction.

The whistling of the kettle draws me away. I pour steaming water into the waiting maw of the filter cone and savor the aroma as the black brew trickles into the mug.

I grip the cup and return to the window, like Mom used to do on a summer morning, eyeing the vibrant fuchsias she'd hung in baskets at the front of the house. The house that Dad built. For us. His family. A family now fading into a dusky memory, like the fuchsias' violet blooms fallen to ground, their color, their life, drained out.

What the hell happened?

What forces had converged for my family to end up this way?

We'd been a normal family, hadn't we? Once upon a time? I always thought so.

Except we weren't. Otherwise, my parents—Loren and Jody Edwards—wouldn't have windmilled to the bottom of the ocean, fodder for bottom feeders.

I sip my coffee and gaze into the lukewarm sky, recalling the last time I saw them.

November 16, 1977

I plodded down the ramp to the transient boat dock at San Diego's Shelter Island. Only a few vessels remained in the slips, among them the Spellbound, my parents' fifty-three-foot sailboat. Most of the other boats had already departed for points south.

I took my time, motivated not by a sense of rejoicing but a sense of duty. Delays had led to a protracted going-away. Three parties in four days had left me not just numb, but resentful.

No, let's be honest. I was pissed off. I should've been on that boat, not my brother.

I just wanted them gone.

I had relished the trip down the coast from Puget Sound, sailing out of sight of land. Especially at night while the others slept, the only light coming from the dimly lit compass and the stars overhead. The only sounds the whispers in the rigging and the swoosh of the hull driving through black ocean swells limned with blue-green phosphorescence. I had looked forward to crossing the ocean to Tahiti and points beyond, like the seafarers of old. But when my brother, Gary, joined us in San Diego for the final preparations, childhood patterns resurfaced and camaraderie drained out of the scuppers like cold seawater washing over the deck—his sarcasm over the fate of empty paint cans, a pointless debate over how to slice cheese, and, the final straw for me, our dustup in the galley.

Now they were leaving—leaving me behind.

My clipped steps on the dock signaled my approach and elicited a glance but no welcome from Gary, who stood on the aft deck of the Spellbound. The boat that Dad built.

Kerry, the youngest of my three sisters, hovered over a smoking Hibachi. She offered a weak wave of recognition. Or had she merely swatted smoke out of her eyes?

I grabbed a lifeline stanchion and hauled myself aboard, then peeked into the main cabin. It had been tidied up since I'd last seen it. The stacks of canned food and other supplies had been stowed in the bilge. Items not permanently fastened down—potential projectiles once the boat began pitching and rolling at sea—had been secured.

My father grinned and held up a beer. I nodded, then waved to Mom, who stood in the galley, dicing potatoes. She looked up and smiled, slicing the air with a quick wave of her own. At forty-three she had staved off middle-age spread, although streaks of gray silvered her cropped brown hair and the crow's feet at her eyes would not be denied.

Dad joined me in the cockpit and handed me a cold brew. He stood nearly six feet, the tallest member of our family; he'd be turning fifty in eight days. His graying hair, normally a crew cut, had grown almost to the point of needing a comb. He lowered his gaze and said, "I wish you were going with us."

I stared at him for a moment before muttering, "Yeah," and took a long pull at the bottle. I wished I were going, too.

My father had envisioned the voyage as the vacation to end all vacations. The Edwards family—Dad, Mom, and the five kids—sailing to the South Seas. But it took him a few years longer than planned to build his ark, and the crew shrank in size. Aileen and Bobbie remained in the Seattle area, and just days earlier I had told him that I, too, would not be going. Not as long as my brother was aboard. Lori Oskam, the daughter of a family friend, had filled my empty slot.

The aroma of seared beef drifted past. "The steaks'll be ready soon," Dad said. "I'll grab the plates."

Twenty-year-old Kerry knelt before the grill and pushed a strand of blond hair behind an ear. Lori, a year older, leaned against the lifelines. She looked hungry thin and offered a smile that held little warmth.

"Just scorch mine top and bottom," Gary said. "You know I like my meat bloody." As a youngster, Gary had reveled in the looks of disgust he elicited when eating raw hamburger and bacon, especially the bacon. "But you can make Larry's well-done," he added, turning a smirk on me. "He doesn't like the sight of blood."

I locked eyes with him until he looked away. He had gathered his shoulder-length hair in a ponytail. A wispy beard clung to a languid chin. He raised a hand to narrow lips and gnawed a fingertip. Gary, at twenty-seven a year younger than I, had bitten his nails for as long as I could remember. Dad and Mom had tried everything to break him of the habit. Even when they dabbed fiery Tabasco sauce on his cuticles, he just lapped it up, grinning and asking for more. Eventually, they gave up, figuring he'd grow out of it.

He glanced back at me, curling a contemptuous lip as he wiped his hand on his jeans. I sipped the Lucky Lager and surveyed the beamy ketch, taking in the deck Gary and I had painted only weeks before, the winches I had disassembled and greased, the ratlines I had built. A point of personal pride. I had laid out the assembly for the ratlines on deck, precisely calculating the angle and diminishing distance between the triangled lower shrouds as they rose to meet the towering spruce spar at the first set of spreaders, twenty feet off the deck. When I fastened the wooden rungs to the stainless steel cables, they fit perfectly.

"Amazing," my father said.

"Rudimentary algebra," I replied.

"Even so, I would have done them one at a time to be certain I didn't make a mistake."

Had he paid me a rare compliment? Or suggested that I got lucky?

My gaze drifted upward. Palm fronds rustled in the cool breeze. In the adjacent marina, masts of boats going nowhere pointed to the stars.

Will I now be stuck here, too, an empty dream lashed to a dock?

Dad returned with the plates. We forked the grilled meat, then went below. I spooned potato salad onto my plate and took a seat in the dinette.

Mom eyed me. "How's your new abode? I couldn't live in something that tiny," she said, referring to the twenty-one-foot sloop I had purchased to live aboard.

I lifted a dismissive shoulder. "I'm getting there. Bought some lumber to build shelves, added more insulation to the icebox."

Across the table sat Bill Garrett, the son of one of Dad's closest friends. "So, Larry, why'd you decide not to go on the trip?"

Gary scoffed and glanced at Kerry. She rolled her eyes.

I turned my gaze on Dad. His rigid expression begged me not to answer. At least not truthfully.

Kerry filled the silence. "Larry doesn't like us," she said, taunting me with a cock of her head and lifting the corners of her mouth into what passed for a smile.

I said nothing. She didn't know why I'd chosen to remain behind.

I rose to get another round of beers. Nothing like a little booze to improve the mood. But we pretty much finished the meal in silence, other than Dad saying they still had a lot of work to do if they were to leave the next day, "come hell or high water." In a low, off-key voice he began singing one of his favorite Kingston Trio songs, *Gotta Travel On.*

"I'd better go," I said.

Dad, Mom, and Kerry joined me on the walk to shore, each step echoing off the water. Mom's bagful of quarters, dimes, and nickels jingled at her thigh. From the phone booth at the head of the dock she and Dad would each call their parents, then Aileen and Bobbie. Kerry would call her hapless betrothed.

I croaked a good-bye to Mom and Kerry, giving them quick hugs. Dad put an arm over my shoulder and a familiar scent triggered a childhood memory. A five-year-old sitting on his lap, my head nestled against a broad chest clothed in a T-shirt smelling of dried sweat after a day's labor at a construction site, the hint of Old Spice unable to mask the odor.

Our embrace ended quickly. We both choked up and only nodded as we separated. I stepped back and tried to blink away the tears, thankful for the dim light.

What's happening to me? I want them gone! Yet I'm about to start weeping like my grandmothers when they said good-bye in Port Townsend, fearful they'd never see their children again. I had dismissed their worries as silliness. Must I now admit that I, too, harbor the same fear?

Dad finally spoke: "You'll get that money in the bank for me?"

I stared at him, incredulous. Inside, I screamed: *That's all you can say right now? That the only thing you care about is a penny-ante bit of money you think I owe you?*

I said only, "Sure, soon as I get a job."

I shuffled head-down toward the parking lot, kicking a lone shoe lying on the asphalt, then heard a knocking behind me. Over my shoulder, I saw Mom, handset to ear, rapping her knuckles on the phone booth's glass wall. She grinned and waved.

I returned the gesture, swallowing the frog in my throat and calling out, "Fair winds!"

2

Friday, February 24, 1978

I sat at a forlorn, military-issue desk in a windowless office divided into cage-like cubicles—who designs these dismal swamps, anyway? When the phone jangled, I glanced at the clock and winced—10:46 A.M. My fingers resumed their frantic dance, typewriter keys slamming to paper, five whacks per second, hoping the call wasn't for me. I'd told my customers their work would be ready by late afternoon. Until then, leave me the hell alone.

"It's for you," my boss called out. "Sounds urgent."

"Urgent, my ass," I muttered, reaching for the extension. I summoned my nice voice and picked up. "Hello, this is Larry."

"It's Linda. Are you sitting down?"

My cousin, phoning from Woodinville, near Seattle.

"Always the nurse," I said. "It's Grandpa, right?"

Our Grandpa Edwards had been diagnosed with cancer two weeks earlier and given at most a couple of months to live. The thought of never seeing him again stabbed my conscience. "I should have—"

"It's not Grandpa," she said.

"Tell me it's not the plane reservations. I have deadlines coming out my ass." She said nothing, and I heard her sniffling. "Linda, what is it?"

"It's your father."

"So, it is about the tickets," I replied, my derisive tone conveying the annoyance I felt. Dad would fly from Tahiti to Los Angeles, where I'd meet him. Together we'd go on to Seattle to bid adieu to the family patriarch. Linda, staying with her parents while recuperating from a tumble on the ski slopes, had been coordinating the airline reservations for us.

"Larry, there's been an accident!" she said, like a mother scolding a lippy child.

My neck prickled. "On the boat?"

She drew a deep breath and said, "I'm so sorry . . . He's dead."

My breath left me as if I'd been whacked with a two-by-four. I stared at a picture of my father thumbtacked to the wall over my desk. Dad at the helm of his beloved Spellbound, master of his floating domain. I'd been looking forward to seeing him, hearing about the trip. He had sent letters from the Marquesas Islands, and I'd had second thoughts about not going with him.

"Are you OK?" Linda asked.

"Yeah, sure," I said and sucked in a lungful of air.

"There's more," she added, choking on the words. "Kerry's unconscious."

My throat lumped up and I could only manage a froggy "What happened?"

She said an amateur radio operator had patched a call from my brother through to her parents' house earlier that morning. "Gary said they were hit by the boom."

I imagined the boat's heavy spruce spar sweeping across the deck like the arm of a giant sea monster, taking out everything in its path. Why hadn't Gary contacted me? I answered the question myself: He wouldn't have even tried.

I'd heard about a typhoon ravaging the southwest corner of the Pacific. "Were they hit by a squall?"

"That's what we thought, but Gary said there wasn't much wind. They were motoring."

"Then how the hell could they have been hit by the boom?"

"I don't know! I'm just telling you what he said."

I apologized, and she said Gary, along with Mom and Lori, were OK.

"How'd Grandpa take the news?" I asked.

"We're not telling him."

"What?"

"He's going to die in a few weeks anyway. Why not just let him go on believing his son is alive and happy and fulfilling his dream."

"But you told Grandma."

"She's devastated."

Neither of us spoke for a moment, then Linda said she had more calls to make; she'd get back to me as soon as she heard anything new. I hung up and slammed a palm on my desktop, sloshing coffee on pages I'd have to retype.

My boss's chair creaked. I swiveled around and told him what I knew, my voice nearly inaudible. He snatched a tissue from atop a file cabinet and handed it to me. "You go on home," he said. "We can take care of things here."

I nodded and dabbed at the tears. But I needed to make a few calls of my own. I tried to reach Aileen, then Bobbie, and only got busy signals.

Dad still smiled at me from the wall. I fought to breathe in the cramped cubicle, framed by the room divider on one side and khaki file cabinets on the other, the air laden with the scent of inked paper. The only sound the clacking of electric typewriters.

I worked as a writer at Action Resumé Service, which specialized in preparing SF-171 job applications for federal civil-service positions. After a week of ten- and twelve-hour days, I'd been looking forward to a weekend of well-earned R & R.

A second attempt to reach my sisters failed, but I couldn't just sit. As I drove across the high arch of the Bay Bridge to Coronado, my watery eyes gave me an impressionist's view of my little sloop anchored near the public golf course.

A postcard world. Sailboat anchored in San Diego Bay. Perpetual summer.

I had teased family and friends living in the Pacific Northwest about the chilly, rain-sodden climate they endured. But as I slipped the boat's mooring, I yearned for a blustery, Puget Sound day, to be pummeled with wind, pelted with rain, the boat heeled hard, wrenching the tiller as I struggled for control of my craft, seeking proof that I was still alive. Instead, I suffered the insolence of a balmy afternoon.

I drifted northward near the airport.

A plane jet-screamed on takeoff.

I screamed with it.

And screamed again.

I had wished Dad out of my life, if only temporarily. Now he was gone. Forever.

For years Dad had scrimped his pennies as he and Mom labored to build and outfit the Spellbound, a big ketch easily recognized throughout Puget Sound by its yellow hull and glistening spruce spars. The dream they had begun to live, scuttled.

An act of fate? Or something else?

My cousin's explanation didn't make sense. How could Dad be killed and Kerry knocked unconscious by the boat's boom if they were motoring? Surely, the boom would have been tied down.

I sailed back to the anchorage, moored my boat and returned to the office. I called Aileen, hoping she would have more details of the accident. She didn't.

"I really need to talk to Mom, to know she's all right," Aileen said.

"She'll call you tomorrow," I said. "Things have got to be pretty crazy right now."

"Do you think they'll get to Tahiti OK?"

"They'll manage. Things can't get much worse."

But things did get worse.

THE NEXT MORNING, I rose at first light and went to the beach. There I walked along the narrow strip of sand bordering the Coronado golf course, where duffers were already chasing their little white balls. I picked up a bit of riprap and rainbowed it over the water, toward the spot where the Spellbound had lain at anchor while the final preparations for the trip were made. A splash, and ripples circled outward across the still water as tears coursed my cheeks.

I returned to my boat and made coffee, then heard a voice hailing me. I peered out and spotted Melissa Garrett* on the beach, waving an arm in a wide arc. Her father and mine had become lifelong friends as boys growing up in Seattle.

I rowed ashore and Melissa squeezed me in a tight hug. I stepped back, my eyes questioning. "It's Kerry, isn't it?" I said.

Melissa swallowed before answering. "My dad just said to come and get you."

As she drove north to Rancho Bernardo, I tried making small talk, but we drifted into silence. Morgan Garrett* met me at the door and led me to the family room. His wife, Nan, sat on the couch, red-eyed, a wad of tissue in her hands.

"Is it Kerry?" I asked.

Morgan hesitated and his face contorted. "Larry, you'd better take a seat."

"Just tell me, damn it! What the hell's going on?"

He pulled me to him, gripping me so tightly I could hardly breathe. "It's your mom . . . she's dead, too."

I pushed away and walked to the patio door, where I stared into the sunlit backyard. Buds had formed on the shrubs, signs of life returning as winter waned.

First Dad, now Mom.

I felt Morgan's hand on my shoulder. "We're all in shock," he said.

"Maybe they were caught in that typhoon after all," I said, still gazing into the yard.

"We were told that she died during the night."

A silent movie flickered through my mind: Gary and Lori standing at the lifeline, grinning in anticipation of the adventure ahead . . . Mom and Kerry waving from the phone booth . . . Dad's torqued face the night we parted.

Morgan and I made a big dent in a half-case of Lucky Lager while taking phone calls from family and friends in the Seattle area. Gary had said Mom died of shock. But we got no update on the Spellbound until that evening, when we were told the boat had been found adrift north of the island of Rangiroa.

I booked a flight to Tahiti.

3

_____

Sunday, February 26, 1978

Midnight approached as the Boeing 747 lifted off from Los Angeles International Airport. I had dozed only a few hours over the previous two days, yet sleep eluded me still. In the darkened cabin, I reread the letters my parents had sent from the Marquesas Islands, where they spent the final two months of their lives. Through their terse words, they lived again.

The voyage from San Diego—two thousand eight hundred seventy-five miles across the open ocean—had taken nearly a month. Some days had been fun, others downright miserable. They suffered from sea-sickness and equipment problems; they had to motor through the doldrums. At one point they rode out a squall packing fifty-knot gusts. But the legendary trade winds lived up to their centuries of renown:

> *We arrived on Wed., Dec. 14, after 27 days. The island was right where Gary said it would be. . . . The trades are fantastic! Set the sails and did not touch them for five days. . . . Warm rain, it just felt good to stand in it and get rinsed off. . . . We caught two fish on the whole trip. Both the last day. A small albacore and 42" mahi mahi. Beautiful fish and good eating. Lori likes fish now.*

The islanders had welcomed my parents and offered fresh bananas, pamplemousse (a variety of grapefruit), coconuts, and wood carvings in exchange for music tapes, *Playboy* magazines, and .22-caliber bullets. The islanders also invited the Spellbound crew to a wedding feast:

> *What a celebration. They have a roofed-over area about 150 feet long. Pits to cook food in, racks above ground to cook meat. They served beer, wine, punch. The guests were playing guitars and singing when we got there. I wish I'd recorded it. Then they stopped and the rock band with big amplifiers started.*
>
> *Wish you would have come.*

Had I made a mistake by not going? Pangs of envy needled within. The Marquesas, a sprawling group of volcanic islands some two thousand miles southeast of Hawaii, seemed to be an earthly Elysium. But could I have prevented my parents' deaths? Could anyone have?

In another letter, they wrote:

> *The mayor of Nuka Hiva let us use a pavilion Christmas day and we had a potluck with all the other boaters. Boats from England, Holland, Australia, 2 Canadian, Panamanian and 3 American.*
>
> *The Monday after Christmas we took 26 people to the north side of the island. Four boats took part in the operation. Eighty people in all. They gave us a feast, and we all stayed overnight with them.*
>
> *New Year's Eve we went to see a woodcarver and his wife and had dinner with them. They fed us lobster, raw fish, fruit salad and a cooked banana dish. Mom ordered some things, so we may never leave.*

As I returned the letter to its envelope, a group of giggling children paraded up the aisle in a game of follow the leader.

How can you laugh? My parents have just died.

Yet, their smiles and laughter evoked memories of my own childhood, of carefree days exploring the woods that surrounded my family's home in semirural Juanita, northeast of Seattle: Playing naked in the ravine behind our house with Gary and boyhood friends as we reenacted *Lord of the Flies*; deer hunting with Dad; swimming at Aunt

Betty's beach; Dad's laughable first attempt at sailing the dinghy he had built.

I yearned for those days. Of course, they weren't all carefree.

My biological mother—Birth Woman, I call her—abandoned my father, brother, and me when I was four, Gary three. In the years that followed, images of her leaving haunted me. Birth Woman slams out of the house, vaporous memories ghosting through the mind, teasing clarity, then bowing to obscurity: Pouting, shouting parent . . . swinging skillet . . . swirling skirt . . . rattling the windows of a little-boy mind as she spins through the door and slips from view, trailing family detritus in her hedonist wake.

Torment lay in words left unspoken, transmitted instead through a look of disdain, a slam-banged door, her absence. The Little Boy formed his worldview, his sense of Self, in those hate- and fate-filled Sprang days—his toddling mind distorted, his life's well poisoned. Betrayed by one he loved. Betrayed by his own befuddled brain. Confusion leading to conclusion, however irrational it may have been.

After she left, we never saw her much. But I sense her leaving to this day as I stumble over a swayed mind-set, voice shrilled then silenced by a constricted throat, companion to unembargoed tears. Her chaotic exit triggered a rockslide that crushed my Self and left our family battered, like a storm-tossed vessel at sea.

One night she stopped by the house, near my bedtime, wanting to take Gary and me out for an ice-cream soda. Another pouting, shouting affair.

Three months after the divorce became final, my twenty-eight-year-old father married Joanne Howatson Peet (everyone called her "Jody"), a twenty-two-year-old widow with two young daughters. Matchmaking friends had paired them up at a New Year's Eve party, and they embarked on a whirlwind romance.

Jody's first husband had died on her twenty-first birthday, following a car wreck. Struck by a drunk driver. She, six months pregnant with Bobbie, emerged with a broken arm and multiple cuts that required more than one hundred stitches. Nine-month-old Aileen suffered from a broken collarbone.

Gary and I met them on a wintry day at the house in Preston where

Jody lived with her parents. As Dad pulled into the driveway, I spotted a small figure swaddled in a heavy coat standing near the front porch. I climbed out of the car, and Dad urged me forward as the bundle of wool waddled toward us.

Dad kneeled and said, "This is Aileen. She's going to be your sister."

Her eyes sparkled with curiosity. I smiled, pleased with the notion of having a sister, yet wondering what it meant. Jody stood on the porch and beckoned us into the small farmhouse.

As I stepped inside, the heat from the woodstove sucked the breath out of me, and someone stripped off my coat. Gary pushed me from behind, then ran toward the kitchen, shouting. My father went after him, and I stared at the unfamiliar adult faces gazing down at me. A whiff of baking cookies scented the air. Somewhere a baby cried.

When Dad married Jody that June, I was six, Gary five. Aileen had not turned two, and Bobbie was six weeks shy of her first birthday. My father formally adopted them shortly afterward. Kerry arrived a week before our parents' first wedding anniversary. For Gary and me, Jody became "Mom." For Aileen and Bobbie, Dad was the only father they ever knew.

We lived in a three-bedroom house in Seattle, but Mom and Dad, country folk at heart, wanted out of the city. They bought a parcel of land in Juanita where Dad, an apprentice carpenter, would build us a bigger home. Now an upscale bedroom community, at the time Juanita was a sleepy crossroads derided by city dwellers as being out in the boondocks.

When the Seattle house sold, we took up temporary lodging in a two-bedroom farmhouse in the outskirts of Woodinville. We four older children slept in bunk beds in one bedroom, while our parents and baby sister shared the other. The bunk beds sat so close together, Mom and Dad had to turn sideways to squeeze between them.

That summer, with school out and construction of our new home under way, we moved into an even smaller abode—an army-surplus wall tent set up near the building site and shadowed by the towering fir, spruce, cedar, and alder trees that forested the hillside acreage. Mom cooked on a Coleman camp stove fueled by white gas, the outdoor kitchen sheltered only by a sheet of plywood draped with Visqueen. We drew cold water from a single spigot; an outhouse sat back in the trees.

Dad later planted a lilac bush on the tent site, and, fittingly, established a compost heap where the makeshift kitchen had been.

We had few neighbors, and until we got to know them, they were faceless voices echoing faintly through the woods. The back of the property dropped into a deep ravine, its steep, damp slopes carpeted with sword ferns, Oregon grape, elderberry, red huckleberry, and delicate maidenhair ferns. The ravine had a small, nameless creek running through it that emptied into Lake Washington.

Each morning, when my chores were done, I explored ever farther into the woods. One day, I returned to the building site at a run, my brother on my heels. "Mom, mom!"

She was bending over a bucket, rinsing out a cloth diaper, and straightened. Alarm crossed her face.

"Guess what?" I said.

She sighed as the diaper dripped water into the dirt at her feet. "What is it?"

I spread my arms wide. "A great big log with stairs chopped in it. On the other side of the gully. Can I climb them?"

"*May* I climb them," she said, ever the grammarian.

"Can I?"

She chuckled and ruffled my hair. "Let me talk to your father first. Now go wash your hands. It's almost time for lunch."

As those summer days passed, Gary and I spent hours each day in our idyllic playground. Before long, we befriended the neighborhood boys, who also found a second home in the sylvan estate. We became swashbuckling Robin Hoods—no Maid Marians allowed.

The setup was far from ideal for my parents, however, especially my new mom. She endured primitive conditions while caring for five children, two still in diapers. But she and Dad both came from farming families and knew the rigors of self-sufficiency. They shared a vision of a better life ahead, for them and their children.

THE KIDS PLAYING follow the leader in the airplane's aisle broke my reverie. I snapped an icy glare at the girl heading the pack. She wrinkled a defiant nose at me and continued on. I closed my eyes and ignored their further forays. They eventually tired of the game, and I drifted back into the past.

Dad told me about his plan for the South Pacific cruise when I was in high school. That morning he munched his Cheerios, while I spooned the Breakfast of Champions. I put my empty bowl in the dishwasher, then started back to the quiet of my basement lair.

"Wait a sec," he said. "I want to talk to you about something."

I rolled my eyes as I turned to face him, certain that he'd tell me I spent too much time with sports and too little time doing things around the house.

"You'll like this," he said.

I'd heard that before, too.

A grin creased his face. "I'm going to build a sailboat and the whole family will go on a cruise to the South Seas. We'll be gone two years, maybe three."

He'd never mentioned it before. I only knew of the flying lessons he'd taken before I was born. I had studied some of his workbooks on aerial navigation.

"We'll catch fish from the boat, eat coconuts right off the trees. What do you think?"

I couldn't tell him what I thought. It had nothing do with fish or coconuts and everything to do with the bare-breasted *vahines* I'd read about in *Mutiny on the Bounty*. My teenage imagination conjured up visions of voluptuous young women wearing flimsy grass skirts and little else. I returned to my chair at the table, smiling at the prospect. "Will we go to Hawaii? Tahiti? Pitcairn Island?"

"You bet," Dad said. Then his smile faded. He leaned forward, arm on the table, as if taking me into his confidence. "I want you to tutor the girls. They'll need schooling while we're on the trip."

I shrugged, not thrilled with the prospect. I'd already tried helping Bobbie with her reading, and that had been a disaster. We both lost patience because what came so easily to me was so difficult for her. "How soon will we go?" I asked.

"In three years or so." When I frowned, he said, "It'll take that long to build the boat. It's the only way we can afford it."

I pursed my lips and stared through the kitchen window into a gray dawn. Rainwater gurgled in the downspout outside.

"What's the matter?" he asked. "A second ago you were gung-ho."

"What about college?"

"What of it?"

"You want me to go, don't you?"

"Of course," he said, "but what's a couple years? Besides, you'll learn things on this trip they'll never teach you in that ivory tower." He paused, his face crinkling with amusement. "You know what PhD stands for, don't you?"

I rolled my eyes again, already knowing the answer.

"Piled higher and deeper," he said, chuckling at his time-worn joke.

"Who'll live in our house while we're gone?"

"We'll have to sell it."

Dad seemed to have no sentiment for our home in the woods. But the prospect of never being able to return to the place I so enjoyed as a youngster saddened me.

My father descended from a family of pioneers. His great-grandfather had joined the westward migration, first traveling by flatboat from east Tennessee to the Iowa frontier, then moving on by covered wagon to southeastern Washington, where he built the region's first grist mill. Dad was born at home, on the family farm. Perhaps that pioneer heritage sparked his desire to push westward and cross the ocean in a sailboat, just as his forebears has crossed the sea of grass in a prairie schooner.

Fiscal realities being what they were, the project took longer than Dad first thought. I had graduated from college and begun teaching school in Tacoma by the time construction began. Gary had joined the army. Our sisters were teenagers.

Nonetheless, Dad held fast to his dream. My parents had built a comfortable home in a world removed from the problems associated with city life, which included the rising tide of teenage drug abuse. But that blight followed them to the increasingly urbanized Eastside and caught up with my sisters. Bobbie started smoking cigarettes in sixth grade, Aileen soon thereafter. Then came the "wacky tobacky" and a variety of controlled substances ingested in the woods behind Redmond Junior High School.

Yes, I wrecked the family car as a nineteen-year-old and later was caught with fake ID, but I was a good student and never touched alcohol or toked a joint until I reached college. Gary started earlier but maintained acceptable grades and graduated from high school. My parents were not prepared for Aileen's and Bobbie's academic shortcomings, truancy, and blatant rebellion.

I heard tales of shouting matches, loss of privileges, and bedroom confinements. Aileen and Bobbie ran away from home and were jailed multiple times, in some instances forcing Mom to drive out of state and bring them home. Aileen and Bobbie ended up in a rehabilitation program for teens.

Thus, the boat took on a new dimension for Dad. It was no longer just a sailing trip. The boat became a means of reuniting his family. Our troubles would be left behind. Or so he thought.

I BLINKED AWAKE as the airplane's cabin lights came on and we began the descent to Tahiti. A flight attendant addressed the passengers in French, reminding me that I was about to arrive in a foreign land. As passengers raised the window shutters and the morning light streamed into the cabin, I peered into an uncertain future.

What does it hold for my family? For me?

4

Monday, February 27, 1978, 5:30 A.M.

The taxi wound through narrow, tree-lined lanes, a bucolic setting that belied the purpose of my mission. The driver didn't speak English; I spoke only a few words of French. I didn't know if he was taking me to the right hospital, but he seemed confident of our destination, L'hôpital de Mamao in Papeete, Tahiti's largest town. I reassured myself that Kerry would be there, along with . . . I tried not to think about it, but my mind conjured up images of bodies lying in caskets.

What will happen now?

As the youngest, Kerry had always been Daddy's little girl. We older children had resented her for it. That underlying tension resurfaced aboard the Spellbound. We fell into familiar patterns as we sailed down the coast to San Diego—small problems magnified by the childhood baggage we still carried. Even so, Kerry and I had been on good terms and shared a few laughs at our parents' expense.

Until Gary arrived.

The prospect of seeing him again worried me most. As boys, we shared a bedroom and argued over territory, at times using a measuring tape to define our boundaries. A seam in the floor tiles became our Maginot Line. Still, when we were young we generally got along and played together in the woods surrounding our home.

By high school, however, we'd become competitors. Gary tried besting me athletically as well as academically. He rarely succeeded. To compensate, he exaggerated his own accomplishments while putting others down, me in particular. I went on to college and became a schoolteacher, he into the army. We saw little of each other over the ensuing decade. When Gary joined the boat in San Diego, nothing had changed—he found fault in everyone and everything around him.

By comparison, he and Kerry got along well, at times flirting like school kids, although even she fell victim to his barbed tongue. One evening, while fixing hamburgers for dinner, these alleged adults got into a shouting match over how to slice cheese. It ended with Gary declaring, "See, I was right." Kerry pouted the rest of the evening.

But he reserved most of his venom for me. One afternoon, a man from a nearby boat asked if we had any trash to go ashore. There were two near-empty paint cans on deck. I didn't know if our penny-pinching father, who squeezed every molecule from a toothpaste tube, wanted to keep them.

I called out to Gary. "Does Dad want these cans tossed out?"

Gary sneered. "No, we're going to hang them on the lifelines for decoration."

"A simple 'yes' would have sufficed."

"You ask a stupid question, you get a stupid answer."

A few days later, we were alone on the boat, stowing supplies in the galley. He made a comment I didn't understand, and I asked him to clarify it.

"Can't you even understand plain English?" he said.

I glared at him for a moment before saying, "You know, I've had enough of your horseshit."

He flashed his patented smirk. "What are you going to do, just stand there like a big gorilla?"

Years of Gary's sarcasm and put-downs spilled into my mind. In the weeks and months to come, it would only get worse—emotions amplified by the cramped space and lack of privacy aboard the boat. At that moment I knew I could not go on the trip. My parents wanted, and deserved, a pleasant voyage, not a running battle between bickering children. One of us had to leave. Gary would not go voluntarily, and Dad would not—could not—choose between his sons. That left me to make the sacrifice. Bile rose in my throat as anger seared within.

I lunged at Gary. Grabbed a handful of shirt. Slammed him against a bulkhead, fist cocked. "What do you have to say now, smart-ass?"

He flinched, his eyes wide with fear. I scoffed, recalling his boasts of being a karate expert as he peacocked in his *gi*. After savoring his cower for a moment, I let him go—just as I had done when we fought as boys. But my decision had been made.

I gazed through the taxi's window at Tahiti's verdant foliage, which seemed to mock my parents' fate. Gary and I needed to make our peace for the sake of family unity, not to mention our individual sanity. Dad's grand plan hadn't worked out. But in the wake of his and Mom's deaths, perhaps that goal of uniting our family could be achieved, at least in part, as we children gave each other the emotional support we needed.

I vowed to make it happen.

The driver broke my reverie as the taxi lurched to a stop at the hospital. My spirits flagged at the sight of the aging, run-down building. What kind of care could this place provide? Inside, a dim light suffused sleepy corridors. A lone janitor mopped the floor. Not a medical professional in sight.

"Kerry Edwards? American?" I inquired.

The aging Tahitian's sad eyes directed me down the hall. I peeked through open doors into the rooms I passed, hoping for a glimpse of my sister. Dark-skinned women, half-dozing in chairs, shot me menacing looks. The church-run facility served the poor and itinerant.

I found Kerry asleep in the end room and tiptoed inside. The space stretched long and narrow, with four beds placed evenly like piers in a dockyard. Kerry lay in the first bed; she had a bandage above her right eye. Lori Oskam lay fully clothed atop the bed next to Kerry's. The other two beds sat empty. A bathroom cubicle occupied a corner at the exterior wall. Thick air hung heavy with institutional distaste, the room's walls coated with the apparently universal green pastel.

At the far end of the room, a door to a patio and garden stood ajar. Through the adjacent window I saw bright-colored birds flit among broad green leaves of plants I'd seen only in pictures. The birds' piercing scolds mimicked my mood. A Tahitian woman cradling a child in her arms stepped into view, then retreated. Like the birds, she paid us no mind.

Lori's eyes fluttered open. As recognition sank in, she sat up and I moved toward her. She wrapped her arms around my neck, pulling me close in a desperate embrace. "I'm so glad to see you," she said. "It's been an unbelievable nightmare."

"I know. Now we need to get you two safely home."

She stood and I stepped back to examine her. She'd always been thin, but she had acquired an almost emaciated look. A tank-top drooped from boney shoulders, her long hair and ankle-length skirt accentuating the effect. She looked more than exhausted; she looked frightened. "How are you doing?" I asked.

Her eyes misted over. "Not too good."

We sat on the bed and I extended an arm across her shoulders. "Are you hurt, too?"

"No, I'm here to help with Kerry. There aren't enough nurses."

"How's she doing?"

Lori stared at Kerry before answering. "She has a fractured skull."

An ache formed in my head. "Shit."

Lori told me they only learned of the fractured left temple from X-rays taken at the hospital. On the boat, Kerry had complained about the wound, but Mom thought the cut over her eye was more serious because it had bled so much. The doctors wanted to operate, but Kerry had said no. She'd wait until she got home.

From the looks of the hospital, I didn't blame her. But was it safe to travel?

"The doctor says it's OK," Lori said. "I talked to my dad last night, and he's getting tickets for us to fly home on Wednesday."

I glanced at Kerry. An IV tube snaked like a power cord from her forearm, but its infusion of energy appeared minimal. Her chest rose almost imperceptibly under the loose-fitting hospital gown.

Lori explained that Gary had stayed with the boat at Rangiroa, an island northeast of Tahiti. The Spellbound had been directed there after the crew of an airplane spotted the boat adrift north of the island.

Despite keeping our voices at a whisper, Kerry's eyes opened, fearful and disoriented. They softened as they fastened on Lori, then me. I leaned over to hug her, but she held up a restraining hand.

"I want to," she said, "but—" She gestured at her head.

I squeezed her hands instead and neither of us spoke for a moment. Her blondish hair, in need of a wash, splayed across pillows that propped her into a half-sitting position. Her blue eyes were sunken and dull. She, too, looked thinner than I remembered. From the tray next to the bed, she picked up a glass and sipped some water.

"These past few days have been hell for you," I said.

She nodded, dabbing her eyes.

"Are you sure you want to go home right away? Head injuries are nothing to fool around with."

She nodded. "I don't want to leave here like Frankenstein's monster."

I stifled a laugh. Her skull might be cracked, but it had not softened her tongue. "I'm going out front to see if anyone has showed up for work yet," I said. "I need to make arrangements for Mom and Dad's bodies."

Kerry and Lori glanced at each other. Kerry swallowed.

"What?" I asked.

"They're not here," Kerry said.

"Aunt Vivian told me . . ."

She turned her head toward the window. "They were buried at sea."

"I don't understand."

"Gary said that was the best thing to do. That the bodies were decomposing."

I stared at her as my mind wedged this new piece of information into the expanding puzzle of my parents' demise.

Kerry's face reddened. "Gary took care of it. He wouldn't let us look at them. He said it would be too shocking. So Lori and I stayed in the cabin. It was hotter than hell, and we were lost, and we didn't know how long it would be before we got to an island."

"And that was it?" I asked, my voice rising. "He just tossed them over the side like bags of garbage?"

Kerry covered her face with her hands. "Don't yell at me, Larry. There was nothing we could do."

I took a deep breath, then spoke in a calmer tone. "Did you catch the tail end of that typhoon?"

Kerry shook her head, wiping away more tears. "No, there wasn't much wind. That's why we were motoring. Dad wanted to get to Tahiti as fast as possible so he could fly home and see Grandpa Edwards."

"Then how'd you get hit by the boom?"

"I didn't."

"But Gary said—"

"I know, but that's not what happened."

"Then what—"

Kerry lowered her voice to a whisper. "I don't remember. I must have gotten up to get some water, then fallen and hit my head on the corner of a cabinet or something. All I remember is laying down on the settee to go to sleep and then waking up with my head hurting like hell and I couldn't breathe."

"You were knocked unconscious?"

"I think so, but I don't know for how long." She said no one else had seen or heard anything. It had been dark and everyone but Gary was asleep. "He was outside steering the boat. And you know how loud that engine is."

"Don't I though," I said. "How'd you get back to the settee?"

"I guess I crawled back and just don't remember it. The doctor said I have a concussion."

My skin tingled in alarm. "So Dad was still OK at that point?"

"Yeah, he got hurt a little later when he fell."

"He wasn't hit by the boom, either?"

She shook her head, then uttered a soft moan.

"Were there big seas?"

"I only know what Gary told me. I was in the cabin, and Mom was with me, and Lori was asleep. He said Dad was stepping up onto the deck and then lost his balance and fell over backward."

"Why didn't Gary say that in the first place?"

"You'll have to ask him."

I looked away. Outside, a gust of wind rustled the wide leaves of what looked like a banana tree; rain spattered the window. Lori stood and walked to the bathroom.

I asked Kerry, "What happened to Mom?"

She swallowed again, hesitating before responding. "She . . . she killed herself."

"But Gary said—"

I gazed unseeing at the wall behind the beds, conscious of my shallow breathing and pounding heartbeat. I had pictured a battered and wind-blown Spellbound pitching and rolling in heavy seas, the decks awash, the main boom swinging out of control, as they all fought for their lives. But as I heard a story so different, my mind raced to catch up, to assemble the jumble of pieces into a coherent picture.

"It doesn't make sense," I said.

"For the second time, her husband had been killed in an accident."

"Still . . . with you hurt. Was she despondent? Did she leave a note?"

"No note, and she seemed all right, under the circumstances. She told me and Lori that everything would be OK. That we'd get to Tahiti and sell the boat and fly home."

"Something changed."

She spoke without inflection, like an actor in a B movie. "Obviously she was upset about Dad, and having his body—"

"Did she overdose on painkillers?" I asked.

Kerry gazed out the window. "Gun."

"She shot herself?"

Still looking away from me, Kerry nodded.

"Where?"

"In the head, where do you think?"

"I mean where on the boat?"

"In the cockpit. She was steering."

"Not in their cabin?"

"I just said she was in the cockpit, didn't I?"

"Where were you?"

"I was laying on the settee, and Lori was in the galley," Kerry said. "Gary was on deck, reading or something. I heard a gunshot, and I jumped up and looked out the window. Mom's face was covered in blood. Gary said he found the gun next to her."

"The shotgun?"

"His pistol."

I stared at her, incredulous. "How'd she get hold of that?"

"I don't know! Why are you picking on me? You're acting like I did something wrong."

"I'm just trying to make sense of it. First you, then Dad, then Mom . . ."

I paced the length of the room. At the rear door, I stepped outside and gulped the moist air. The smattering of rain had turned into a downpour and drummed a battle march on broad leaves.

After a moment, I returned to the room as Lori stepped out of the bathroom. "This is unbelievable," I said. "There's no way Mom killed herself, especially with a gun."

"She had told me she might leave the boat when it reached Papeete," Lori said.

"What?"

"Because of Gary."

Hands clenched, I started to swing a fist at the wall, then spotted a small wastebasket and kicked it instead. The scapegoat arced toward the interior doorway, then smacked to the floor as three uniformed men entered the room. Two were middle-aged and appeared to be of European descent, the third a young, tawny-skinned Tahitian. Scenes of *Casablanca* flickered through my mind. The lead man looked at the wastebasket, then at me, his lips pursed. He issued a command in French.

I shrugged and shook my head. Frenchy repeated his command to the Tahitian, who translated it into English. He identified the speaker as Lieutenant Something-or-other and interpreted the ensuing exchange:

"You must leave," the lieutenant said.

"What's going on?" I demanded.

"Who are you?"

"Larry Edwards, Kerry's brother."

"We must talk to Kerry—alone," he said and turned to Lori. "You are Lori Oskam?"

She nodded.

"You must leave also."

"I don't understand," I said.

"It is an investigation. It will be explained later." When I didn't move, he raised his voice and waved toward the door. "Go! Report to the Gendarmerie at four o'clock."

I glared at the man for a moment, then said to Kerry, "We'll be back as soon as possible."

Tears moistened her eyes; fear incised her face.

Lori and I left the room. In the corridor, she leaned against the wall and sobbed. "I'm so scared," she said.

I put a hand on her shoulder. "All you have to do is tell the truth."

5

Monday, February 27, 1978, 3:45 P.M.

Lori and I trudged up the hill to the police station, the Gendarmerie, a cluster of tin-roofed structures. Trees and leafy undergrowth surrounded the colonial-style buildings, and the compound's gates appeared perpetually open. No one had stormed that bastille in years. I glanced over my shoulder. Lush vegetation blocked the view of the harbor below and the dozens of sailboats lining the quay. A sullen sky glowered overhead, the air steamy.

The double doors of the central building stood open, like a pair of sentinels. I paused on the veranda and Lori looked at me, her face taut with anxiety. I squeezed her hand. "We'll get through this, then you and Kerry can go home."

She sucked in a chestful of air, then exhaled in a whoosh. We stepped into the narrow foyer, and I told the clerk who we were. He waved at a pair of wicker chairs. A moment later, the lanky interpreter we'd met that morning led us to a small office at the right side of the building.

The lieutenant who had ordered us from the hospital sat behind a wooden desk and shot us an accusatory glance. I guessed his age at about forty, his features unremarkable other than his Gallic nose. The interpreter, about my age but a head taller, directed us to a pair of cushionless wooden chairs. As the interpreter closed the door, Lori shivered. Never mind the sauna-like atmosphere.

I touched her arm. "It's going to be OK. It's just a routine inquiry so they can fill out their reports in triplicate." I failed to convince even myself. Still, maybe the lieutenant could elicit more satisfactory answers than I had.

The lieutenant, through the interpreter, asked where I had been at the time of the deaths. He also wondered if, while I crewed aboard the boat before it left San Diego, there had been disputes or had everyone gotten along. The only significant problems were between Gary and me, and I didn't see how that had any bearing on my parents' deaths.

"Have you talked to my brother?" I asked.

"I ask the questions," he said and continued his inquiry into the relationships on the boat. I didn't have much to tell him. My parents' letters had indicated they were having a good time.

Lori endured the brunt of his interrogation and sobbed as she repeated what she had told me that morning: She saw and heard very little because she was asleep when Kerry and Dad were injured, and she was in the galley getting Kerry a glass of water when Mom killed herself.

"How convenient for you," the lieutenant muttered. He shook his head as he jotted down her answers. Then he looked up and glared at Lori. "There was drinking on the boat, disagreements, fights, a melee," he said.

"No, nothing like that. We all got along."

"Lies!" he shouted and slammed his fist on the desk. His pen bounced to the floor.

I shouted back. "Stop bullying her!"

He turned to me and narrowed his eyes. "*Allez!*" he said and pointed toward the door.

I went, hoping I hadn't made things worse for Lori. I wondered why we'd been questioned together in the first place.

In the foyer, Tom Rutherford*, a friend of my parents and fellow cruiser, sat in one of the wicker chairs. His white hair and mustache stood out against his dark skin, tanned from many months at sea. He rose to his feet and shook my hand, offering his condolences.

"What's with the fireworks?" he asked.

"I called the lieutenant a bully. Now he's browbeating Lori without any interference from me."

"I tried to visit Kerry at the hospital, but the gendarme at the door gave me the bum's rush."

"We're not allowed to speak to her either."

"Why the third degree?"

"He's insisting that my father's death was not an accident, that my mother didn't kill herself. He says they were a bunch of drunks and things got out of hand."

"That's crazy! Your folks—and the girls," he added with a wink, "liked to have a good time, but who doesn't? If it wasn't for your dad, I'd be stuck in Nuka Hiva, and your mom nursed everybody's cuts and scrapes and no-no bites. It's an unfortunate tragedy. End of story."

"I think these guys are bored. This is probably the biggest thing to happen here in years. They won't tell me anything about my brother, either."

"Why don't you ask him yourself?"

"What do you mean?"

He glanced around before whispering, "He's out back," then pointed toward the rear of the building. "Go into the courtyard and turn left toward the *toilette*. You'll see him."

I found Gary in a small room that served as a temporary jail cell. Vertical bars ribboned the open window, but the room had a conventional door that stood open, allowing air to circulate. A burly Tahitian sat on a stool outside of the cell. Gary paced like a zoo lion, his sun-bleached hair a tangled mane. A white T-shirt hung from his shoulders, faded blue jeans clung to narrow hips. He had the gaunt look of a shipwrecked sailor. Gary and I had our differences, but things had changed. Sure, I had questions about what happened on the boat, but seeing him caged by ill-tempered cops sparked a raw animal instinct and put me in a defensive frame of mind. We had to close ranks.

"Gary!" I said.

When he saw me, relief flooded his face. I stepped toward the door, but the guard motioned for me to leave. I retreated to a safe distance and called out, "When did you get here?"

"They picked me up at the airport this afternoon."

The fuckers. Wouldn't even tell me they had him in custody.

Gauze swaddled Gary's right forearm and hand. "What happened to you?"

Before he could reply, the guard uttered a command. It required no translation.

"I'll be waiting out front," I said.

I rejoined Tom in the foyer and sank into the empty chair. "The gorilla ran me off, but at least Gary knows I'm here."

"I didn't want to mess with that guy, either," Tom said. "He could be a middle linebacker for the Dallas Cowboys."

We sat for a moment without speaking. In the deepening twilight, bugs fluttered around the lights on the veranda. The wind had died, leaving the air dank and oppressive.

"I'm sure gonna miss your folks," Tom said. "A couple of the nicest people I ever met, always willing to lend a hand to others. Your dad fixed my generator and repaired my mast after it cracked. Wouldn't take a penny for it, either. Then he got word about his father. How's he doing? Your grandfather, I mean."

"Not well. My dad and I were supposed to meet in L.A. next week and—" I choked up and couldn't finish. The interpreter reappeared and summoned me back to the interrogation room.

Lori still sat in the hot seat, eyes red-rimmed and puffy, fingers shredding a tissue in her lap. The lieutenant wanted to know where we'd be staying. I told him, and he emphasized that we were not to visit Kerry. As Lori and I left the room, I whispered to her that she should ask to use the restroom. When she returned, she said the guard had chased her away, but not before she'd said hello to Gary.

Tom escorted her to the quay, where a family had invited us to stay with them aboard their sailboat. I remained at the Gendarmerie to find out whether Gary would be released or not. After three days with almost no sleep, I nodded off, my mind swirling with images of Gary, like Papillon, trying to escape from Devil's Island.

The sound of feet on the hard floor startled me awake. I rubbed my eyes, then poked my head around the corner as the guard led my brother to the door of the interrogation room.

Gary stopped and we exchanged worried looks. "I'll wait for you," I said.

He nodded and stepped into the room; the door closed. I could hear muffled voices but couldn't understand what was said. I wanted to put my ear to the door, but the guard had taken a seat at a desk outside the room. I pulled a chair up to a small table near an open window and wrote an entry in my journal:

> *Nightmare City! I'm at the Gendarmerie, Fr. Polynesia. One of the men is "interviewing" Gary. He finished with Lori and me about 7:00 P.M. The bastards are accusing the three of them, especially Gary, of murdering Mom & Dad! They'll finish with Kerry tomorrow morning.*

Exhausted, I fell asleep with my head on the table, my journal for a pillow. Later, an opening door woke me: a bathroom break. As Gary walked to the rear of the building, the interpreter approached me. "A long way to go," he said. "No need to stay."

My shirt clung to hot, sticky skin, muscles cramped, joints ached. I wanted nothing more than a soothing bath and twelve hours of uninterrupted sleep. "I'll wait," I said. Gary returned a few minutes later and paused, looking my way. "How are you holding up?" I asked.

"I'll have a nervous breakdown when I get home."

The guard nudged him into the room. I fell asleep again and didn't wake until the four-hour interrogation ended. The little hand of the wall clock pointed to eleven. I had been in Tahiti for eighteen hours. It felt like eighteen days.

They released Gary, although we were to return the next morning. The lieutenant, after playing bad cop all evening, offered us a ride to the quay, about a half-mile away. "We'll walk," I said.

The air had cooled, and the hike down the hill would give me a chance to talk to Gary alone. He stood next to me on the veranda and gnawed on a fingernail. I started down the stairs.

"Where're we headed?" he asked.

"The Weavers* invited us to stay with them until we go to Rangiroa to get the *Spellbound*," I said. "They say they met Mom and Dad in the Marquesas."

"I know the boat. Eighty-five-foot ketch."

I fell silent. I wanted to ask him so many things, but I wasn't sure of the best way to begin. I opted for the back door. "Did you know Kerry has a fractured skull?"

"Yeah, the Gestapo told me about it. Wanted to know if I got drunk and beat her up. Or if Dad did it, and did I get hurt trying to defend her. Did see her?"

"This morning. Then the gendarmes arrived and kicked Lori and me out. She seemed to be holding up pretty well, all things considered."

"Did you call Aunt Vivian?"

"I called Aileen. She'll get in touch with Vivian," I said, then nodded toward his arm. "What happened?"

"A spinning winch handle."

"Have you seen a doctor?"

"It's not broken, but I think I tore some ligaments in my wrist. Hurts like hell. The heavy bandage is in case I bump it against something."

"When did it happen?"

"A couple days before Dad died."

Rather than look directly at Gary, I kept my eyes on the pavement, in part to keep from stumbling in the dark, in part to appear conversational rather than accusatory. "The gendarmes believe it happened during a fight. A 'melee,' they called it."

"I told them exactly what happened a thousand times," Gary said. "But those assholes want to make this the crime of the century."

I nodded. "They're looking for inconsistencies in your stories, between you and Kerry and Lori."

"They won't find any."

"You said Dad and Kerry were hit by the boom, but Kerry said that wasn't true."

Gary sighed. "The whole world was listening to those radio calls, and I wanted to wait until I got to an island so I could talk privately on a landline before giving all the details."

I had more questions, but I kept quiet as we continued down the hill, conscious of the badgering he'd endured. When we neared the quay, however, I wanted one more explanation while we were by ourselves. "I'm still puzzled by Dad's accident. After years of living on the boat and safely crossing the ocean, how the hell did he fall in the cockpit?"

"Didn't the girls tell you what happened?"

"I'd like to hear it from you."

"You'll have to wait. I haven't slept in three days, and I don't feel like being interrogated again." He turned and continued on toward the quay.

Stunned by his answer, I stood motionless, staring at his back as he walked away.

I'm trying, Gary. I'm really trying. But you're still an asshole.

After a moment, I followed him to the Weavers' boat. The Pegasus exemplified the type of craft I had dreamt of owning. I preferred a schooner rig, but the big ketch still showcased a classic sheer line and had an expansive teak deck, fine woodwork, and varnished mahogany trim gleaming under the streetlights. The plank-hulled yacht of 1920s vintage bespoke of wealth I'd be unlikely to experience firsthand.

I watched Gary go aboard. Lori rushed out of the cabin and threw her arms around him. He parried her questions, saying they'd talk later. I joined them, and Pam Weaver* led us to the crew quarters. It consisted of four narrow bunks shoehorned into the bow, along with bulging sail bags, coils of line, and the ubiquitous foul-weather gear draped over pegs. Nonetheless, compared to the Spellbound it was spacious.

The next morning, Tom Rutherford hailed us as we relished coffee and croissants on the aft deck. He held up a newspaper and said, "Have you seen this?"

I didn't read French, but the headline and photo of Gary on the front page were self-explanatory: "*La Tragedie du 'Spellbound': Gary EDWARDS a Tahiti depuis hier.*"

"Fuck," I muttered, imagining a lurid description of my parents' deaths.

I accepted the paper and turned to the full-page story inside. It had more pictures of Gary's arrival at Faa'a Airport. One image showed him walking on the tarmac, briefcase in hand, as if on his way to a business meeting.

Gary had taken French in high school and translated the gist of it for Lori and me: Bad luck aboard the Spellbound had resulted in the tragic deaths; the yacht Tarvana had gone to aid the Spellbound and led it back to the island of Rangiroa in the Tuamotu Islands; Loren Edwards had died in an accident, and his wife, Joanne, increasingly despondent over the sight of her husband's dead body, had taken her own life; the gendarmes were investigating but saying little about it.

When he finished, Gary scoffed. "They're saying the boat is made of ferro-cement. Can't they tell the difference between cement and fiberglass? The dumb shits couldn't even get Kerry and Lori's names right—'Corey' and 'Susan Hoskam.'"

I granted him a cursory nod, but the use of "despondent" to describe Mom's mental state had caught my ear. Neither Kerry nor Lori had characterized her as despondent or suicidal. I asked Lori about it.

"I don't know where they got that," she said. "Like I told you—"

Just then, two uniformed officers arrived. They ordered us to go with them to the Gendarmerie. I tensed, anticipating another shouting match with Lieutenant Bableonaneaux, or whatever the hell his name was. Instead, they took us to a woman, a government attorney, who instructed us to read and sign our statements.

"The investigation is over?" I asked.

She nodded. "Sign and you may go."

"What about my sister?"

"She will be released from the hospital tomorrow."

6

Wednesday, March 1, 1978

"That lieutenant, I swear his favorite phrase was 'Lies! Lies!' " Kerry said. We were in a taxi on our way to the airport. "And those yokels at that so-called hospital—Mom did a better job caring for me than they did."

I shot a recriminating glance at my sister, her glib tongue violating the sanctity shrouding our parents' deaths. When she caught my squinted gaze, her breezy tone dissolved to a murmur. "I can't get out of this hellhole soon enough."

I sighed and touched her arm. "You've earned a moment of levity."

After seeing Kerry and Lori aboard their flight home, Gary and I purchased tickets for our comparatively short hop to Rangiroa on Friday. A wave of anxiety passed through me. Would the yellow ketch be red with blood or other signs of death? Then the thought of sailing the boat home with Gary distressed me more. I had abandoned the trip in San Diego because of him—when our parents were still alive. Could I spend a month at sea with him, without their moderating influence?

Things are different now. We'll pull together. We have to.

When Gary and I returned to the Pegasus, a man standing nearby introduced himself as Al Prince, editor of the *Tahiti Bulletin*, an English-language weekly. "I'm sure you had a rough time with the gendarmes," he said to Gary, "but do you mind answering a few questions?"

"I don't mind," Gary said, "but you better get the story straight. Not like those idiots with the French papers. And I want to read it before it goes to press. Otherwise, if there are any errors, I'll have to sue you."

Prince thought a moment, then nodded. We went aboard the boat and Gary laid out the story. Pretty much what I'd heard from Kerry and Lori, but with more detail about being low on fuel and not knowing where they were. It sounded plausible, although Gary gave evasive answers to questions about how he got lost in the swarm of islands known as the Tuamotu Archipelago.

After the editor left, I asked Gary about the events following Mom's death, but he refused to answer. "Like I said, I've been interrogated enough by the Keystone Cops. You just heard everything I have to say."

Prince returned that afternoon with a draft. Gary lingered over it, occasionally scoffing as he had while reading the story in the French-language paper. "You'll have to correct these mistakes," he said. "Some of the dates are wrong; Lori is a family friend, not my girlfriend; and my stepmother was forty-three."

We went to the newspaper office to oversee the changes. I had hoped Gary might reveal new information to the editor. But I learned nothing substantive, and I tired of Gary's haranguing—he insisted that he be quoted word for word, not paraphrased.

I went to the post office, the only place in town that offered international telephone service to the public. From there, I called Aileen, who said she and Bobbie, along with Lori's parents, would meet Kerry and Lori at the airport. I told her about Gary and the newspaper editor, and said, "The French-language papers already have it plastered on the front page."

"It's front-page news here, too," she said and read me the headlines. "The *Post-Intelligencer* says, '2 Deaths: A Mystery in Tahiti,' and *The Seattle Times* has 'Confusion Clouds Deaths on Yacht.' The reporters call me every day."

My parents had hoped to write a book about their trip. Sadly, their story was being written for them, and not with a happy-ever-after ending.

Aileen and I said good-bye, and I wandered through town, in no hurry to return to the Pegasus. Small shops in aging colonial buildings lined narrow streets, reminiscent of Tijuana, Mexico. I stopped at a café for a sandwich and coffee—tiny cup, no refills. Abandoned newspapers littered the tables, my brother's picture on prominent display. I understood Gary's desire for accuracy in the news stories, but, in the words of the Bard, doth he protest too much?

I left the café in search of the public market, hoping to find some fresh fruit, but the market had closed for the day. A bar with a neon sign in the window advertising Tahiti's Hinano beer looked enticing. I could drown a few sorrows there. Then I thought better of it and retraced my steps to the quay.

I found Gary sitting in the cockpit of the Pegasus. When I clambered aboard, he glanced my way but said nothing.

"Get everything you wanted?" I asked.

"Meaning what?"

"From Jimmy Olsen, cub reporter."

"Of course," he said, then picked up a French-language paper, different from the one we'd seen earlier but with a familiar headline.

"Anything new?" I asked.

"Same ol' shit," he said.

I waited to see if he had anything to add. When he said nothing, I went below for a glass of water. As I returned to the aft deck, I heard a "*bon jour*" from the quay.

"Tati!" Gary responded and stood to greet a Tahitian man. Gary offered a hand and helped the man aboard.

Francis Sanford, known to friends as "Tati," had met my parents in the Marquesas Islands, where he'd been campaigning for reelection as a deputy in the territorial assembly. My father had ferried him and his entourage between the islands. In exchange, Dad received 80,000 French Polynesian francs, or about eight hundred U.S. dollars, which Dad planned to use for the flight home to see his dying father. Tati had paid my father under the table, since local regulations forbade foreign vessels from taking inter-island passengers for hire.

The slender man defied the burly Polynesian stereotype and wore a silk shirt neatly tucked into pleated slacks. He looked around the boat. "Bigger than Spellbound," he said, spreading his arms. "Maybe less sick, oui?"

I shrugged. "Perhaps."

"You come my house, meet family, we eat," he said, looking from me to Gary.

"*Oui*," Gary said.

At Tati's house, situated on the outskirts of town, we met his wife and teenage daughter. Both looked like models for a travel brochure. Their home sported a modern Euro-style living room and kitchen, but the bedrooms recalled the more rustic island accommodations of yesteryear: thin mattresses lying on the floor, tented in mosquito netting.

We sat around the dining table and Tati's wife served *poison cru*, curried beef, and the trademark French baguette, which we washed down with wine and beer. I thought it was dinner and did not hold back, only to learn we were eating appetizers. Dinner, Tati explained, would be at a restaurant in town. There we would join his two sisters and their families in a celebration of his election victory.

He refilled our wine glasses and said, "Your father and mother, very nice people, friends to me. I sick on boat—" He put a hand on his belly and leaned over, as if vomiting, then laughed. "They help me. Is very sad."

I nodded as the fountain refilled my eyes.

The meal at the restaurant began with a tasty soup, never mind the hot, humid weather. Platters of grilled vegetables, shrimp, duck, octopus, and rice filled the broad table, along with crusty bread and bottomless bottles of French wine.

I gorged myself, abandoning any attempt at self-control. With the investigation behind us and Kerry safely homeward bound, I wanted to put the heartache of my parents' deaths behind me, if only for a night. I drifted into a euphoric never-never land where all was right with the world, abandoning any thoughts of why I had been obliged to visit the exotic port.

The next morning aboard the Pegasus, my head punished me for the previous night's sins. I gratefully accepted a cup of coffee from Pam Weaver and watched the shoreside activities in silence as Gary regaled her about our night out with Tati. She listened politely but fidgeted in her seat, as if she were thinking, didn't your parents just die? Before he could finish, a pair of gendarmes pulled up in a Jeep-like vehicle and beeped the horn.

I groaned. "I thought we were done with them."

The driver spoke: "*Demain, vous allez à gendarmerie à quatre heure.*"

"We're supposed to go back up the hill at four o'clock," Gary said.

I turned to the driver. "*Pourquoi?*" Having heard "why" used so often during the preceding days, I could speak at least one French word with authority.

He shrugged. "*Apportez vos passeport.*"

Gary translated. "He said to bring your—"

"Passport, yeah. I figured that much. What about you?"

"They confiscated mine on Monday."

"*Vous comprenez?*" the gendarme inquired.

"*Si, si. Yo comprendo,*" I said, reverting to Spanish as I waved him away.

AT THE GENDARMERIE, Gary and I took seats opposite a man who introduced himself as Captain Michel Bereze. At least we'd moved up a rung. The door stood open to better circulate the sea breeze coming through the open windows. Again, the interpreter translated for us.

"I must have your passport," Captain Bereze said to me.

"Why?"

"You are not to leave Tahiti."

"What about Rangiroa?"

He shook his head.

"But we have tickets to fly there tomorrow—*pour le bateau*, to go to the boat. Besides, Gary needs clean clothes. He's been wearing the same shirt for the past four days." I pinched my nose for emphasis, trying to lighten the moment.

The captain offered a faint smile. "Is not my problem."

"This is bullshit!" I shouted. "Our boat is sitting up there unattended. For all we know, it's being looted."

"The gendarmes watch the boat. It is sealed."

"Sealed? I thought—"

"You cannot leave," he said and handed me a telegram—from the Honolulu office of the United States Federal Bureau of Investigation.

7

Saturday, March 4, 1978

Three American agents came by the Pegasus, two from the FBI, one from the U.S. Coast Guard. They instructed Gary and me to meet them at the Gendarmerie the next day.

The trio had dressed casually in shorts and flowered shirts, as if on their way to a beach party. But these were not your friendly neighborhood cops on a meet-'n'-greet. Their narrowed eyes focused mostly on Gary, predators sizing up their prey.

If it had any effect on him, he didn't show it. After they left, he said, "I have nothing to hide."

I rescheduled our flight to Rangiroa, then walked to the post office. Phoned Aileen. Asked her about Kerry and Lori.

"We were mobbed at the airport by reporters," she said.

"We're getting harassed by them here, too."

"TV cameras, flashbulbs, microphones shoved in our faces. Like running a gauntlet."

"Vultures."

"*The Seattle Times* has a huge picture of us on the front page and the headline says, 'Survivors Voted for Sea Burial.' The *Post-Intelligencer* has a front-page article, too."

"Did you speak to them?"

"Lori's dad did, but he's the only one."

Aileen said Kerry's surgery had gone well and the doctor assured Kerry that she'd be as good as new. But before the surgery, an FBI agent had visited Kerry at the hospital and spoken to her alone. "Kerry says the agent asked her the same questions as the police in Tahiti, and she gave the same answers."

"We're meeting with the Feds tomorrow afternoon," I said.

"I wonder what's going on. The *Times* quoted an FBI guy who says, 'There is no evidence of foul play.' "

Sunday, March 5, 1978

I rose before dawn, having tossed in my bunk most of the night, wrestling with uninvited cacodemons.

I shuffled along the quay as Ol' Sol peeked over the eastern horizon. The boats sat motionless, their denizens below deck, asleep or downing their first swallows of wake-me-up. The odd burgee fluttered in the sputtering breeze, and drying laundry, that universal symbol of humanity, draped lifelines. The homeports painted on the boats' transoms offered a lesson in global geography—Darling Harbour, Australia; Newport Beach, California; Gig Harbor, Washington; Nuku'alofa, Tonga; Victoria, British Columbia; Veerhaven, The Netherlands; Sète, France. A strange brew of wealthy vacationers, hedonists, and the disenfranchised—escapists all, running from their own demons. Their common denominator a boat: some ornate yachts, others rust-streaked derelicts. Whatever the condition, that floating platform punched their ticket to paradise.

I imagined the Spellbound moored there, "Kirkland, Washington," stenciled on its yellow transom, my parents on deck, beaming self-satisfied grins, morning coffee cradled in their hands, chatting with new acquaintances.

The wail of a siren, a shrieking icon of my presence at the remote rendezvous, shattered the image.

THE GENDARMERIE, YET again. I thought I'd finished with that unhappy enclave of officialdom. I had anticipated my departure from

Tahiti and putting the ugly chapter behind me, only to be yanked back as authorities from two countries whipsawed my emotions: anguish to relief to fear.

At one-thirty, the FBI agents ushered Gary and me into an unfamiliar room. A large table occupied most of it, leaving only narrow spaces for the chairs. My brother and I squeezed into seats against the exterior wall, where a refreshing breeze wafted through open windows. The agents sat opposite, their flinty orbs pinning us to the wall.

The man in charge—I dubbed him Steely Eyes—had exchanged his Hawaiian shirt for a starched white that set off a weathered face taut with authority, his short dark hair parted to perfection. Stoneface, the sidekick, had selected blue Oxford cloth, his sandy hair windblown. The burly Coast Guardsman—did he say his name was Cookie?—wore a regulation pale-blue, short-sleeved shirt and navy-blue trousers. Their semiformal attire contrasted with my T-shirt and shorts, and Gary's ratty shirt and blue jeans. At least Gary's clothes had been laundered.

We settled into our chairs and faced off across the table. A divided loyalty clawed my gut, on the one hand pulling me toward Gary, to protect him against the assault of implacable authority figures. Yet, part of me wanted to join the interrogators. Ultimately, though, I had no choice. I had to side with family.

Steely Eyes opened a manila folder containing a stack of documents and set out a pad of lined paper. He examined Gary with a penetrating stare that softened a degree as his eyes shifted to me. "We're sorry about your parents' deaths," he said.

"Thank you," I replied. "But why are you here? We signed off with the gendarmes on Wednesday."

"It was determined, by what your brother told the French authorities, that this incident took place aboard a boat traveling in international waters. When that happens, the vessel's country of origin has jurisdiction and, in this case, that's the United States of America."

I rolled my eyes at his bureaucratese. "I understand the juris-diction, but one of your guys told *The Seattle Times* there's no evidence of foul play."

"That's what we're here to find out."

"Either you believe there's something amiss or you don't," I said. "We were told the investigation was over, that we're free to go. Now we're being treated like criminals."

The earlier hint of compassion vanished. "Mr. Edwards, we invited you here as a courtesy, to explain to you that we have serious questions about how your sister was injured and how your parents died. We are not here to debate the merits of our presence with you. You'll have to leave while we interview your brother."

His ferrous gaze drilled deep and I shivered. As I stood, I slammed the chair against the wall, but it elicited no response from the agents. Stoneface opened the door for me.

I stopped in the doorway. "How long will this take?"

"Several hours, I'm sure."

I looked at Gary, slouched in the chair, his face blank, staring at the ceiling as if bored—but his nail-biting told me a different story. "Will you let him go when you're done?"

"Depends."

"On what?"

"On what he tells us."

OUTSIDE, I LOOKED for a way to lurk below the windows and listen, but shrubbery grew close to the building and the windows were too high to hear anything more than an occasional word. A stern glance from a passing gendarme warned me away.

I wandered up the road that led past the Gendarmerie toward Tahiti's mountainous interior. Ramshackle structures with rusted, corrugated roofing perched on the steepening hillside—doubtless the homes of underpaid natives working at the posh tourist hotels lining the lagoon.

"Paradise. Yeah, right," I muttered. I kicked a fallen breadfruit, a pimpled green globe the size of a volleyball, scattering chunks of white pulp in the foliage. A bird chuckled at me from a tree branch. I picked up a bit of pulp and pitched it in his direction. "Fuck you!"

I closed my eyes and consciously breathed. Mom had always said, "Count to ten when you're mad." But what do you do when you're clobbered by another roundhouse punch: the possibility that she and Dad had died under suspicious circumstances?

It couldn't be happening.

Not to my family.

I sensed rivulets of tears on my cheeks and in my beard. The bird again squawked from its perch. I picked up another piece of breadfruit and cocked my arm. But the creature's flamboyant colors and sidelong gaze deflated my impulse. I let the chunk of fruit slip from my grasp.

Beyond the tree, La Diademe, the basaltic upthrust that had forged the island in a fit of fiery eruptions eons past, rose nearly eight thousand feet. The vulcan summit played peekaboo among the wreath of clouds prancing around it. I glimpsed a cave high up the mountain—at least I imagined that dark spot to be a cave—and I yearned to crawl deep inside, away from the heartache.

I plodded back to the Gendarmerie and was sitting on the front steps when Agent Steely Eyes emerged. I looked up but said nothing.

"Let's take a walk," he said.

He led me through the gate and stopped in the shadow of a leafy tree. "I don't know how close you are to Gary . . ." he began, then paused.

I shrugged. "We're brothers. Sometimes we get along, sometimes we don't."

"A half-dozen French and American doctors have examined the X-rays of your sister's wound," the agent said. "They all came to the same conclusion: Kerry did not have an accident."

Numbed by his words, I stared into the distance.

He continued. "The fracture was caused by a forcible blow with a blunt instrument. A gun butt, maybe a wrench. Your brother said Kerry found a large Crescent wrench under a cushion on the settee."

A lump filled my throat and I struggled to breathe.

"I suggest you have a heart-to-heart with your brother," Steely Eyes said. "Maybe he'll tell you more than he's telling us."

My heart pounded like a fist on a locked door, as if trying to escape. I balled my hands, ready to smash the man's marble mouth and silence the ugly words. He would drive a wedge between me and my brother, pit us against each other, force me to turn coat and help them, the inquisitors, wring a confession from Gary. But what about *my* soul? Did that mean nothing to them? Was I merely an expendable lever with which to tighten their torturous rack?

I shifted my eyes to meet his. "What's he telling you?"

"I'm not at liberty to say, but I'm sure you've heard most of it. Between you and me and this tree, we're concerned about the bodies being dumped over the side and his banged-up arm and why it took so long to get to an island."

"You think he's lying."

"Let's just say it raises a lot of questions to which we are getting less than satisfactory answers," he said and walked away.

I slumped against the tree and sagged to the ground, forehead on my knees. My mind reeled with the implications. Could it be true? Did Gary hit Kerry? Was it one of the others? Certainly Dad or Mom wouldn't attack their own daughter, would they? And Lori? She was a mouse.

Could someone from another boat have come aboard? Modern-day pirates were a genuine threat. That's why Dad had taken the rifle and shotgun with him—and, ostensibly, why Gary had brought his pistol aboard. But if they had been attacked by others, Gary and Kerry would have said so. That left someone aboard the Spellbound.

Gary?

But why? What could have provoked such an attack?

The Fibbies must be lying, throwing shit at the wall. Having participated in Vietnam War protests, I had a knee-jerk distrust of authority figures. Even so, didn't I have my own doubts about what Kerry and Gary had told me? I wanted to believe them.

But could I?

Could I trust Gary?

I returned to the Gendarmerie, a tornado of possibilities whirling my mind. I settled into the familiar wicker chair, again waiting for an interrogation to end. My world had become a Picasso painting; I wished for Gauguin.

I nodded off. When I woke, full dark cloaked the island. Nearly six hours had elapsed since the "interview" began.

I thought about going aboard the Spellbound the next day and not seeing Mom and Dad. Tears welled up. Would they ever stop?

I rose and stepped outside onto the porch. Through the trees, I could see the yellow glow of streetlights that paralleled the quay.

A few minutes later, Captain Bereze joined me. He wore civilian clothes, officially off duty but no doubt curious about the interrogation. "*C'est bon?*" he asked.

I stared at him, failing not only to comprehend his words but his apparent attempt at polite conversation.

"*Excusez-moi* . . . it is good?" he continued, making an effort to speak English.

I shook my head and looked back toward the harbor. "No, it's not good," I murmured.

He nodded. "*Non, je suppose pas.*"

I looked at him in the faint light. He blushed and fidgeted. I almost felt sorry for him. He had tried to make a conciliatory gesture, but the language barrier left him sounding foolish. He turned, offering his hand. "*Bonsoir*—good evening," he said. I shook his hand and he descended the stairs.

Another hour passed before my brother and the agents emerged, grim-faced. Gary's trademark swagger had vanished, along with his sneer. I checked for handcuffs but saw none. I raised my eyebrows, questioning. He went outside without responding, filling his lungs with the cooler night air.

Steely Eyes stopped beside me. "We're through for now. We'll see you at the airport in the morning." He left the building, his two colleagues at his heels.

I stepped onto the veranda and stood beside Gary. I looked into his face but kept quiet, giving him a moment to relax. He glared at the agents' backs as if, by sheer will, he could vaporize them like an extraterrestrial foe in *Star Trek*.

"There's a reception aboard the Pegasus," I said and started down the stairs. "Let's go have a drink."

He fell in step and we walked in silence, the mood decidedly more subdued than when making the same trek five days earlier, when we thought the investigation was over. But after several minutes, the suspense got to me. "How'd it go?" I asked.

He took a moment before answering. "I guess they don't get enough excitement in Hawaii. Probably because Jack Lord solves all their cases for them."

I stopped, my jaw clenched. Would I ever get a straight answer from him? Did he feel nothing? Our parents were dead, yet his flippancy continued unabated. I had not seen him shed a grieving tear.

Gary moved on and I quickened my pace to catch up. When we reached the quay, I spoke again, trying to be calm and nonjudgmental. "One of the agents talked to me."

"So?"

"He says Kerry's injury was no accident."

Gary stopped and faced me, his features taut. "That's bullshit! Those fucking pigs just made that up to scare me."

"They also wonder why you dumped the bodies over the side, unless—"

His eyes flared, his lips curled. He jabbed a finger at me and said, his voice rising, "You weren't there. You don't know what it was like. We had two dead bodies laying on the deck in the sweltering sun, and they were decomposing. Rotting. They were beginning to smell. Then the boat ran out of fuel—or at least I thought we were out of fuel—and after drifting around, I didn't know where we were or how much longer we'd be stuck out there. What was I supposed to do, chop them up and stuff them in the icebox?"

I had hoped that if no other good came of the horrific tragedy, it would bridge the chasm that had separated my brother and me for so many years. But he didn't seem to want any part of it. Still, I had to weigh my desire to wring his neck against the need to gain his cooperation.

"Gary, I'm on your side here," I said. "I'm just telling you what he told me. That doctors will testify—"

"They're just guessing."

"Even so, it makes the FBI suspicious, and with the bodies buried at sea . . ."

"Yeah, yeah. Heard it all a hundred times."

"And your arm—"

"Wrist."

"Whatever. The point is—"

"I told you, I hurt it two days before Dad died. If you don't believe me, you can read his journal and see for yourself."

Gary spun about and strode toward the Pegasus. I wanted to tackle him, take him down, sit on his chest like I did when we were boys and subject him to The Torture, dribbling spittle on his forehead, then nose, as I inched it toward his smart-mouth.

I looked around. Looky-loos had stopped to stare, point, whisper. A man on a sailboat stepped to its stern and grasped the backstay, looking intently at me, then toward Gary. My family not only had to endure outrageous accusations from ruthless cops, we had become a spectacle, a public drama titillating insatiable voyeurs.

I shambled toward the Pegasus, recalling my conversation with Gary about Birth Woman, how he had described her heavy drinking. That had been years earlier, our most adult conversation ever.

Arriving in Tahiti, I had hoped, if naïvely, we could return to that moment, that we could reasonably discuss the grievous events that had taken place aboard the Spellbound. Was that even possible? I had assumed Gary had done nothing wrong. But he had been defensive from the start. At my echo of the Feds' concerns, he had become more so, as if I, too, were making warrantless accusations. I was supposed to shut up and take him at his word, no questions asked. Yet, if he had nothing to hide, why not be civil and talk to me?

8

Monday, March 6, 1978

Gary and I stood in line at the airport waiting to board the flight to Rangiroa. Al Prince, the newspaper editor, joined us. "Good morning," he said.

"It was," I replied.

"Look, I understand how you feel . . ."

I started to tell him that no, he didn't understand, but he continued.

"Your family sent a telegram to my office."

"About Kerry?"

"Sorry to be the bearer of bad news," he said, "but your dad's father died yesterday. I thought you'd like to know before you left for Rangiroa."

Through misty eyes, I looked at Gary, his face telling me nothing, then I glanced around. French tourists and Polynesians made up most of the passengers grouped on the tarmac. Smiles and laughter animated their conversations. I hated them for their nonchalance, their blithe disregard for my pain.

The morning sun pierced my face and arms, and I felt beads of sweat on my forehead as the humidity ratcheted upward. The thought of never seeing Grandpa Edwards again came as another kick to the gut. I blinked back tears and thanked Al for tracking us down.

He held out his hand, and I shook it. "Good luck," he said. "When do you think you'll get back here?"

I tilted my head toward the federal agents. "It's up to them, isn't it."

Aboard the plane, Gary and I sat together, a few rows behind the Feds and Coast Guard officer. The plane leveled out above the blue-gray Pacific. An occasional speck of white indicated a sailboat, a piece of lint afloat at Poseidon's whim.

I let my head fall back against the headrest, relieved to put Tahiti behind me. After a week of dealing with French officialdom and inquisitors from my own country, the fabled island left me with no pleasant memories.

For a moment, the prospect of being aboard the Spellbound again excited me. The boat lying at anchor at a tropical isle. Would it be as I had fantasized? Then Guilt knifed my conscience: *Have you forgotten why you're here?*

Had the fact of my parents' deaths truly sunk in? I hadn't seen their bodies. *Maybe they aren't really dead.*

I gazed down at the featureless expanse of ocean. What in hell could have caused this horror?

There had been tension before my parents left San Diego. But mostly that had been between Gary and me. I'd left the boat, hoping it would defuse things. But how did it end like this?

I looked at the man sitting next to me. My brother. Yet a man I didn't truly know. I think he sensed my eyes on him, for he blinked several times, but he looked straight ahead. We didn't speak during the hour-long flight.

As we came in for the landing at Rangiroa, the airplane's window framed the palm-studded atoll like a travel poster. Again, I imagined arriving as a vacationer, the anticipation of carefree lounging on the beach, umbrella drink in hand, and snorkeling in the world's second-largest lagoon. But seeing the bare masts of the death ship jolted me back to the reality of why I was there. My mind's eye filled with bloody bodies lying crumpled in the cockpit. I shook my head to clear the thought and focused on the forest of palms sprouting like a green mustache above the narrow lip of the submerged volcano.

After touching down, we went to the Kia Ora Village resort hotel. Gary and I waited in the hotel's open-air lobby while the agents checked in—my brother and I would be staying on the boat. Then we joined the agents in the parade to the dock, where we boarded the hotel launch.

Among the half-dozen boats anchored in the lagoon, I recognized the Fair Winds, a forty-two-foot ketch owned by Phil and Lisa Brower*, friends of my parents. As we motored past, I hailed the Browers and said I would talk to them later.

The Spellbound's yellow hull loomed large, seeming as if we were approaching a ghost ship adrift at sea. The launch nudged the hull, and I waited while the others boarded, then joined them on deck. Besides Gary and me, there were the two FBI agents and the Coast Guard officer, and two French gendarmes who came to observe. The Fibbies again had shed formality, donning shorts and flowered shirts.

On deck, I glanced around, apprehension winding my body spring-tight. The ocean crossing and tropical sun had weathered the boat. Varnish cracking here, canvas fading there. But I saw no obvious signs of death. No red-black trails of dried blood in the scuppers or gear strewn haphazardly about. Only a vibrant-red police seal on the cabin door hinted of anything amiss.

An FBI agent broke the seal and entered the cabin, a bloodhound on a scent, eyes darting about. But the boat had been cleaned by hotel housekeepers. Just a few stubborn blood spatters remained.

The agents confiscated anything deemed useful in piecing together what had transpired aboard the Spellbound: the boat's logbook as well as the diary and journals kept by Dad, Mom, and Kerry. Gary told them he hadn't kept a journal because "everyone else was, so what was the point?"

The Feds snatched up a fourteen-inch adjustable wrench, which they thought may have been used to bash in Kerry's head, as well as a weighty, stainless steel winch handle, which they thought may have been used to club my father. And the guns, of course.

Gary produced his pistol easily enough—the gun he said Mom had used to shoot herself. The gun Mom had insisted not be allowed aboard the boat. *Had she suspected something the rest of us hadn't?*

Gary once bragged to me that while in the army, he wasn't sent to Vietnam because "they said I'm too crazy to carry a gun, so they assigned me to the motor pool."

Procuring the rifle and shotgun were another matter. Gary confirmed they were below the dinette, the same place we'd put them before the boat left San Diego. Dad had hidden the guns to keep them from being taken by foreign customs officials and possibly having the boat impounded. Once away from port, the guns could be unpacked and kept at hand for sport shooting, target practice, and for defense, if threatened by pirates. But before entering French Polynesia, the guns—including the pistol—would have been placed in the hold again.

Steely Eyes asked me to retrieve them. I opened the hatch at the forward end of the dinette and removed a steel basket that slid drawer-like under the deck, where fresh fruit and vegetables had been stored. When I pulled the basket out, it shrieked like a dying rabbit, an ear-piercing sound I remembered only too well. My bunk, when I'd been aboard the boat, lay just a few feet away. The screech of bare, unoiled metal could be heard throughout the cabin, and it had jerked me awake a number of times.

No way Mom could have gotten in here without someone noticing.

I dropped to my knees in the confined space. Before me were the water and fuel tanks. Only a few inches separated them from the deck above. The guns had been wrapped in blankets and placed in plastic garbage bags, then sealed with duct tape and wedged atop one of the tanks, near the hull.

I crawled to the starboard water tank and reached into the black space, probing with my fingertips for the telltale shape of a gunstock. I gripped one, then the other, and pulled the guns toward me, then handed them up to Agent Stoneface before exiting the claustrophobic space.

"What about the ammunition?" he asked.

"I didn't see any," I said. "Only the two guns."

Gary had leaned against a bulkhead with a thumb hooked in a pants pocket. He sneered and said, "You must be blind."

I turned to him. "OK, Superman. You find it."

His face paled. I could imagine the gears spinning through his mind. The agents shot him questioning looks.

Gary straightened up and said, "Oh, right, I forgot. We took the ammo out when we were plinking paint cans and shooting skeet on the trip over here. I kept it in my cabin."

"Along with the pistol?" Steely Eyes asked.

Gary glared at the man but said nothing.

As the Feds continued poking around the boat, the Coast Guard officer looked at me. "Not the most comfortable boat in a seaway, is it? The visibility forward is limited."

Ire rose within as I thought to defend the design of the boat. It was my father's, after all. But the officer was right. The Spellbound's cabin, with its spacious, house-like windows, had a high profile. It made for comfortable living quarters, but it restricted visibility from the cockpit and increased the rolling motion of the boat at sea, abetting *mal de mer*.

I shrugged. "It's a floating condo. That's the compromise Dad made so Mom would agree to live on the boat during Seattle's long winter months and go on the trip."

He nodded but seemed unswayed by my explanation. I knew he thought Dad had his priorities back-assward—I had felt the same at times—but surely that wasn't what got my father killed. Or had it played a role? Had discomfort of the crew increased the tension between family members?

Back on deck, Steely Eyes called Gary to him. "We want you to walk us through the sequence of events," the agent said, "and show us where you were when you first learned Kerry was injured, when your father fell, and when your stepmother shot herself—as you claim she did."

Gary sighed. "I already told you a dozen times."

"Yes, but we didn't have the benefit of being on the boat. Humor us."

My brother leveled an icy stare at the agent. When Steely Eyes didn't flinch, Gary turned toward the cockpit. I moved closer. I'd heard his explanation to the newspaper editor. Would he tell the same story to the FBI? In hindsight, I believe the agents had me on board so I'd know exactly what Gary was telling them. No doubt they wanted to gauge my reactions as well.

Gary spoke in a lifeless monotone, as if bored with the proceeding. He said that it had been early morning, before dawn, and he was at the helm while everyone else slept. Then he heard someone moaning and went into the main cabin to investigate. He flipped on a light and found Kerry lying on the settee, which sat crossways against the cabin's aft bulkhead, just inside the cabin door. A pillow covered Kerry's face. He lifted the pillow and saw blood oozing from a wound over her right eye. Dad appeared, apparently awakened by the sounds, and wanted to know what was going on. Gary told him Kerry was hurt, but he didn't know why. Then Mom came into the cabin and began tending to Kerry's wound.

Gary went back on deck and resumed his position at the helm. Not long afterward, he thought he saw a light in the distance and was concerned it was an island they needed to steer clear of, so he called Dad on deck. As Dad stepped up onto the cockpit coaming to get out of the glare of the cabin light, he lost his balance and fell backward, striking his head on one of the spokes of the steering wheel. It left him lying in the cockpit, unconscious and bleeding.

"He'd been having trouble with his balance," Gary said. "He'd fallen a couple times and injured his leg, and it was infected. He was going to see a doctor while he was in Seattle."

I interrupted him. "Kerry said that, too, but—"

Steely Eyes raised a hand and stopped me. "You can observe. You don't get to comment or ask questions."

I nodded, and he motioned for Gary to continue. Gary said Mom, having heard Dad fall, had called out through the open door, asking what had happened. Gary told her and, because it was dark, they moved Dad inside the cabin to better examine him. Gary said blood was spurting from the back of Dad's head, then Dad's heart stopped. Gary said he tried to staunch the blood flow while Mom administered CPR.

How could he apply pressure to the back of Dad's head when Dad was lying on his back?

Gary said he got on the radio and made the Mayday call, but because they were in the middle of the ocean, the odds of getting medical help in time to save Dad were zero. At some point they realized they were not going to revive Dad. He had lost too much blood and did not respond to the CPR. They moved his body up on deck and to the back of the boat.

"Where was Lori during all this?" Steely Eyes asked.

Gary said she had been asleep, but either he or Mom, he couldn't remember which, woke her and told her to steer the boat from the inside steering station.

I had to bite my lip to keep from asking a question, but Stoneface asked it for me. "So you're saying that Kerry's moans were heard by you out on deck, and by your parents, who were asleep in their cabin at the back of the boat, and lights came on, and there was the commotion around Kerry in the cabin, then your father fell, and you dragged him into the cabin, creating more commotion, and Lori, lying fifteen feet away, slept through it all?"

"She had a late watch," Gary said. "She was tired."

Stoneface considered the answer for a moment. "Then what?"

Gary said he returned to the helm while Mom tended to Kerry and Lori fixed them some breakfast. Once Kerry was resting comfortably, Mom took the helm, sitting in the cockpit, and Lori sat with her. After eating, Gary tended to other matters and sorted out the navigation. At one point, he went forward to make sure everything was secure—the anchor, the furled sails. He stayed there for a while, alone with his thoughts. Then he heard the gunshot and ran toward the back of the boat. He found Mom slumped in the cockpit, his pistol lying on the deck below her outstretched arm. He moved her body to the aft deck, beside Dad's.

"How did you know she was dead?" the Coast Guard officer asked.

Gary shot him the are-you-an-idiot look and snorted. "Half of her head was blown away."

"Where was Lori when this happened?" Steely Eyes asked.

Gary shrugged. "I guess she was in the cabin because she and Kerry were looking out the window, and I told them to get down, not to look."

"Why did you do that?"

"There was blood everywhere. I thought it'd be too much of a shock."

"But not for you."

Gary stood silent for a moment, then sighed as if dealing with a petulant child. "Somebody had to take care of it."

"Did you find a suicide note?" Steely Eyes asked.

"I didn't see one."

"Why did you wait until the next morning to report the death?"

"Like Kerry and Lori, I thought it would be too shocking for the folks back home, having told them about my father's death already."

The three agents looked at one another, brows furrowed. Stoneface shook his head. "So, Loren and Joanne are both dead. What'd you do then?"

Gary stared across the lagoon and yawned. The agents waited, saying nothing. Gary finally spoke, at first without looking at them. He said he tried to get the boat to the nearest island, but Lori had allowed the boat to wander off course while he tended to Mom's body. Then they ran out of fuel, or he thought they had. He spoke by radio to other boats in the area, but none were within sight, and because it was overcast, he couldn't take a sun sight to establish their position—no mention of his injured wrist. They drifted all night.

The Coast Guard officer stepped forward. "But this is a sailboat. Why didn't you set sail?"

"There wasn't much wind and the sails would have just banged around."

"So that's when you decided to bury the bodies at sea?" Stoneface asked.

"What else was I supposed to do? We were lost and their bodies were starting to decompose in the heat. I didn't know how long it'd be before we got to an island."

"But before you ran out of fuel, weren't you keeping track of your progress, noting speed and distance traveled?" the Coast Guard officer asked. "By calculating the current, you'd have had a rough idea of where you were."

"In all that chaos, I forgot to write it down, and I didn't see the point after Lori got us lost," Gary said.

The agent pursed his lips and looked to Steely Eyes, who prompted Gary to continue. "You decided to bury the bodies at sea."

Gary nodded and assumed a somber look. "We talked it over and voted on it, and I took care of it."

"How, exactly, did you take care of it?"

"I put the bodies in sleeping bags, and then weighted them down with chain and rolled them over the side."

"Was there a ceremony of any kind?" Steely Eyes asked.

Gary shook his head.

"Where were Kerry and Lori when you did this?"

"I told them to stay in the cabin."

"So you did this by yourself?"

"That's what I just said, isn't it?"

I rolled my eyes. *This is no time to be a smart-ass, Gary.*

"What about your injured wrist?" Stoneface asked.

Gary raised his arm slightly and glanced down at it. "It hurt, but I managed." He said that later on he realized he could switch to another fuel tank and get the engine running again, which he did, and got the boat under way.

I blurted out a question: "But if you were lost, how would you know which direction to go?"

Steely Eyes glared at me. "If you can't keep quiet, I'll put you on the beach."

"Sorry," I said.

Gary, tight-lipped, looked at me with narrowed eyes, then at the agents.

Steely Eyes nodded at Gary. "You got the boat moving again . . ."

"That's about when the search plane found us, then the sportfishing boat showed up and led us back to Rangiroa, which I think was about sixty miles away."

Stoneface said, "The pilot of the search plane says that when he spotted the Spellbound, it was 'maneuvering erratically.' "

Gary held up his bandaged arm again. "Like I told the Frogs, I couldn't steer well."

"But you could wrap two bodies in heavy chain and get them over the side."

Gary stared at the agent for a moment, then turned away to gaze across the lagoon. The three agents again looked at each other, shaking their heads.

I stood frozen in place, astonished by what I'd witnessed. Much of what Gary had said made no sense. I had a volley of questions for him, beginning with the timing of events associated with Dad's death. If it was dark when Dad fell, that meant it was about 4:30 A.M. or earlier, and he died soon after. Gary didn't make the Mayday call until about 6:45. Yet, what Gary had just said made it sound as if he'd made the call while Dad was still alive or immediately after he died, leaving a two-hour discrepancy.

And what of Dad's fall? How could someone be so badly injured from a fall of a few feet? Granted, if he struck his head on a spoke of the wheel, as Gary claimed he did, it's likely that would have injured him to some degree. But the spokes did not have sharp points; they were rounded. Surely the wheel would have turned when Dad fell against it, diminishing the impact. Also, he would have instinctively put back his arms to break his fall. A broken arm seemed more likely than a head injury so devastating that Dad bled to death in a matter of minutes.

The location of the pistol also concerned me. If it had been stored with the other two guns, as Gary said it was, how could Mom have retrieved it without anyone being aware of it? And if the pistol hadn't been stored with the other guns, where was it? The logical answer, it being Gary's gun, would be that he kept it in his compartment, a cubbyhole that doubled as a workroom. Yet, how could Mom have retrieved the gun without Gary knowing it? Yes, she could have done it while he was on deck and Lori sat with Kerry, but would Mom even know where to look? The longer it took, the greater the chance of detection. Yet, Gary, Kerry, and Lori had said they had no clue that Mom had the gun or intended to take her life.

And how did she load it? She'd never learned how to use a gun, not even a simple bolt-action rifle, let alone a semiautomatic pistol. It could have been loaded, but how would she know?

How did she conceal it to get it on deck? In the hot, humid weather of the tropics, they lived in swimsuits and shorts.

Moreover, Kerry and Lori had said Mom assured them everything would be all right; they would get to Tahiti and fly home. Lori had said she sat with Mom in the cockpit, and there was never any indication of depression.

These thoughts raced through my mind as I looked from Gary to the agents, then back to Gary. He moved to the aft rail, gnawing at a fingernail as the Feds huddled beside the cockpit and spoke in low tones.

I caught some of their words, and from the questioning looks, hand motions, and finger pointing, I deduced they suspected Gary of calling Dad out to the cockpit, then clubbing him from behind with a winch handle. That could have caused the injury Gary had described. It also helped explain the sizable chink in the edge of the cockpit roof and the loud thump that Kerry reported, possibly caused by the winch handle glancing off Dad's head and hitting the cabin top and making the loud noise Kerry had mentioned.

The fuel situation seemed dodgy, too. Lori had told me they didn't run out of fuel, that they had problems getting fuel to the engine, so the boat just drifted. And the batteries were way down because of using the radio. Then, suddenly, the engine started, about the same time the search-and-rescue aircraft appeared. Gary had done something, but she didn't know what.

My gut coiled like a diamondback, its tail rattling a warning. I tried reassuring myself. *There's a simple explanation for this. There's got to be.*

But Gary's story didn't add up.

What did add up was that when Kerry allegedly fell, Gary was the only one awake. When Dad allegedly fell, Gary was the only one on deck. When Mom allegedly shot herself—with the pistol Gary had brought aboard over her vehement objections—Gary was the only one on deck.

I looked at my brother, who stood staring into the distance. *Is it possible? Did he cause this horror?*

Steely Eyes, Stoneface, and the Coast Guard officer gathered their plunder and readied to leave the boat. I asked about the logbook and the journals. Stoneface confirmed an entry in Dad's journal about Gary injuring his wrist, but he refused to let me read it or the logbook.

"You think he killed them," I said.

He hesitated for a moment, looking toward his companions, then turned back to me. "Let's just say we have a lot of questions about what happened aboard this boat and how your parents died."

I had a lot of questions, too. Still, the mounting evidence notwithstanding, I refused to accept that Gary could have killed them, his own parents. He couldn't have. But his explanation had inconsistencies, contradictions. Too many holes.

The law-enforcement contingent left the Spellbound. Their bodies shrank to miniature as they reached the shore. I wrote in my journal:

> *Who hit Kerry? What if Gary did do it? But why? And what of the bodies? True, in the heat, not knowing exactly where they were or how long till they could put into port, it would almost make sense to dump them. Yet, was there another motive?*

That night I huddled in the forecastle, the tiny cabin that had served as Kerry's sleeping quarters when in port. Because it was in the bow of the boat, it had a triangle shape. It consisted mostly of a V-berth, layered in four-inch foam, the standing room barely large enough to turn around in. Overhead a clear hatch let in light and offered deck access. A pair of louvered doors with a puny hook latch provided scant privacy, or safety.

I curled up as far from the door as I could get, a large pair of channel-lock pliers at my side. Yes, I could have stayed at the hotel, but I needed to save what little money I had to get the boat back home. Besides, I didn't want to leave the Spellbound in Gary's hands. Not for even one night.

I had asked Stoneface if I'd be safe staying on the boat. He said, "I don't think your brother would be so stupid as to try anything. He has to keep up his charade."

Nonetheless, at one point I woke up to a moment of terror. Did the rattle of the doors wake me? Had Gary tried to open them? My hands trembled as I gripped the pliers.

9

Wednesday, March 8, 1978

"Red sky at morning, sailors take warning," I said, thinking that the real threat lay not overhead, but down below, where Gary had yet to stir.

As I sipped instant coffee from my perch on the foredeck, the magenta clouds faded to primrose, yellowed, then turned gray-white as dawn marched into day. Overhead, seabirds squawked.

I wondered if Gary had actually been at the forecastle door or if I had dreamt it. No, I had been fully awake, senses finely tuned to danger, certain he was standing outside the door, peering through the louvers. I could smell his sweaty T-shirt.

I rose and went below for more coffee to lift my leaden eyelids.

The FBI agents had scheduled a final interview with Gary that morning. Surely, they would have fresh questions after being aboard the boat. Would my brother have any fresh answers?

Gary and I went ashore together, with few words exchanged, and the agents led him to a table in a corner of the hotel's covered patio. If nothing else, they had silenced his insolent tongue and reduced his strut to a shamble. I watched from the other side of the patio as they settled into chairs, and Steely Eyes leaned forward, elbows on the table, speaking to my brother. Stoneface jotted notes on a pad of paper. The Coast Guard officer had his eyes on Gary, who sat back in his chair, arms crossed on his chest. They were too far away for me to hear what was being said.

"Larry!" The low but insistent voice startled me. I turned to see Phil Brower approaching. "Still giving him the third degree?" he asked.

"I wish I was a fly buzzing around them," I said.

Like my parents, Phil Brower and his wife, Lisa, hailed from Seattle. They were a fun-loving couple, and I had liked them from the moment we met in San Diego. I found them practical and more cognizant of the realities of life on the ocean than my parents had been.

Gary and I had dined with them the previous evening, but after they expressed their condolences, we talked about their trip and better times, avoiding any further discussion of the deaths.

Standing there on the patio, Phil put a hand on my shoulder. "Come on, there's nothing you can do here. Let's take a walk."

We headed for the palm-fringed shoreline on the ocean side of the atoll. Blue lorikeets chattered overhead as I gazed out over the Pacific. Small breakers rolled ashore, the only visible motion on the unbroken expanse of ocean; the arc of the horizon stretched beyond my field of vision. A sense of loneliness gripped me and my hands trembled.

"I just want to find out what the hell happened on that boat," I said.

"Gary hasn't told you?"

I turned to face him. "He's told me a lot of things. But between him, Kerry, and Lori, none of it makes a whole lot of sense. The FBI thinks he killed them."

Phil's jaw tightened and he glanced downward. "What do you think?"

"It's hard to know what to think. The Feds are saying the X-rays of Kerry's head show that she was whacked by something, like a wrench or gun butt. Her skull fracture was no accident."

Phil's eyes widened. "We saw some problems on your parents' boat, but that's true of every cruising boat out here," he said. "It can't be helped. People are crammed together in a small space. Everyone gets cabin fever, personalities clash. God knows, there are times I've wanted to throttle my wife and kids. But they don't kill each other. They just jump on another boat. Happens all the time."

"Yeah, well, something else happened on the Spellbound. I want to believe there's a rational explanation, but I may be kidding myself."

Phil sighed and began walking along a beach littered with broken coral that had been ripped from its foundation and worn smooth by the relentless motion of the sea. "There were not two nicer people," he said. "Always willing to lend a helping hand. Like the time your dad helped me fix that water pump. Your mom sewed our torn sails. She treated infections and small cuts. She shared food."

I nodded, wiping my cheeks with the back of a hand.

"But . . . and this is why I wanted to talk to you alone . . . Lisa is really upset. The cops are right. Gary and the girls are not telling you everything. There were serious problems on the Spellbound."

I stopped and stared at Phil.

"Your mom threatened to fly home because of Gary."

Goose bumps pimpled my arms. Lori had said that at the hospital, but I hadn't given it much credence.

"It may have just been wishful thinking," he said, "but she was pissed off. No question about that. And your dad said he wished they had a smaller boat that just he and your mom could handle by themselves so they could continue on in peace, 'without the kids.' " Phil punctuated his final phrase with waggling fingers.

"I'm not surprised," I said.

We continued along the beach and Phil added, "Your parents didn't go into particulars. They just seemed unhappy with the situation. We told this to the FBI agents when they interviewed us yesterday."

I wished I could read my parents' journals, but the agents had taken them as evidence. I could only speculate, but Mom being upset with Gary came as no shocker. After all, that's why I left the boat. Why not Mom? Except that it was her boat as much as Dad's. She was supposed to be having the time of her life, not wanting to jump ship.

Phil stopped and touched my arm, his eyes glistening. "Lisa and I are really broken up by this. Your parents were good friends and to have this happen . . ." Phil suppressed a sob and cleared his throat. "If there's anything we can do, just let us know."

I nodded. "I appreciate everything you've already done. Helping to clean up the boat, packing up their things."

"It's the least we could do. That boat was a mess. All that blood . . ."

Emotion overwhelmed him again. "But surely it was an accident of some kind. Your dad, I mean."

I stopped and looked into his eyes. "It's getting harder and harder for me to believe that."

"I have to believe it," Phil said.

I nodded. "I want to."

"One more thing. I doubt it's important, but on Sunday morning, before Kerry and Lori flew to Papeete, the three of them were on the beach together, away from the hotel. I could see them standing close together, talking, but I couldn't hear what they said."

"You mean as if they were trying to get their stories straight?"

He shrugged and after a moment we walked back to the hotel. Phil invited me to go diving, but I demurred. "I need to get the boat ready to sail to Papeete, then home."

When we reached the patio, the agents stood in their perpetual huddle. Steely Eyes spotted us and signaled for me to join them. "We're taking off in a few minutes, but before we go I want to let you know where things stand," he said.

I glanced around, a knot forming in my gut. "Where's my brother?"

"Using the facilities."

"Are you taking him with you?"

"No."

"So he didn't confess?"

The agent spat out a near-laugh and shook his head. "It was pretty much the same story, but there are inconsistencies."

We spoke for a moment longer, and his final comment left me brooding. I caught a glimpse of Gary as he returned from the restroom and gestured toward him. "Does he know about this?"

"No," Steely Eyes said. "We think it will have more impact coming from you."

I stared at him for a moment. *You calculating bastards.*

"Good luck," he said, then extended his hand. I ignored it.

Gary stopped a few feet away and fired a defiant glare at the agents, then said to me, "The train's leaving the station, unless you want to swim back with the sharks."

I sniggered, thinking it might be safer to swim.

After we boarded the Spellbound, Gary went directly into the cabin. He hadn't said a word on the trip back. I'd hoped he would spout off about his chat with the FBI agents, but his bravado had evaporated.

I stood in the cockpit, thinking of the months I'd spent on the boat . . . and why I'd left, the final straw being the scuffle with Gary.

I had to confront him again.

I stepped into the cabin and crossed to the galley, where he stood fixing a sandwich. I gripped my thighs to stop my hands from shaking. "What did they say?" I asked.

He looked at me with a soulless gaze, then turned back to his sandwich.

"OK," I said. "Then I'll tell you what they told me." I paused, but he kept looking down. "If you don't come up with a more plausible explanation, the case will be presented to a grand jury in Seattle, and you'll have to testify . . . under oath."

Gary did not, as I expected, proclaim his innocence or what idiots the FBI agents were. Instead, his features froze and he swallowed. His Adam's apple bobbed like a cork on the sea.

I continued: "Even if you've done nothing wrong, you know what happened on this boat. And it's not the story you've been feeding me and the Feds."

He turned his head and looked straight at me, his ice-blue eyes as predatory as an arctic wolf. "Yeah, I know a lot of things. I know math, economics, accounting . . ."

My body jerked as if I'd been hit with a stun gun, and I wondered: *Am I standing face-to-face with my parents' killer?*

My hands flexed. I imagined wrapping them around his scrawny throat to still that bobbing Adam's apple forever.

Yet, I refused to let go of the fading hope for a more palatable explanation. *There has to be.* I tried to come up with something that did not contain the word "murder." That nagging guilt surfaced again: *Had I stayed on the boat . . .*

"You need to go home and face your accusers," I said. "If you're innocent, as you claim you are, you'll be cleared and it'll be over."

He didn't look up. Just kept munching his sandwich as if I didn't exist.

You heartless son of a bitch! I started toward him. I'd pound that disdain and condescension until his face frothed into bloody pulp. But what would that get me? Twenty-five to life.

I turned away and went on deck, my heart pounding. I took several deep breaths to calm down. *What do I do now? Do I dare remain on this boat . . . with him?*

Steely Eyes had said Gary couldn't risk blowing his cover. And, as naïve as it may sound, I wanted to talk with him, to learn the truth behind our parents' deaths. I hoped that his conscience would get the best of him, that he'd confess, that he'd ask for my help, if not forgiveness.

But I wasn't betting on it. I pinned my faith on the grand jury. Surely the pressure of being in the witness box, grilled by a relentless prosecutor in a room of questioning eyes, would break him down.

Meanwhile, I had work to do. There were a number of mechanical problems with the boat that needed fixing—problems I *could* solve.

10

Thursday, March 9, 1978

    I scanned the main cabin, trying to get into my father's head.

Where would he have hidden it?

    Aunt Vivian, Dad's older sister, had not found a current will among my parents' effects. She and Aunt Verney, one of Mom's younger sisters, had been named co-executrixes of my parents' estate. Before I left Tahiti, Vivian had told me that the document might be in a secret compartment on the boat.

    Gary had said he knew nothing about the will. Yet, why would my parents have the will on the boat and not in a safe on dry land? Nonetheless, Vivian had insisted, so I began a systematic search. If not the will, perhaps I'd find something—a clue, some evidence—that the FBI had missed.

    At least I had the Spellbound to myself. I could explore the boat in its entirety without Gary peering over my shoulder at every step. He had accepted an invitation from Phil Brower for an overnight diving excursion. I thought Phil crazy to take him along, but Phil needed a diving partner.

    In the main cabin, the navigation station sat to starboard, a peninsula jutting into the room. Dad's World. In front of the nav table stood the captain's chair he'd used while writing in his daily diary, the boat's logbook, and his journal. The relevant charts lay at hand. Under the table, I had built the shelf that housed the brass sextant. Dad had complimented me on the design and construction. Even as an adult I'd blushed with pride at his praise.

In San Diego, Dad had practiced his Morse code while seated at that table, listening to the dots and dashes with headphones and jotting down the corresponding letters on a notepad, preparing for the ham radio licensing exam. But in the Rangiroa lagoon, the radio sat silent and unusable, as if it had died along with him. Gary had told me it was no longer tuned properly, so we couldn't use it to communicate with family members back home. I didn't know whether to believe him or not, but I recalled Dad's frustrations. It wasn't like a transistor radio; the antenna had to be tuned as well, and I had no idea how to do it.

I poked through various compartments within and below the nav station, finding nothing other than the expected charts and navigation instruments. On the adjacent outer bulkhead, tiny spots dotted the wooden panel. Dried blood? I shuddered and turned away.

Overhead, the laminated beams Dad had so lovingly crafted spanned the width of the cabin. Alternating light-colored ash with deep-red mahogany, they formed a graceful, candy-stripe arc that shaped the cabin top and the deck above.

If only his life's path had matched that gentle arc.

Against the cabin's aft bulkhead was the settee. Mom's World. At sea, she had slept there, read there, made herself at home there. I opened the storage bins underneath. They contained household items—games, pens and pencils, pads of paper. Yellow cylinders caught my eye. Exposed but undeveloped film. The photos my parents would have shared with the rest of the family upon their return.

Flashlight in hand, I peered into the vacant space behind the bins. Bits of sawdust, remnants of the construction days, and that familiar musty boat smell, but no revelations.

More storage lay under the walk-around on the port side. A few Christmas ornaments and sundry items someone would have to inventory eventually.

I moved on to the galley, forward of the main cabin, although I couldn't imagine finding the will there—too much moisture and open flame. I heated water for coffee on a single-burner kerosene stove, more appropriate for the tropics than the diesel cookstove, which I doubted had been used since the Spellbound left San Diego. I would have welcomed a cool, iced drink, but I had no ice or refrigeration unless I ran the engine, and the boat was low on fuel. Besides, performing the coffee ritual softened the bricks of tension that stiffened my every move, colored my every thought.

Cup in hand, I went to the adjacent dinette. Pots and pans, dishes and linens. I sipped the scalding brew, then left the cup on the table and went on to the forward section of the boat. To port was a bathroom, or head, as it's known on a boat, with toilet, sink, and shower. To starboard lay a single bunk. My "bedroom" when I'd been aboard, although it wasn't a room. Just a single bunk with a bookshelf overhead and a small port that seeped a dismal light. No door of any kind. Only a privacy curtain that hung limp in the stifling air. It reminded me of the sleeper cars on the Great Northern Railway when Grandma Jane took Gary and me to Indiana one summer to see the old family homestead. Below the bunk, open storage held some of Lori's things but no hidey-holes.

The passageway ended at the forecastle, with the V-berth I had claimed as my refuge since returning to the Spellbound. It had been Kerry's abode and doubled as the sail locker. The bunk had to be dismantled to retrieve a sail, eliciting no small degree of whining from her.

I removed the cushions and opened the locker. The sails sat atop the keel and against the hull. No space for a secret compartment. As I shoved the bags aside, Dacron sailcloth crinkled. Sailcloth that Mom had sewn. In preparing for the trip, she had worked at Shattauer Sails, where she learned the basics of the craft. During the trip, she traded sail repairs for food, fuel, and other necessities in the barter economy that characterized the cruising life. As I replaced the compartment cover, a tingling coursed through my body, as if I were closing the lid to her coffin.

Below the main cabin lay the engine room. As with the galley, I couldn't imagine my father hiding anything so important as a will down there, but I had to check it out. I opened the small hatchway, dropped to hands and knees, and crawled into the broad but shallow space. The only standing room was in the narrow bilge, forward of the massive Detroit

Spellbound, right, in the Rangiroa lagoon, French Polynesia, March 1978. *Photo: Larry Edwards*

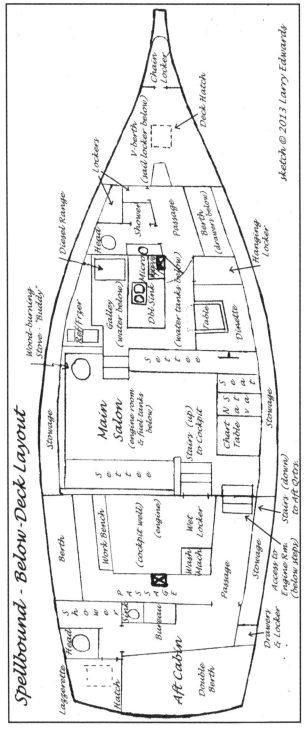

Spellbound - Below-Deck Layout

sketch © 2013 Larry Edwards

Chain Locker

Deck Hatch

V-berth (sail locker below)

Lockers

Shower

Passage

Berth (drawers below)

Hanging Locker

Diesel Range

Head

Micro

Wp...

Dbl Sink

(water tanks below)

Table

Dinette

Wood-burning Stove - "Buddy"

Ref/Frzer

Galley (water below)

s e t t e e

s e t t e e

Stowage

Main Salon (engine room & fuel tanks below)

Stairs (up) to Cockpit

Chart Table

N a v S t a t

s e a t

Stowage

Stairs (down) to Aft Qrtrs

Berth

Work Bench

(cockpit well)

(engine)

Wet Locker

Wash Mach

Passage

Stowage

Access to Engine Rm. (below steps)

Stowage

Head

Sink

Bureau

S h o w e r

P A S S A G E

Lazzerette

Hatch

Aft Cabin

Drawers & Locker

Double Berth

diesel engine—the "iron genny" Dad had called it. Water and fuel tanks sat atop the curvature of the hull. A maze of pipes and tubing—water, fuel, and drainage—traversed the compartment. A bank of marine batteries huddled at one side. We'd replaced one in San Diego. It had been a sweaty, elbow-and-head-banging effort for Dad and me, skidding its one hundred pounds across the compartment and out the hatch. A diesel-powered generator sat perched on a shelf, providing comforts beyond the imaginations of seafarers of old.

Relieved to be out of the closeted space, I stared the length of the narrow corridor that led to my parents' cabin at the stern of the boat. The most likely hiding place.

Why hadn't I started the search there?

I inched along the passageway. On the right, tucked under the cockpit well, sat a mini-clothes washer. On the left hung coils of line, foul-weather gear, and other equipment, at easy hand for immediate use. My foulies had hung there once upon a time.

The cabin doorway stood open, beckoning. I tensed. I couldn't go inside. Not yet.

I turned into Gary's cubbyhole on the port side of the cockpit well. On his bunk sat a large, wedge-shaped foam pad that propped him up while he slept.

The year before, he'd been in a car accident. He claimed he couldn't lie flat because it bothered his back and neck. He also had brought aboard a neck brace, along with an assortment of painkillers. He had sighed a lot, as if in perpetual agony. Funny, though, how it never seemed to keep him from scuba diving or sailing the boat. The pain seemed apparent only when expediency demanded it. Maybe he suffered, but I saw no sign of it. Nonetheless, he had sued the other party and won a handsome settlement that gave him funds for the sailing trip.

The confined space doubled as the workroom, where a drill press sat atop a workbench, along with an assemblage of woodworking tools. But I found no secret compartment or any sign of important documents. Only one place left.

As I returned to the doorway to my parents' cabin, my gut twisted and I stopped.

What am I afraid of?

While growing up, my parents' bedroom had been their sanctuary. They rarely allowed us kids inside. I marveled that it still left me uneasy. I'd been on the boat for two days but had not set foot inside the cabin.

I stepped in, then exhaled in a whoosh, unaware that I'd been holding my breath. The only true "stateroom" on the boat, it boasted a double bunk, a private head with a shower and tiny bathtub (knees under the chin), a clothes locker, and an antique chest of drawers with a large mirror that Mom had insisted on having aboard. A fore-and-aft bulkhead divided the space, and a stained-glass window set into the bulkhead added a sense of tranquility.

Cardboard boxes sat on the bunk, as if my parents were moving in, not out. I lifted a corner of the comforter and held it to my face, inhaling my parents' last vestige, then shivered and let it fall.

Books sat on the shelves above the bunk. Mostly sailing books, but also works of fiction, among them Ernest Gann novels. One of Dad's favorite authors, although Dad would read most anything. Dad liked "Ernie," as he called him, because Gann wrote about flying, Dad's first, and lost, love.

I lifted the foam mattress and peered underneath—painted plywood but otherwise bare. I checked the storage space under the bunk and found nothing unexpected, then, one by one, I removed the drawers from Mom's dresser. Taped to the back of one of the drawers I discovered an envelope. I eased the bulging container away from the wood and opened the flap.

Not the will.

Rather, a wad of gaily colored French Polynesian francs totaling about eight hundred dollars—the money Tati had given them for ferrying him and his political entourage among the Marquesas Islands.

I put it back for safekeeping. Or so I thought.

I returned to the main cabin. Sweat trickled from my forehead, stinging my eyes. All the ports and hatches were open, but without a strong fan, air did not circulate well. I abandoned the search and stood in the cabin doorway, maximizing the flow of air across face and body.

I scanned the lagoon, which lay rippled in a morning breeze laden with salty odors of decaying sea life. Frigate birds swooped and screeched overhead. Nearby bobbed a twenty-eight-foot sloop belonging to the American marine biologist who had participated in the search-and-rescue effort. Beyond it lay the Tarvana, the sportfisher that had gone to the Spellbound and led the boat back to the lagoon.

On the Tarvana's aft deck, a woman of apparent European descent appeared to be disrobed. I snatched the binoculars from the nav station for a better look. She wore a bikini bottom but no top, and I watched her settle into a chaise lounge. Oolala!

Had Mom or Kerry done the same? Nah. At least not Mom. Too much of a prude.

I ducked into the cabin and slumped onto the settee, needing a shield from the merciless sun. I nursed what remained of the tepid coffee, trying to grasp the magnitude of the tempest that had swept over me—and my family.

Steely Eyes had asked me why, after leaving a good job as a schoolteacher in Tacoma, I left the boat in San Diego, just three months into the cruise.

"Too much tension," I told him. "I knew there would be problems. Of course, I never imagined this horror."

It wasn't as if I'd been obsessed with the trip, like my father. Dad had taken longer to finish building the boat than planned, and I had pretty much given up on it. After I graduated from the University of Washington, I taught junior high school health—sex and dope, I called it—and coached track. By the fifth year, however, my enthusiasm had waned, and the boat was ready to go. I had no wife or steady relationship. The timing melded perfectly, like Dad's joinery. I could always go back to teaching when I returned, more worldly wise.

Even so, I never fully committed to the trip. I retrieved my journal from a duffel bag and read what I'd written about those early days aboard the boat.

Port Townsend, August 6, 1977
   The start of the "great adventure." What I'm feeling the most is curiosity. It's the games I want to watch. This will be an interesting study

of the human being and family relationships. Five people aboard this boat, with a projected 3-year cruise. We will lose one within 6 months, possibly me; the others I anticipate staying at least a year. I have doubts about the trip ever being completed.

A chill coursed my spine. Had I unwittingly predicted their deaths?

During the voyage down the coast, the realities of crossing the ocean on a small boat had surfaced. Mom and Kerry fell victim to seasickness and stretched out at opposite ends of the settee, their legs overlapping. The boat's high profile exacerbated their woes. Kerry also took medication, which left her drowsy and useless as crew. She and Mom preferred being in port, shopping and socializing, to being out of sight of land. Sailing was a means to their end.

For me, sailing was an end in itself. Being on the open ocean, I felt liberated. Nothing in sight but water stretching to the horizon, sliced by rolling, white-crested swells that surged under the boat, first lifting, then easing the vessel into the trough as a wall of gray-green—driven by thirty-knot winds descending from the Gulf of Alaska—rose above our heads, poised to crush us under its curling brow, then, as if playing cat-and-mouse, lifting us out of harm's way, to be repeated again and again and again. No two swells were alike, creating myriad variations on the theme and requiring constant adjustments of the helm to keep the boat on a steady course.

Not so enchanted, my fellow crew members. Mom tried to stand her first watch at sea, but she soon ordered me to take over "for a minute" while she puked over the lee rail. Then she went below and rejoined Kerry, leaving me at the helm.

We had no autopilot or steering vane—that was on the San Diego list—so we needed a hand on the wheel at all times. Dad revised the watch schedule to a three-man rotation: Him, me, and the airline pilot whom Dad had asked to crew and help navigate. He and Dad also suffered, but either they were not hit as hard as Mom and Kerry or they just toughed it out.

Mom defined the term *trouper*, so when she stayed below, I figured she must really be hurting. Yes, she vented woe-is-me sighs to accompany her actions, but she'd always done her share. Not so, this time. She laid herself out like a corpse. But with Kerry, I had my doubts. Being "Daddy's little girl," I suspected her of milking the ailment for every drop.

I did not get sick. I seemed immune to it. I adopted an air of loftiness toward my shipmates that I later regretted. I had not appreciated the extent of their suffering.

Then again, there were moments I thanked them. I fell in love with Mistress Night. While they stayed below, lying in their bunks, I had the cockpit to myself. Alone with my thoughts under a canopy of stars, the cool green glow of phosphorescence in the wave tops lighting my way. The only sound the rush of the swells rolling under the hull.

I'd written in my journal:

When I look across the water, I know I've been here before. It doesn't frighten me; I'm comfortable out here. That scares me a little, because I could be careless. Yet, I respect the tremendous power that lies below me. A power that unleashed could toss this boat like a twig in a tornado.

As we progressed southward, the conditions fell to dead calm and a nearly flat sea, and we motored. Dolphins pranced at our bow, flashing in and out of the bow wave like a precision drill team. That improved the mood aboard the boat.

I declared a truce with Kerry. We needed a snack for the night watch. Having a sack full of green apples, we settled on apple bread. We only found a recipe for nut bread, so we improvised, adding sunflower seeds to the mix and dubbing it Apple-Sunflower Surprise. In the days that followed, Kerry and I took over the galley. One afternoon we made a great pot of chili for dinner. Mom still pretty much sat, read, and napped, although one day she did take a couple of watches.

The weather warmed as we passed the Channel Islands and doglegged to San Diego, where we'd make our final preparations before sailing for French Polynesia. One evening in port, my parents went out to dinner with the Garretts. Rather than fix a proper dinner, Kerry and I opened a can of corned beef, dumped it on a paper plate, and scooped it up with crackers. We washed it down with cold beer.

Kerry laughed. "Mom would have a fit if she saw us eating like this."
I grinned and clinked her bottle with mine. "I'm not telling."

BACK ABOARD THE Spellbound and reviewing my journal, I hoped to unearth clues to the source of the troubles that had spawned aboard the boat—the tiny, festering wound that went untreated until it became a gangrenous boil. But Gary had not sailed that first leg to San Diego, and I wasn't on the boat for the ocean crossing or the two months they spent in the Marquesas. I slammed the journal shut and dropped my head into my hands.

That evening, not wanting to loll around the boat feeling sorry for myself, I dinghied ashore and went to the hotel bar. I immediately spotted Inga, the blonde woman from the Tarvana, her breasts spilling out of a tight-fitting halter top. She flirted shamelessly, and the Tahitian boat captain plied her with champagne, spending his meager earnings on his wealthy guest, his eyes brimming with lust as they danced. Her drunk husband, sitting at the bar, watched the *pas de deux* with bleary-eyed amusement.

I ordered a gin and tonic, then scanned the room looking for a likely prospect of my own. Nothing. Every woman in the place coupled up. I convinced the captain to take a breather and danced a few numbers with Inga, who taught me to rumba.

The sortie over, I nodded at the barkeep, ordering another over-priced drink, then opened my wallet and stared at the shrinking bankroll. My brain, even in its inebriate fog, signaled restraint, in terms of funds and booze. But Fool elbowed aside Good Sense, and I tossed more money on the bar. Drink in hand, I swiveled to watch the merrymakers.

The cacophonic hotel bar, set on stilts over the lagoon, shook from the throbbing music and heavy feet of the dancers. "Have your fun, you fucking bastards. You'll all be dead soon enough."

I drained my glass, clanked it on the bar, and pushed through the dancers. Outside, the lagoon lay dark and forbidding, the Spellbound a faint silhouette against the starry night. I staggered against a palm tree ringed with a metal collar. I ran my fingers over the slick surface. It kept rats from climbing to the fronds and gnawing into the coconuts.

Mom and Dad should've had a rat collar on the Spellbound.

"Pardon?" A woman spoke from the shadows.

Apparently, I had uttered my musing aloud. She stepped into view, a strapless *pareu* clinging to free-falling breasts. A *bon vivant* about to join the *soirée*. I leered at her. "To bee or not to bee, the eternal conundrum of the hive."

"Bonsoir!" she retorted, then performed a cartoonish dismissal, snapping her head forward and continuing her march to mayhem.

"Out, damned spot," I called after her, wondering if Lady M had had an ill-tempered dog. I snickered at my joke, pushed upright and shuffled toward the dock where I had moored the Zodiac. I tumbled into the inflatable dinghy, just catching my balance before caroming into the black lagoon. A wetting would have done me good, but what if I couldn't climb back into the boat? The thought of sharks having a late-night snack at my expense had kept me dry. I yanked the starter cord on the outboard motor and shoved off.

"Lay on, MacDuff!" I shouted and gunned the motor.

Back aboard the Spellbound, I went to my parents' cabin where I could sleep in a spacious bunk. But even in my drunken state I couldn't do it.

The next morning, I awoke lying on the settee, my head throbbing. Sunlight streamed into the cabin, the harbinger of another hot, humid day. I had not bothered to undress, just flopped down and snoozed. But I had slept through the night. A good ten hours with Morpheus, and not while caged in the forecastle, fear and cold steel for cellmates. Hangover notwithstanding, with Gary gone I felt the most relaxed since my arrival in Polynesia.

But Gary would return.

What then?

11

Tuesday, March 14, 1978

I stood at the helm and steered the Spellbound in broad circles near the entrance to Tiputa Pass, waiting for Gary. I had weighed anchor and got the boat under way while he went ashore to get our papers stamped at the Gendarmerie. With me were Chris Peters, an Australian, and Richard Tuttle*, an Englishman, on loan from the schooner Sundancer. They had agreed to help sail the Spellbound to Tahiti.

Felix Homer, the skipper of the Sundancer, had taken Gary to the beach, and they approached in an inflatable dinghy. I let the Spellbound drift while Gary climbed aboard, then put the engine in gear and began a slow turn toward the pass. But Gary rushed to the cockpit, shoved me aside, and spun the wheel. The bow arced to port, followed by a shout of alarm from Felix. Gary, in his frantic maneuver, had nearly run him down.

I ran forward to see if Felix was all right.

"Bloody hell," he said. "That's the thanks I get?"

"Are you OK?"

"Yeah, you missed me, but only just." He then waved dismissively and shouted "bon voyage" in a tone laced with sarcasm.

I stormed back to the cockpit. "What the hell? You could've killed him."

Gary gave me a blank look. "We have to get through the pass with the outgoing tide; otherwise we're stuck here for another day. He should have gotten out of the way."

"Oh, he's a mind reader?"

Gary stared straight ahead. "The anchor needs stowed."

"You're the expert. Maybe you should do it."

He sneered. "And you're going to take us through the passage?"

"Why not? You've never done it before," I said, arching my lips into a faux smile.

Gary feigned concentration on the task at hand. Chris and Richard glanced at each other with questioning looks. I felt guilty about having asked them to crew, considering the allegations against my brother. But I needed the extra hands. I also enjoyed the camaraderie, having relished meals and laughed over drinks with them during the days spent waiting for clearance from French officials to leave Rangiroa. Most of all, though, I felt safer.

I looked at Gary, reminding myself that I had to get the boat to Tahiti. If he wanted to be in charge, it wasn't worth wasting my breath to argue with him. It should be a simple, two-day passage, and once we reached Papeete he'd be extradited. I went forward and lashed the anchor to the inboard end of the bowsprit, Chris and Richard lending me a hand.

We hit a rough patch as we crossed the reef. Enough to give us the thrill of a carnival ride, but nothing like the beating we'd have taken had we tried to leave the island any later. Twice a day, as the tide reversed course, eight- to twelve-foot waves thundered through Tiputa Pass, creating a frothy chaos of whirlpools. Divers risked their lives if they didn't get out of the pass during that phase.

Porpoises, however, frolicked in the devil's playpen. The coltish creatures escorted us into open water, prancing at the bow and lifting our spirits with their lightning-fast maneuvers. The clear water sparkled from thousands of fish darting about, their iridescent colors flashing in the bright sunlight, ample evidence of why divers flocked to the atoll. If only I could have fully enjoyed it.

Once we cleared the pass, we set the sails. The soothing sounds of the boat slipping through the sea replaced the mind-numbing rumble of the diesel engine.

We established a watch rotation of two hours on, six off, then settled into a typical passage-making routine: talking, reading, eating, writing in journals, and cocktails before dinner. With any luck, it would be an unremarkable forty-eight hours.

I went below to examine the chart and lay out our course. Gary stepped up and pressed against me, forcing me to sidestep to maintain my balance.

"Think you know what you're doing?" he said.

"It's pretty much a beeline to Papeete," I replied.

He jabbed me with an elbow and slid the parallel rules across the chart. I glared at him, then backed off, again reminding myself of the overarching goal. If I pressed him, it could quickly escalate, and it didn't take much to imagine what he might do.

It soon became clear, however, that Gary didn't know what he was doing. I wrote in my journal:

> *Very light breeze and Gary decided to run before the wind. We set the whisker pole and not 30 seconds later it pulled away from the mast. The bracket holding the inboard end of the pole broke. Then he said to run the staysail and main wing-and-wing, so down came the genny. While I stowed the sail, he changed the setup again, this time setting the main, mizzen and stays'l to the same side of the boat, but he only let them out about half enough. Useless. With the light wind and swells, air dumped from the sails, and the booms (all 3 of them) slashed about. In the meantime, our "skipper" had gone below to play backgammon with Richard and had not reappeared once to see what all the racket was about. In 2 hours, we had gone only 2 miles! I dropped the mizzen and stays'l, rehoisted the genny, and slightly altered course. We were soon making three to four knots. I've handled the sails ever since with no questions from Gary.*

Darkness settled in while I manned the helm. Chris kept me company and provided a second set of eyes. Gary had given us a heading and I looked forward to a peaceful night at sea. We were making good time in the southeasterly breeze. Richard and Gary had gone below.

"I see a light," Chris said, gesturing toward a position a few points off the bow.

I stood and saw the dim, white light where there should have been no light, unless it was the stern light of another vessel. But we had not seen any other boats or ships in the area before sundown. The alternative meant a light on shore, but there wasn't supposed to be any shore ahead of us, only open water.

Flashes of my father's death flickered my mind. He had died, according to my brother, while stepping out of the cockpit, in the dark, to look for an island ahead.

"Let's keep an eye on it," I said.

At the top of the hour, Chris and I swapped places. A quarter moon rose to starboard, highlighting the indolent sea in its ethereal glow. I went forward to get away from the glare of the cabin lights to see if the light had moved relative to our position. We appeared to be closing in on it. I looked for a red or green running light indicative of a vessel of some kind. Nothing. I focused on the areas on either side of the light. In the faint moonglow I discerned a black, irregular line directly in our path—palm trees.

"Shit!"

I hustled back to the cockpit. "Chris, please go forward and tell me what you see. I'll take the helm."

"No worries, mate." He returned a few minutes later. "Looks like an atoll."

"Yeah, we're headed for a fucking island." I handed the helm back to Chris, then instructed him to fall off to port twenty degrees while I eased the sheets on the main and genoa. The change in the angle of heel, combined with the groans of the lines winding through the blocks, brought Gary on the scene.

"I heard something happening, so I thought I should be on deck," he said without a trace of irony.

"Something happened all right," I said. "We were about to shiver our timbers on a coral reef."

"Oh, yeah," he said. "We were supposed to change course about an hour ago. I forgot to tell you." With that he went back into the cabin.

I went to the nav table and examined the chart where Gary had plotted the course. We should have made a southerly dogleg into the passage between Rangiroa and Tikehau. I mentally kicked myself for having left it to him. We were sailing in the Tuamotu Archipelago, also known as the "Dangerous Archipelago" due to its tricky currents and low-lying atolls—the coral-encrusted peaks of undersea volcanoes. Because the atolls lay only a few feet above sea level, they were hard to spot during the day and almost invisible at night. Over the years, they had caught many a mariner unaware. Had the moon been obscured, we could have run up on the reef. The boat, along with its crew, would have been pounded to bits by the surf.

Did Gary actually forget? Or was "accidentally" beaching the boat his way of tossing a monkey wrench into the FBI's investigation?

THE NEXT DAY, Gary discovered that a fitting on the stays'l stay had loosened. He shouted for tools and winch handles and halyards and the like.

"With all that drama, you'd think the boat was sinking," Chris said.

I shook my head and laughed.

The problem solved, Chris, Richard, and I took over the cockpit. Except when taking his watch, Gary sequestered himself below, while the three of us, young men from different countries, told tales and swapped ribald jokes.

Chris, like me, had a curiosity about the world and people around him, and we talked for hours at a time. I told him as much as I knew about the deaths of my parents, whom he had met at Nuka Hiva three months earlier. He confided that even then Gary had made him uneasy with his superior demeanor.

"Gary spoke disparagingly about having 'the girls' on board, as if they were a useless nuisance," Chris said.

He later sent me an account of how he met my parents at Taiohaie Bay, his observations at the time, and his thoughts while aboard the Spellbound with Gary and me:

> *Our week's visit to Nuku Hiva was a festive one, with many parties on the various vessels moored in the harbor. One of the parties was on Spellbound, where we met the Edwards family, watched a slide show of*

their vessel's construction, and heard stories of their uncomfortable crossing to Nuku Hiva. I was not convinced that the boat was suitable for lengthy ocean cruises, and this seemed to be evident from the comments of the crew.

We got to know the crew fairly well over a seven-day period and heard that relationships had been less than cordial during the sail from San Diego. We assumed this had been due to the discomforts of the long crossing. All of the crew seemed to be normal and happy, everyday, suburban Americans, except for the son, Gary, who struck me as particularly surly. There appeared to be friction between Gary and other members of the crew that related to his view of their sailing skills. These factors gave me little confidence in the future success of the Spellbound's cruise of the Pacific.

Weeks later, as we sailed into the lagoon at Rangiroa, my vague misgivings about the Spellbound crew were confirmed in the most brutal way. As we anchored in this beautiful setting, we noticed Spellbound anchored in the harbor with the American flag flying at half-mast. One of the other yachtsmen rowed over and broke the shocking news.

According to Gary, they encountered a storm. The father, Loren, fell from the deck into the cockpit, hit his head, and died soon after. Only two hours earlier, the daughter, Kerry, while alone in the forward cabin, fell and fractured her skull. Nobody saw the incident and (after seeing her cabin and sleeping in that bunk) I believe it is almost impossible that this could have happened. The next day, as reported by Gary, Jody was so distraught that she committed suicide.

Meanwhile, Gary's brother, Larry, had flown out from the U.S. to assist the family. I got to know Larry very well. He was a remarkably positive person who took charge and arranged for the Spellbound to be sailed back to Tahiti, and asked me whether Richard and I could swap over temporarily and crew on the Spellbound for the passage to Tahiti. We were happy to assist.

On the morning of the 14th March 1978, we sailed out of the harbor of Rangiroa, one of the most beautiful islands I visited in my travels—a scene of almost mocking contrast to the bleak story surrounding this yacht.

While sitting out at night, Larry confided that he didn't believe his brother's story. However, he would not speculate on what he thought might have happened. As I stood at the helm, I thought of Gary sleeping down below. I wondered what he must be thinking at night, what stories were left untold.

TWO DAYS AFTER leaving Rangiroa, Tahiti came into view. Clouds enshrouded the mountainous island, casting a gray pall over what the tourism industry had dubbed "Heaven on Earth." With La Diademe hidden from view, the most distinguishing features were the hulking cargo ships and skeletal pier-side cranes in the commercial port.

"Not really an exciting island, is it," said Richard, who had the helm at the time.

"Definitely not a picture for the travel brochure," I said.

Gary came on deck, so I went below to write in my journal. I had just settled in the dinette when the boat heeled sharply, gathered speed, and rain drummed the deck. My coffee mug slid across the table. I grabbed it, set it in the galley sink and ran topside. A squall had struck and its sudden gust caused an accidental jibe, leaving the genny backwinded and the boat out of control. Gary and Richard were trying to reel in the big jib but to no avail. The gust had overpowered them. I spun the helm and headed the boat into the wind, dumping the air from the sails and giving the crew the leverage they needed.

Crisis over, we reset the sails and Gary charted a broad reach that eliminated the risk of another accidental jibe. But the new course would take us past the harbor entrance, requiring us to come about and tack upwind to make port. I suggested we simply tack downwind. Gary's solution? He started the engine.

The day's real fun, however, began inside the harbor, where boats moored Mediterranean style, or stern-to, with an anchor securing the bow. We found only one slot wide enough for the beefy Spellbound, and that would be a tight fit, making the maneuver a tricky one. Sailboats are hard to back up, and although the wind was light, it also came abeam, as did the current, leaving little margin for error. And since the Spellbound had become a macabre celebrity, a crowd of thrill seekers, newspaper reporters, and photographers gathered for a closer look, adding to the tension. I didn't envy Gary the task, grateful that he had insisted on being the skipper. Had his ego allowed it, I was certain he would have handed it over to me, hoping I'd fail. Instead, I, like the other yachties along the quay, stood ready to take his measure as a yachtsman.

He told Chris, Richard, and me to stand by the anchor as he backed into the mooring. Never mind that another boat was about to pass between us and the quay. Boat be damned, he asked me if I was ready.

"No, we're not," I said. "The dinghy has to go in the water, fenders need to be over the side, and the mooring lines need to be laid out."

His reply: "You're a big boy now and shouldn't have to be told everything to do."

"The point is, you don't know what you're doing and refuse to admit it," I said.

He'd been so anxious to prove his brilliance as a boat handler by whipping up to the quay and mooring the boat in record time that he'd jumped the gun.

Meanwhile, the Spellbound had drifted perilously close to the boat on our downwind side. I chuckled as he gunned the motor and shot the boat away from the quay and into clear water. His merry crew then completed the preparations, our not-so-subtle yo-ho-hos belittling his ineptitude.

Gary scowled at me, then repositioned the boat and ordered us to drop the anchor. Except that he chose the wrong place for the set. Because of the length of the scope, it would not keep the bow from drifting into the boat on our downwind side. We had to set a second anchor. Meanwhile, the Spellbound drifted sideways, and we had to fend it off of the adjacent boat. No small task, pushing a thirty-ton behemoth against wind and current. With the help of volunteers on the quay, we finally got the stern lines tied off and the boat secure.

I poured three Scotches and handed one each to Chris and Richard, then raised mine. "I cannot thank you enough," I said, my voice low. "Not only for crewing, but for providing a buffer between Gary and me. Had it been just the two of us . . ."

Grim-faced, they nodded and touched their glasses to mine.

12

Thursday, March 16, 1978

A pair of gendarmes appeared quayside within an hour of our arrival. I looked at Gary. Apprehension crossed his face as the policemen pushed their way through the crowd of onlookers and stopped at our boat.

Good, they've come for him.

Then one of the gendarmes motioned to me. I crossed the deck and kneeled at the transom. He told me to report to *le capitaine* at eight o'clock the next morning.

What now?

With that shackling my mind, I phoned Aileen to let her know Gary and I, and the Spellbound, were in Papeete. She said Kerry was recovering nicely from the surgery.

"That's great," I said, "but from your tone, it sounds like there's something else."

"That woman, the FBI agent. She thinks Kerry's lying, or at least not telling them everything."

I told her about the grand jury.

"I heard," she said, "but no date's been set. Kerry said the FBI might give her a lie detector test."

"I wish they'd give our brother a lie detector test."

~

The next morning, I reported to the Gendarmerie. Chris Peters, who spoke passable French, accompanied me to translate. I figured Captain Bereze must have an update on the investigation, but he merely told me to report to a government office, where there were administrative matters to deal with. I asked about the FBI and whether Gary might be extradited. He said there were no new developments.

I went to the government office as instructed, but shortly after my arrival the bureaucrats left without explanation. I drummed my fingers on the arm of a chair and watched the clock for what seemed like a more-than-reasonable amount of time, then we returned to the quay. There the Browers invited us aboard the Fair Winds for coffee. As Chris and I settled into the cockpit, a gendarme hailed the Spellbound. I saw him talk to Gary, then Gary disappeared. I hollered at the man and waved him over. He said I was to return to the government building.

"I just came from there."

He insisted.

"I'm gonna finish my coffee," I said and sat down.

"What do they want now?" Phil asked.

I shrugged. "They just say, 'Report here, report there,' then I sit on my ass for a couple hours while they dick around."

After finishing the coffee, I trudged back up the hill, Chris in tow, and found Gary already meeting with a government official. I hadn't noticed his leaving the Spellbound, but he'd obviously gotten the word. The official was outfitted like a member of the French Foreign Legion.

Chris leaned toward me and whispered in my ear, "Inspector Clouseau." I stifled a laugh, thinking I felt more like Rick Blaine in *Casablanca*. I looked at Gary. *At least they had rounded up one suspect.*

The official presented us with a bill for nearly $3,500 for search-and-rescue services and Kerry's medical expenses. And, oh by the way, the Spellbound had been impounded.

I snapped forward in my chair. "You're taking *le bateau*?"

He shook his head and explained that the boat could remain at the quay, and we could stay aboard, but neither the boat nor Gary, as the vessel's captain of record, could leave Papeete until we paid the bill in full.

Gary looked at me and grinned.

I examined the invoice line by line. It included charges by the doctor who had tended to Kerry's wounds at Rangiroa. Among his expenses were drinks.

"We're not paying his bar tab," I said.

"These are legitimate expenses."

"I suppose a round of golf would be a legitimate expense as well."

The man did not respond.

"This is bullshit! He can get drunk on his own dime."

The official agreed to exclude the drinks and several other items, reducing the bill to $3,300. As we stood to leave, he said, "*Bon chance.*"

"My ass," I muttered.

On the way back to the boat, I stopped at the post office and phoned Aunt Vivian, who had initiated probate for my parents' estate. I asked her to wire funds so I could pay the bill and make repairs to the boat before sailing home. She agreed but said it would likely be weeks before the funds were available.

"Weeks?" I said.

Vivian sighed. "These things take time. I'm just glad that you and Gary are back in Tahiti, and you're both aboard the boat, keeping it safe."

"Yeah, well, without money from the estate, I can't afford to stay here much longer. These phone calls alone are costing me a fortune. Besides, I heard that a big storm blew through San Diego and boats were lost in several marinas. I don't know if my boat survived or not."

"I understand, but my hands are tied."

We said good-bye, and I banged the receiver into its side hook. Sweat trickled into my eyes, and I swiped at it with a forearm.

I stepped outside, where the sea breeze offered some relief. I could see the tops of masts of the sailboats lining the quay. The people around me went about their business, oblivious to my troubles. I started down the steps, then stopped.

There's got to be a better explanation.

I located Chris and he agreed to go back to the Gendarmerie with me, where I asked Captain Bereze about it. He said the official got it wrong, that it didn't matter whether Gary or I remained with the Spellbound. It just had to be one of us.

Back at the boat, I explained it to Gary. "So?" he said.

"So you need to go home. Don't you get it? They're saying you assaulted Kerry and murdered our father and our mother, for chrissake."

He gazed out a window. "She wasn't my mother."

"What?" I felt heat rise in my neck and face. "The woman who raised us, who was the only mother we ever really had?"

He said nothing.

"She was more of a mother than that alcoholic who abandoned us. You even testified against her when her second husband divorced her."

Gary lifted a hand to his mouth and pried away a bit of cuticle.

"That's your answer? You're not denying that you killed her?"

"She killed herself."

"I want to believe you, but you've contradicted yourself so many times. Kerry and Lori, too. I don't know who or what to believe."

When he didn't reply, I added, "You need to go home and face your accusers and give them a plausible explanation for what happened on this boat. Our grandparents have a right to know. Aileen and Bobbie and I have a right to know."

He turned to me and scowled. "You don't want to know."

I stared in disbelief as he went to the galley, opened a drawer, and withdrew a carving knife. I flinched. Then he began slicing a baguette.

I left the boat and walked around Papeete until the tension began to drain away. On the way back, I passed a newsstand. The Spellbound had returned to the front pages of the local papers. I bought copies and returned to the boat, where I scanned the articles. As far as I could tell, the reports stated the obvious, that *le bateau de la mort*—the death ship—had arrived in port and the investigation continued. But the news articles offered nothing new.

Gawkers trailed past the boat at all hours, pointing and snapping pictures. I remained out of sight or away from the boat as much as possible.

I had to do something, but what? Without money from the estate, I couldn't stay much longer. I had no way of forcing Gary to leave. He had money from his insurance settlement and nothing to lose by staying. He just sat there, smoking cigarettes, chewing his nails, and staring into space. No doubt counting the minutes until I left.

I hoped Kerry would say enough to the FBI that they'd have Gary detained by the French. But no word came from Seattle.

The next day, after a refreshing cold shower at the public restroom, I talked to other boaters about the need for crew and the recommended sailing routes to the States. When I returned to the Spellbound, it looked as if it were lying low. I went aboard and found the bilge filled with seawater. Gary said he had opened the wrong valve. The water intake had stopped, but he didn't seem concerned about the saltwater sloshing around inside the boat. The electric bilge pump had quit, and pumping the water out by hand would take all day, if I didn't collapse from exhaustion first. I pulled a submersible electric pump from the shower and jury-rigged it to pump out the bilge before the water damaged the engine or shorted out the electrical system.

The crisis over, I confronted Gary again. "You need to go home. I'll take care of the boat."

"As if you know what to do or could even sail the boat out of the harbor, let alone to Seattle," he said.

"Uh-huh. And you nearly sank it today."

"That was an accident."

"Yeah, just like when we almost ran up on the reef. And your stellar performance while docking at the quay is evidence of your superior seamanship."

His cheeks flamed. "That was your fault."

"Keep telling yourself that, buster."

He snorted and said under his breath, "Dumb shit."

"What'd you say?"

"You heard me."

His eyes taunted me, daring me to press on. Memories of our boyhood battles entered my mind. Battles I invariably won. But my options were limited. And if he had assaulted Kerry and killed our parents, who could predict what he might do? I was not dealing with a reasonable person. The guns were gone, but the boat had plenty of weapons on board in the form of knives, wrenches, and winch handles—and a Polynesian war club designed for a single purpose.

Needing a new bilge pump, I went to my parents' cabin to retrieve some of the cash I'd discovered earlier. The money had vanished. I returned to the main cabin and questioned Gary about it. He responded with his trademark shrug, again taunting me with a smirk-and-stare.

I had to get away. From him, from the boat, from the haunting images of my dead parents. I walked to a part of Papeete I hadn't yet explored and found a small restaurant, where I sat at an outdoor table under a large, leafy tree. I ordered a pizza, and when it arrived, a cockroach the size of a mouse fell from the tree and landed on the table next to the pie. I swept the giant insect to the ground where, once back on its feet, it waddled up the path to the front door and, without hesitation, entered the restaurant.

I shook my head and looked down at the pizza, then frowned. The culinary customs in Tahiti were as foreign to me as the language. I had ordered it *avec l'oeuf* (with egg), figuring the term referred to a scrambled egg. Not so. A single egg had been cracked over the center of the hot pizza, cooking the egg white but not the runny yolk. Not exactly finger food, especially when one sports a beard.

When I finished eating, I wandered around town as the sun set and the air cooled. Anything to keep me away from the boat—and my brother. I ducked into a small bar two blocks from the quay. A pair of sullen Polynesians glanced my way, then returned to their drinks. Other patrons watched an angry exchange at the pool table, smiling and nudging each other in anticipation of a fight. Cigarette smoke and the pungent odor of stale beer hung in the air.

I moved to the far end of the bar where I'd be out of range of swinging cue sticks. No one spoke English that I could discern, most of the conversations being in Tahitian, accompanied by a smattering of French. Tourists, after dark, did not frequent that part of town, a world away from the glamour of the resort hotels near the airport. But I only needed to say "Hinano" and dole out the coins for a bottle of beer.

In one corner, a band played songs not unlike country music back home, with a recurring melody reminiscent of "She'll Be Comin' 'Round the Mountain." I wished I had my fiddle or bass so I could join in.

I nursed several beers, clapping at the end of each song, and at one point one of the guitar players caught my eye. I smiled and lifted my beer in salute. He nodded as they struck up another tune.

When I judged that sufficient time had passed for Gary to be asleep, I slid off the barstool and stepped into the humid but refreshing outside air. The street lay empty. The public market, a boisterous exchange every morning, sat dark and silent. I strolled past several closed shops, then heard steps approaching from behind. Before I could turn to see who followed me, a heavy hand gripped my shoulder and spun me around. As I turned, I had a vision of Gary poised to club me. When I saw the burly guitar player, a sense of relief washed over me. But only for an instant. Glaring at me with red-rimmed eyes, he thrust out a hand and spat out a demand in Tahitian. I didn't need a translator.

I dug into a pocket, pulled out a few coins and deposited them in his open palm. He glanced at the coins, then spoke again, his voice rising. I considered telling him to go fuck himself, but since he bore a striking resemblance to Manu Tuiasosopo, UCLA's renowned defensive lineman, I reached deeper into my pocket and gave him all the coins I had, about four or five dollars' worth.

"I gather you're not from the Tahitian tourist bureau," I said, praying he didn't expect me to empty my wallet as well.

He examined the coins, gave me a curt nod and returned to the bar. Only when I was safe did the reaction kick in. My hands trembled, then my knees. I gasped for air and slumped in a shop's doorway, wondering how close I'd come to ending up in the same hospital Kerry had recently occupied.

Monday, March 20, 1978

With no foreseeable way to win the waiting game with my brother, I booked a flight to Seattle two days hence. Ticket in hand, I met with Captain Bereze a final time to retrieve my passport. I apologized for my earlier belligerence and thanked him for his assistance. He demurred, saying, "It is my job."

That evening, Felix and Trish Homer invited me to the Sundancer for "a bit of a rage." They had movies of their ocean crossing and plenty of gin and orange drink, sans ice cubes, as usual. A twinge of guilt stabbed my conscience, but I had to blot my parents, at least temporarily, from my mind. I rip-roared and eventually staggered back to the Spellbound, singing, "Heedy, hidy, Christ almighty, who the hell are we-e-e-e . . ."

The next day—my final full day in Papeete—filming for the movie *Overboard* began at dawn, and it seemed that no matter what route I took to the public market, Angie Dickinson, Cliff Robertson, and the camera crew blocked my way. When I returned to the boat, Gary was standing on the stern, watching the activity.

"Bunch of assholes," I said. "They've blocked off half the streets."

Gary smirked. "A producer came by the boat and invited me to lunch. He wants to use the Spellbound in the movie."

I eyed him with suspicion.

"The money could pay off the debt with the Froggies," he said.

"If it's a reasonable amount, it's worth considering."

He grinned. "Yeah, and I might be in it. I'm supposed to hand Angie a bicycle and tell her when to return it."

"We can't agree to anything without talking to Aileen, Kerry, and Bobbie," I said. "And we should talk to Aunt Vivian and Aunt Verney. The boat is now part of the estate."

Gary's eyes bored into me. Was that hate? Or merely condescension?

I tried to track down the producer and get some details, but no one I talked to knew where he was or could answer my questions.

The following morning, I stepped off the Spellbound's lofty stern and lifted my head for a final look. The light of the rising sun reflected off the upper sections of the boat's masts.

Beacons of hope? Or fiery torches signaling tribulations to come?

13

Wednesday, March 22, 1978, morning

Papeete to Seattle, with a plane change in Los Angeles. Twelve hours parked on my ass, trapped in a torture chamber. The saving grace being that I scored a flight aboard Air New Zealand rather than Air France. The gracious New Zealand hostesses, with a verbal gait somewhere between the Brits and Aussies, were a refreshing change from the flight to Tahiti and the French officiousness in Papeete.

Below, surreal puff-balls polka-dotted the inconceivable expanse of water. Confined to one sense—sound, smell, taste, and touch being held hostage by the cabin interior—it looked more like a work-in-progress from Monet than a world of relentless swells, bow spray, and sudden squalls. And death. My parents lay in that watery deep.

Are we flying over them now?

I put a hand to the window as if I could somehow reach out to them, feel their touch, catch a whiff of their scent, hear them laugh. I thought of my father, born in 1927 in a farmhouse in the Palouse country of eastern Washington, the youngest of three children. During the Great Depression, his parents moved to Seattle, hoping to find work, and Dad spent much of his boyhood in the city's Ravenna district near Green Lake. He attended Roosevelt High School but graduated from Woodrow Wilson High School in Washington, D.C. (one year ahead of Warren Buffett), after his father took a job with the federal government at the end of World War II.

Dad served a two-year stint in the army, then enrolled at the University of Washington on the GI Bill. However, he had to drop out when his life took an unanticipated turn. In early 1949, he met my biological mother, and they married the following August. I was born in November. I never got the full story from him. Anytime I asked about it, he blushed. The closest he came was through a brief aside one night after I'd met a girl at a drive-in movie theater: "Don't stay out late," he said. "You can get into trouble."

I thought I could pry it out of him during a quiet night at sea or a stroll on a deserted beach, but that hope had been dashed forever.

In a similar vein, Mom, born in 1934 and the second-oldest in a family of five children, grew up on a small farm near the hamlet of Preston in the foothills of the Cascade Mountains. Her father felled trees as a logger; her mother worked the farm. Mom graduated from Issaquah High School, where she earned a varsity letter in girls' basketball. Afterward, she worked for the phone company before marrying her first husband. She played volleyball in an adult recreation league in Bellevue.

After I graduated from college, I'd yearned for an adult relationship with her, to move beyond the parent-child rut we'd occupied for nearly two decades. But as with Dad, that wish had evaporated like a morning mist.

I swallowed a sob and wiped my eyes. A hostess stopped and offered me a tissue. "Allergies," I said. "Thank you."

I peered out the window again. If Gary had killed Mom and Dad as the FBI suspected, what led to that grisly result?

Gary had said, "She's not my mother," as if that explained everything. He hadn't killed his mother because the woman who died was not his mother. He had not killed his mother because his mother—the one I called Birth Woman, the one who left us when we were vulnerable preschoolers—lived the life of an alcoholic in Memphis, Tennessee. A woman I hadn't seen more than a handful of times over the previous two decades and with whom I had little contact. Gary had lived with her for a while as an adult, after he was drummed out of the army. When he returned to the Seattle area, he told me about her having a six-pack for breakfast and polishing off a fifth of vodka before the day ended. Some mother.

After Birth Woman had walked out on us, Grandma Jane and her father, Great-grandpa Funk, often watched Gary and me until Dad married Jody and she became "Mom." I'd never truly known any other. But Gary? Maybe he never accepted her. Maybe he clung to a vague memory of that wisp of nothing we never really knew.

Mom, on the other hand . . . I chuckled, recalling Sunday mornings. She took us kids to Sunday School and Dad picked us up. They rarely attended church, except for the occasional sunrise service on Easter—lip-service Presbyterians. One day I figured it out: With the five kids away, Mom and Dad could play.

And why not? With a ready-made family, they'd had little time for themselves. I imagined them saying, "Thank you, Jesus."

I seldom told my friends I had a stepmother. I wanted to be normal, I wanted our family to be normal—a dad, a mom, and five children. End of story.

Of course, there were moments I hated her. Or I thought I did. One time she made me pull my belt from my pants and hand it to her, then she laid into me. I had been in charge of taking care of our dog's puppies, but they got sick and it cost a bundle in vet bills. I hadn't neglected them, really. But she wouldn't listen.

Afterward, I wrote on a scrap of paper: *I hate my mother.* One day she came to my room and riffled through the clothes in my dresser. She found the note—*Idiot! why didn't you throw it away?*—and I watched as she read it, fearful of what she might do. But she just tossed it aside and continued going through the drawers. I had no idea what she was looking for. When she left, I took the note to the basement fireplace and put a match to it.

There were times I didn't think she cared about me, that only her precious little girls mattered. Yet, hadn't she nursed me, albeit it with a heavy hand, after a fall from my bike had scraped the hide, hairline to jaw, from the right side of my face? Using tweezers, she'd picked out bits of dirt and gravel embedded in my flesh, accompanied by commands of "hold still!" Standing at the kitchen sink, she suds'd up a washcloth with a bar of Dial soap and scrubbed my face like a bathroom floor. Then she flooded the oozy wound with hydrogen peroxide. Doctoring, farm-style.

Hadn't she comforted me when I failed the test for my driver's license? Hadn't she gone with me to the police station after I wrecked the family car? And again after I got caught with a fake ID that I'd made to buy beer at convenience stores? Hadn't she taken me to J.C. Penney to buy the suit I wore to the junior prom?

And there was the time, while home for a weekend, that I'd been out with friends and returned about ten o'clock. I said goodnight to my parents and went to my bedroom in the basement. I saw the door to the backyard ajar, so I slammed it closed. It had to be shut hard to get it to latch. My father the carpenter never found the time to fix it.

The next morning, when I went upstairs for breakfast, Mom stood at her usual position atop the heat register, her back to the window, cup of coffee cradled in her hands, nightgown ballooned out by the warm air rising around her feet and legs. She wore her Issaquah High School letter sweater and her brown hair, styled after Jacqueline Kennedy, just touched the collar. Puffy bags framed bleary eyes, as if she'd gotten little sleep.

"Where'd you go last night?" she asked.

"I went to bed. You saw me."

"I heard you leave."

"I didn't leave. The basement door was open. I shut it and went to sleep."

A look of realization crossed her face, and that same sense flooded my mind. She had lain awake waiting for me to return. That touched me. I saw her in a new light. Of course, I couldn't tell her that. Not then.

Through the airplane's window, I watched white clouds billow upward, building fantasy castles in a cerulean sky.

Now it's too late.

Yes, she was my stepmother. Yes, she had passive-aggressive tendencies she used to manipulate Dad and others. But she had a kind, nurturing soul. She'd been a community volunteer, raising funds for the Cystic Fibrosis Foundation and the Children's Hospital Orthopedic Guild. During the summer she taught swimming at Juanita Beach for the American Red Cross. Later, she became a teacher's aide in the local school district's special-education program. Family legend had it that she planned to become a nurse when she returned from the sailing trip.

Even so, aboard the boat, had Mom exploded in a fit of anger? Had years of pent-up emotion—along with the usual injustices and indignities of life—piled high like a rogue wave rolling ashore and unleashed a torrent of violence? Hard to imagine. I rejected any notion that she instigated the attacks aboard the Spellbound. Or took her own life.

I switched planes in L.A. and boarded the flight for Seattle. I welcomed the intonations of a familiar language, yet, as hurried travelers pushed and pressed against me, I missed the languid pace of Tahiti.

When the plane roared skyward, I puzzled over how to tell family members what I knew, how to say that the FBI would make a case for Gary having killed Mom and Dad. Their gut reaction would be, as mine had been, denial. Isn't that always the way people react? "Why, Johnny was the nicest boy. He couldn't have done such a horrible thing."

I'd remind the disbelievers of the willful child who was rarely disciplined—Gary, the vindictive one. One day, when I was about ten years old and Gary nine, I had just finished sweeping the recreation room in the basement. As I was about to sweep my pile of dirt and dust balls into a dustpan, Gary romped down the stairs and scattered it with a kick of his foot.

"You A-hole!" I shouted.

He smirked. "It's your fault. You put it right where everyone walks."

I complained to Mom, and she told him to sweep it up. My turn to smirk, and I went outside, my chores done for the day. That night, as I got ready for bed, I turned down the bedspread. On my pillow I found a present from Gary—a neat little pile of dirt and dust balls. Gary was in the bathroom brushing his teeth, so I returned the favor, then turned my pillow over, climbed into bed, and waited.

When he discovered what I'd done, he picked up the debris and threw it at my head. "That's what you get!"

I jumped out of bed and we faced off. "You started it," I said and shoved him backward onto his bed. He stood and shoved me back, and soon we were wrestling on the floor. Even though he was a year younger, Gary was already taller, but I prevailed in our little scuffles. I soon had him on his back and sat on his chest, pinning his arms down with my knees.

"Get off me, you fat pig!" he said.

"Say you're sorry."

"No! It's your own fault."

I pushed some spit onto my lips and hovered above his face.

"You better not!"

"Say you're sorry."

"I'm . . . not sorry."

I dropped the spit just above his eyes. "The next one goes in your mouth."

"OK, OK. I'm sorry," he said.

"And you'll never do it again."

"I'll never do it again."

I let him up, but as I turned toward my bed, he jumped me from behind, throwing a choke hold on me. I wriggled free and took him back to the floor.

A commanding voice ended our scuffle. "Larry," Dad said, "let him up."

I hadn't heard Dad come down the stairs. I stood and explained what had happened, pointing to the dirt scattered on my bed, pillow, and in my hair.

"You have to learn to get along," he said.

"But Dad . . ."

"I don't want to hear it. Stop fighting and go to bed."

When Dad left the room, I heard Gary behind me, chortling. Gary had gotten away with it—again. I sighed and got back into bed, turning my back to my brother, who obviously was Dad's favorite.

At the time, I didn't understand the preferential treatment Gary received. I just thought it unfair and resented it. Later on family members told me that Gary had "special problems" stemming from early childhood and had to be treated "with kid gloves" so as not to traumatize him further. There had been rumors of abuse. Not physical or sexual, but neglect—Gary left crying in his crib as Birth Woman entertained her male friends.

As we grew older, Gary became a show-off; he took risks. Had he been born several decades later, he would have been first in line for extreme sports. As it was, he had to invent his own. He climbed higher in trees; he rode his bike faster down hills; he raced his car into blind curves.

Dad had told me about the slashed tires on the car of Gary's former girlfriend's new beau, and that the army had given Gary the boot for drug-related charges, and that an employer had fired Gary for unethical behavior. Gary told me about the army incident, claiming he'd been framed, and he said his employer had no cause to fire him but had refused to listen to his explanation.

Later on, one of Mom's sisters told me they'd known for years that Gary was troubled, especially after Mom discovered he'd been taking her underpants. At first I laughed, then my gut knotted as the story unfolded. At about age eleven, she said, he'd begun taking Mom's panties from the clothes hamper in the laundry room and hiding them at the back of a dresser drawer.

I recalled that time Mom had whirled tornado-like through the bedroom Gary and I shared, emptying dresser drawers. Is that what had infuriated her?

None of that explained why violence may have erupted aboard the Spellbound, as the Gendarmes and FBI believed, but it was a reminder that Gary had never been the misunderstood angel he perceived himself to be.

14

Wednesday, March 22, 1978, evening

Aileen picked me up at the Sea-Tac airport and took me to her apartment in Kirkland, where Kerry and Lori awaited my arrival. Hugs all around, but a bittersweet reunion. I inspected Kerry's head. The wound over her right eye had healed. On her left temple, where her head had been shaved, golden fuzz sprouted around the surgical scar, which looked like an upside down horseshoe, the symbol of good luck. The irony did not escape me.

"Does it hurt?" I asked.

"Not anymore. Dad always said I had a thick skull."

"The FBI told me what the doctor said, that it was no accident."

"Sharon Wilder*, the FBI agent, keeps asking me about it. The bitch. But I don't remember how it happened. Like I told you, all I remember is waking up and Gary was talking to Dad."

I nodded and reached for the phone. I called our grandparents and scheduled visits while Aileen opened a bottle of wine.

Glasses in hand, the four of us settled into chairs and on the couch, and I summarized my stay in Tahiti. Then I turned to Kerry. "The thing is, there are conflicting accounts of what happened and when it happened—how Dad died, how you got hurt. First, we were told that he and you were hit with the boom, then it was only his being hit with the boom and you had apparently fallen, then it was that Dad slipped or lost his balance and fell, and finally, oh-by-the-way, he'd been having this pesky little equilibrium problem."

"That's what Gary told us," Kerry said. Her whiny tone grated my nerves.

"And I slept through most of it, remember?" Lori added.

I looked at Lori. Did she truly believe anyone would buy into such a ridiculous assertion? "The bottom line," I said, "is the FBI thinks Gary is responsible, and I'm leaning that direction." I turned to Kerry. "But I wasn't there. You were."

"I was unconscious for a while and slept a lot," she said.

"After you were hit on the head. What about before that?"

Kerry shrugged.

"And Mom shot herself with Gary's pistol? Yeah, right. First, at the crack of dawn, almost exactly twenty-four hours after Dad died. How convenient. Then, in another telling, sometime in the afternoon of the same day Dad died. That, after Gary first told everyone she'd died of shock during the night."

"Lori and I only heard the gunshot," Kerry said. "We didn't see anything. Gary told us what happened."

"I rest my case."

"Rrrrrrr . . . you always say that, like you're smarter than everyone else."

So, I'm getting on her nerves, too.

"I'm not saying I'm smarter. I'm saying there are gaping holes in the logic. Too many inconsistencies, too many contradictions. Like this shit about being lost and out of fuel, and it'll be days before getting to land so the bodies have to be dumped over the side, then Gary discovers fuel just before you're rescued, and," I snapped my fingers, "shazam, a couple hours later, you're all safe at Rangiroa. It's a miracle. Gary's the hero of the day."

I sipped my wine, then said, "What a crock of shit. And when you go before the grand jury, that's probably what they're gonna say, too."

"Yeah, well, I don't need any more of your shit," Kerry said and refilled her glass.

"Maybe it was a meteorite from outer space that hit your dad," Lori suggested with no hint of making a macabre joke.

Lori had never struck me as being the brightest bulb in the box, but a meteorite? I looked at her, incredulous. "What about Mom's threat to leave the boat because of Gary? Threatening to send the three of you home? Lori, you told me that at the hospital. And the Browers said it, too."

She shook her head. Kerry said nothing.

The next morning, Aileen handed me a cup of coffee along with a stack of newspapers. The articles reported Kerry and Lori's arrival from Tahiti. *The Seattle Times* had a large photo of my sisters plastered above the fold on the front page. The *Seattle Post-Intelligencer* had given their return similar treatment.

The headlines blared: "2 Deaths at Sea: A Mystery in Tahiti"; "2 Survivors of Yacht Tragedy Due in Seattle"; "Two Return Home: Survivors Voted for Sea Burial"; "Nightmare Cruise They Don't Want to Talk About"; "Deaths Interrupted Yacht's Urgent Mission."

"This is as bad as the papers in Papeete," I said. "It'd be one thing if these vultures cared about us, but we're just fodder for the morbid entertainment of voyeuristic masses."

I leafed through the papers, shaking my head. "A lot of this is BS, and they got a lot of it wrong. They always like to say someone 'died instantly,' as if it'll make us feel better believing the person didn't suffer. But Dad didn't die instantly."

Then the words "ear infection" caught my eye. I looked at Aileen and held up the article. "That's new," I said. "Gary never said anything about this before. Neither did Kerry or Lori."

Aileen shrugged. "The reporters don't call as much now, but the guy from the *Times* keeps wanting to know when the funeral will be."

"He'll go away eventually."

"He hasn't so far."

I DROVE THROUGH Woodinville and slowed to take in familiar landmarks, in no rush to face Grandma Edwards and Dad's sister, Vivian. I clattered over the railroad tracks and crossed the Sammamish Slough, then stopped briefly at the hamlet's only traffic light before continuing up the hill. The clapboard schoolhouse where I finished third grade had been replaced with a modern brick structure. As I left the hamlet, wind gusts whipped the evergreens bordering the road, and I caught glimpses of skeleton-like alders, willows, and cottonwoods in the valley below, stripped of their leaves and silhouetted against the gray gloom cloaking the region like a death shroud. Drizzle magnified the air's chill, and a feeling of dread descended over me.

I turned off the main road at Steiner's Corner, drove past the community hall where the bon voyage party for my parents had been held, and around the corner toward Aunt Vivian and Uncle Keith's place. Their house, built by my father twenty-odd years before, sat unchanged, surrounded by rhododendrons and azaleas laden with buds but not yet flaunting their spring colors. Beyond the back pasture stood a wall of green-black fir and cedar, the woods where my cousins and I had picked blackberries and red huckleberries.

Uncle Keith, a tall son of Illinois, greeted me with a crushing handshake and hustled me inside to near-suffocating heat, cranked up no doubt for Grandma Edwards. She stood and grasped me tighter than I thought possible for a frail woman closing in on eighty. I'd last seen her the previous August when I waved good-bye from the Spellbound as the boat left the Port Townsend harbor. It seemed like a lifetime.

Aunt Vivian gave me a hug, but it felt half-hearted. Cousin Linda sat at the dining table, one leg in a full cast and propped on a chair. I leaned over and got an enthusiastic embrace. "Details to come," I whispered.

She looked at me with questioning eyes, then nodded.

With the coffee poured, I delivered the sanitized version of my time in Tahiti and the situation with the boat. Then I asked Aunt Vivian to join me for a private conversation. She led me down a short hallway to one of the bedrooms, where we sat on a twin bed. I delivered the news of the FBI's suspicions and that a grand jury could indict Gary for murder.

"I know, but a son doesn't kill his father," Vivian said, patronizing me with a sigh and a weak smile.

I stared at her in disbelief.

"We're so proud of Gary," she continued. "Getting the boat safely to port under such tragic circumstances. Without him, Kerry and Lori might be dead, too."

Her response stabbed my heart. She, and apparently Grandma as well, had bought into Gary's self-aggrandizement, conveniently ignoring his conflicting accounts of the incident. Then I realized she was not aware of the contradictions because Gary had told her only what he wanted her to hear: Dad had died in a tragic accident and Mom had taken her own life.

I started to explain that there were unanswered questions, but Vivian hushed me, took my hand and said, "If we just pray to Jesus, everything will be fine."

I swallowed a sarcastic reply and thought, gosh, wasn't Grandpa Edwards surprised when he arrived in Heaven, greeted by his son and daughter-in-law.

We returned to the living room and Keith offered me more coffee. "I'll get it," I said and went to the kitchen, passing Linda at the dining table. I filled my cup and joined her. "Planning another skiing trip?" I asked.

She laughed. "Yeah, maybe I can break the other one."

Speaking in low tones, I laid things out for her, including Gary's flippant responses to my questions, in particular his knowledge of "math, economics, and accounting."

Her eyes wide, she said, "That sounds like Gary. But why would he do it?"

"I wish I knew."

I rejoined my grandmother, aunt, and uncle, taking a seat on the couch. I told them of the interest in using the Spellbound in the movie being filmed in Tahiti and asked them what they thought about it.

"Gary's taking care of it," Vivian said.

"But this is a family matter."

"I think your father would be proud to have the boat he built appear in a movie, and the money will come in handy."

"How much are they paying?"

"Gary said the details are still being worked out."

"Yeah, I bet they are."

~

FROM THE PARKS' house, I drove to Seattle and walked through the Arboretum, one of my college haunts. I needed a moment of reverie before my next stop. Afterward, I idled past the place I had shared with other runners when on the University of Washington track team. The "Trak House" sign still hung beside the front door.

That evening, Grandma Jane, Birth Woman's mother, fixed me dinner at her home on Queen Anne Hill. I recalled the joyful days spent with her and Grandpa Arnold, before their divorce—camping in summer, the trip to Disneyland, playing in the snow on Mount Rainier. And for the first time I could remember, she actually agreed with the Edwardses on something. "Gary is innocent," she said.

Being a god-fearing Methodist, she rejected the notion that a grandson of hers could commit such an evil deed. I held my tongue as I gazed across the table at her—with permed white hair tinted blue, she parodied herself. Doubts crept into the nether regions of my mind.

What if I'm wrong? What if, as preposterous as it seems, Gary is telling the truth, or at least some semblance of the truth?

Mom's family carried no such doubts. The following day, Aileen and I made the forty-five minute drive to Preston to visit Grandma and Grandpa Howatson in their one-story rambler, another home built by my father.

The small farmhouse I had first visited more than two decades earlier was long gone, replaced with fruit trees that provided filling for Grandma's pies. Smoke curled from the chimney of the newer house, and my mouth watered in anticipation of hot biscuits and the honey from the bees they kept.

Kerry had not joined us. When she'd visited them after returning from Tahiti, Grandma Howatson had told Kerry that she wanted to talk to her alone, to hear what *actually* happened aboard the Spellbound. Kerry kept putting it off.

Once we'd settled in the living room, I told them as much as I knew about the investigation and the FBI's assertion of Gary's guilt.

"Jody did not kill herself," Grandma said. "Not with Kerry badly injured and needing her care."

"I'll shoot him on sight," Grandpa added.

I had no doubt he would. I'd seen his gun, and I'd seen him use it—on a steer about to be butchered.

Saturday, April 1, 1978

Several hundred people crowded into the chapel at my parents' memorial service.

April Fools' Day. Maybe they had been fools.

I sat in the front row, tears cascading my cheeks as family and friends spoke kind words about my parents. Strains of my parents' favorite melodies filled the chapel, including Gordon Lightfoot's "Christian Island."

In the parking lot afterward, Peyton Whitely, *The Seattle Times* reporter who'd been covering the story, approached but I waved him off.

The mourners gathered for a reception at the home of Lori Oskam's parents. Other than a polite offering of condolences, Dad's family and Mom's family stood apart from each other. Friends of my parents commented on it, and I told them about the divergent opinions on the FBI investigation and suspicions about Gary.

Several of them seemed shocked by the news, but not a longtime friend of Mom's. I had a boozy recollection of the remainder of the afternoon, except for her words, which permanently seared my mind: "I recognized long ago that Gary needed therapy, but it was not my place to tell your parents how to raise their children."

I raised my glass and took a long sip.

"I think your father knew it, but he was just too proud to seek professional help," she added, then drilled me with her eyes. "So watch yourself. You could be next."

15

Monday, April 3, 1978

Kerry, Aileen, and I sat in the living room of Kerry's apartment, beers on the coffee table. Kerry lifted her bottle and picked at the label, then looked at Aileen and me for a moment before turning her gaze back to the bottle, as if trying to figure out how to put the genie back in.

I grabbed mine and took a sip. "So . . . sounds like your memory's coming back."

She raised her head. "Yeah, a little."

Aileen and I watched her, waiting. Kerry, who was staying with her current beau, had phoned Aileen, saying she'd recalled more details of how she got hurt.

I tipped my beer again and Aileen followed suit. Kerry looked from one of us to the other. She sighed, then glugged a hit off of the brew.

Cut the theatrics and get on with it.

Talking to her bottle, she said, "I remember sitting up and screaming and someone pushing me back down. It was dark and I couldn't tell who it was."

She paused and Aileen prompted her. "You said there was a pillow . . ."

"Yeah, over my face, and there was a hand on my throat and someone was straddling me. Then I could breathe again. That's when I heard Dad say, 'What's wrong with Kerry?' And Gary said: 'She's having fits or something.' Then Dad told him to go on deck and steer the boat."

"And you were on the settee in the main cabin," I said.

She nodded and sucked on her cigarette.

"And it was Gary straddling you?"

"I guess so."

I cocked my head. Kerry's words and movements had a rehearsed feel to them. Her tone seemed empty, mechanical.

"Where was Mom?" Aileen asked.

"Dad shouted to her, and she came from their cabin. They'd been sleeping."

"So it was still dark," I said.

Kerry nodded again.

"What else?"

"Later on, I looked in the mirror and saw bruises on my neck, and my throat was sore for a couple days."

"You mentioned that at the hospital in Tahiti."

"When did Dad go on deck?" Aileen asked.

"Maybe fifteen minutes later. It wasn't very long. Gary said he thought he saw an island and wanted Dad to come out and take a look."

I turned toward Aileen, brow furrowed, then back to Kerry. "Gary said it was two hours after he found you."

"It wasn't that long. It was still dark outside."

"I'm sure you're right, but that's what he's saying."

"Why don't you believe anything I tell you? No one ever believes me."

Aileen said, "We do, but . . ."

"Kerry, we just want to understand what happened," I said. "These are the kinds of questions you'll be asked at the grand jury hearing next week."

She lit another cigarette, and we sat silent for a moment, nursing our beers. Then Kerry continued. "It was only seconds after Gary called Dad outside that Dad got hurt. I heard a loud noise, like a crash, and the whole cabin shook. Mom yelled to Gary, asking him what happened."

She stopped and I shot her a look of exasperation. "What did he say?"

She glanced at me, then looked down at her cigarette. "He told Dad was hit by the boom," Kerry said, "but in a tone of voice that didn't seem like there was anything to worry about. Mom went to the door and saw Dad laying in the cockpit. She had to order Gary to help her move Dad inside the cabin. Blood was spurting from Dad's head and Gary just stood there, like he didn't care."

Aileen looked at me. "That son of a bitch."

No one said anything for what seemed like a long time but probably was only a few seconds. "Anything else?" I asked.

Kerry knocked the ash off the end of her cigarette. "Afterward, I found a large wrench behind a cushion on the settee, and I remember wondering how it got there. You know how Dad was, always wanting the tools put away."

"So you think Gary hit you with it?" Aileen said.

Kerry shrugged.

"When you called, you said something about powder in a cup."

"Yeah, my head hurt like hell—"

"This was after Mom died?" I asked.

Kerry nodded and took another drag on her ciggie. "Gary handed me a cup of water and told me to drink it. He said it would help me sleep. There was white powder floating on top of it. I tried to drink it, but it tasted awful, so I didn't."

Barbiturates, I thought. Mom had included them in the medical supplies. "What do you think it was?"

"I don't know. It scared me."

"We'll have to start calling you Rasputin," I said.

Kerry touched the spot where her head had been shaved for surgery. "My hair will have to grow back out first."

"That was Rumpelstiltskin."

"No," Aileen said. "It was Rapunzel who let down her hair."

We all laughed, then fell silent.

I drained my beer and asked Kerry, "Why would Gary attack you?"

Her face contorted as if she were about to cry. "I don't know. I keep telling you, I don't know, I don't know, I don't know!"

I glanced at Aileen as she rolled her eyes. What Kerry said was little more than she'd told us before.

"Is that it?" Aileen asked.

"Another boat offered to help us. They had a doctor on board. But Gary turned him down."

"When was that?"

"Not long after Gary made the first Mayday call."

"Why did Gary turn him down?" I asked.

"He said we'd have to turn around, but he wanted to keep going toward Rangiroa, where there was a medical clinic." Kerry stubbed out her cigarette and looked at her watch, then at us. Her eyes begged us to leave.

"Did Mom talk to the doctor?" Aileen asked.

Kerry shook her head.

"Why not? Mom would've—"

Kerry shouted, "I don't remember!"

I touched her arm. "Kerry, it's OK. Maybe you'll remember more later on."

"Maybe. But I've told you everything I can for now."

"Grandma Howatson still wants you to come see her," Aileen said.

"I know."

"I can take you up there."

Kerry said nothing as she extracted another cigarette from the pack and lit up.

I stood and Aileen followed my lead. Kerry set the cigarette in an ashtray and joined us. We hugged good-byes and I promised to call after I got to San Diego.

As Aileen drove us back to her place, I said, "She's stringing us along, feeding us bits and pieces just to keep us off her back."

"Yeah, I don't know what to believe anymore."

KERRY NEVER WENT to see Grandma Howatson, someone she'd been close to when younger, having spent many days, and nights too, at the small farm, gathering duck eggs from around the pond, feeding the cattle, picking vegetables from the garden, and bouncing on the vine maples at the back of the property. Nor would Gary ever contact the Howatsons to express his condolences over Mom's death.

These are the actions of innocent victims of a tragedy?

Given what the FBI suspected—that Gary killed our parents—I could understand Gary not visiting them, but it reinforced the

Howatsons' belief that he was guilty. But Kerry? What was she hiding that she was too ashamed to visit her mother's parents and tell them how their eldest daughter had died? So ashamed that she refused to talk to them about the final hours of the two people who had conceived her, nurtured her and coddled her into adulthood? Or was it that Kerry knew her grandparents would see through her bullshit?

HAVING BEEN AWAY from San Diego for nearly six weeks, I had to get back to my boat and, with any luck, my job. But before I left Seattle, I met with Sharon Wilder, the FBI agent assigned to the case there. She was not much older than I, and her tight dress and heels were a far cry from Steely Eyes and Stoneface in their shorts and Hawaiian shirts. I dubbed her Nattily Attired.

"I wish I could tell you more, but you seem to know as much as I do," she said. I doubted that. "But the pistol, the one your brother had on the boat?" she said, her inflection turning it into a question. I nodded. "He told you it was from his army days, right?"

"That's what he said."

She huffed. "Another lie. He bought that here just a few days before he left."

"In Seattle?"

She nodded. "Bellevue, but same difference."

Had Gary told the truth about anything?

"The grand jury hearing is next Monday," she said. "Kerry and Lori are gonna crack and tell all. Gary will be subpoenaed once he returns to the States. Then we nail him."

She sounded like a TV cop. Or a cheerleader. Still, I wanted to believe her.

Tuesday, April 4, 1978

I flew home, accompanied by the Garretts. We didn't say much, and when Nan and I looked at each other, our eyes misted over. From time to time, she held my hand.

Being squeezed into the narrow seat, unable to fully stretch my legs, I recalled rides in the family car as a kid. Until my parents bought a station wagon, we had a 1955 two-door Ford Fairlane coupe. To create more seating, Dad shaped a piece of plywood that covered the backseat and the leg space, then spread a blanket over the wood. We four older kids sat on pillows and kicked at each other, fighting for leg room—until Dad raised an arm and threatened to slap us. Occasionally, we went to drive-in movies in the same fashion. One night we saw the Western *Shane*. One of the few times I saw Dad cry.

Sunday, April 9, 1978

A travel article mentioning the Spellbound appeared in *The San Diego Union*. Tal and Lee Sturdivant had written about their sail from Tahiti to Hawaii, and said that two days out of Papeete an airplane buzzed their boat, the Little Revenge. The air crew told the Sturdivants, via VHF radio, of the Spellbound's plight. The Sturdivants agreed to lend aid. They soon sighted the Spellbound about eighteen miles from Rangiroa. Tal contacted the Spellbound by radio and Gary responded, saying he had found fuel and didn't need any help. The Sturdivants, who only learned of my parents' deaths after they reached Hawaii, wrote that the Spellbound then "motored away" from them.

So much for Gary's being "hopelessly lost."

Then, almost as if in rebuttal to the Sturdivant article, *The Seattle Times* ran another front-page story on Sunday, April 30. Mom's birthday.

The piece was written by Elouise Schumacher, a travel writer who had spoken to Gary in Tahiti. Aileen phoned the next day and read it to me. The article did not mention the Sturdivants or contain even a "no comment" from the FBI. It read as if Gary had written it himself.

One detail in particular caught my ear. He'd told Schumacher that Mom died at 7 A.M. on Saturday, February 25.

"That's interesting," I said, "since he reported her death by radio at six-thirty A.M. So he's clairvoyant, too?"

That article was the first news we'd had of Gary in weeks. No one in the family had heard from him, not even Aunt Vivian. Her letters and telegrams to him had gone unanswered. Was he too busy schmoozing with reporters and the Hollywood crowd?

Then, in the first week of May, Vivian received a letter from Gary dated April 25. In it he itemized the money owed to the French Polynesian government and requested funds from the estate. However, the most interesting parts were his comments about Kerry and me:

> *I feel sorry for Kerry & Larry for having had to say what they have. I have been asked why I do not go back ASAP and defend myself. I do not have to. I like myself. I feel good with myself and sleep good all night. I think what I did was what I had to do with what was happening at the time to me, and the others on the boat. I do not like what happened, I wish it had not happened—I would have liked to continue the trip and enjoyed the South Pacific w/ mom & dad, Kerry & Lori. Nothing will change what has happened—I do not like what happened—I am working on accepting what happened. I have to live with myself. . . . If you want to know my version of what happened—what I believe to have happened—write and ask me.*
>
> *All I will say now is that 1. if I had tried to kill Kerry—I wouldn't have tried. I would have and she would not be there now. 2. Larry, I can only imagine, must have either had a vision or wishful thinking for another 5% of the estate or whatever.*

He ended the letter with a statement that struck me as odd, yet typically manipulative, considering that Vivian attended church regularly and Gary did not: *May you walk beneath no other Shadow than that of our Lord.*

But the words that left me cold were: *I think what I did was what I had to do with what was happening at the time to me, and the others on the boat. . . . I have to live with myself.*

What the hell did that mean? What, exactly, did he do that he had to live with himself? For me, it was an oblique admission of guilt. Also curious was the way he rationalized it—he did what he "had to do."

And what did he mean by "what I believe to have happened." What did belief have to do with it?

16

Monday, May 15, 1978

Larry Schiller phoned. I had some idea of who he was. He'd contacted Kerry a few days earlier saying he wanted to produce a movie and publish a book about our parents. Kerry and Aileen were to meet with an attorney to discuss it. But Schiller didn't bother to introduce himself to me or offer condolences about my parents' deaths. I asked him to start at the beginning.

"Didn't your sisters tell you what this is about?" he asked.

"My sisters are overwhelmed," I said. "They told me they'd been contacted by someone claiming to be a representative of a Hollywood production company, and this person enticed them with the prospect of a boatload of cash. Frankly, it's moving too fast for my tastes."

Kerry had told me of the big numbers—hundreds of thousands of dollars—Schiller had tossed around. She and Aileen were living on the dole and visions of conspicuous consumption danced through their heads like Christmas sugarplums.

Schiller sighed and filled me in. Yes, he had ties to Factor-Newland Productions, which developed made-for-TV movies, including *Overboard*, the movie being filmed while I was in Papeete. I would receive a contract in a day or two. It called for eighty dollars earnest money, paid at the time of the contract signing, then fifteen hundred dollars at a later date, plus two percent of the net. It sounded like peanuts to me, and Hollywood accounting being legendary, I expected the royalties to be the equivalent of Fred C. Dobbs' treasure of the Sierra Madre.

The Factor in Factor-Newland turned out to be Alan Factor, somehow related to Hollywood cosmetics pioneer Max Factor. But Schiller remained a mystery. Years later, he went on to fame, if not fortune, as the author of a book about Jon Benet Ramsey, the six-year-old girl found dead in her Colorado home, and I also unearthed descriptions of Schiller as a "carrion bird" and "the journalist who dealt in death." But at the time his name meant nothing to me.

Nor did I know anything about Barry Farrell, whom Schiller had tapped to write the book. Farrell phoned me from Seattle a few days later. Aileen and Kerry had signed the contract. He wanted to meet with me after he returned to Los Angeles. The process, he said, would require two or three lengthy interviews. I wrote in my journal:

> *Farrell, like Schiller, sounded as though I ought to not only know him by name, but be glad to speak with him. Never mentioned Mom & Dad, just said something about "the writer" of the "book." I knew what he meant, but he pissed me off when he wouldn't come out and say it.*

I learned only after Farrell's death that he had been a respected journalist, beginning his career with the *Seattle Post-Intelligencer* and later writing for *Life* magazine. He had dubbed Schiller the "carrion bird," which raised his esteem a notch in my mind. Had he bothered to tell me this at the outset, I might have been more receptive.

"Have you signed the contract?" he asked.

"I haven't seen the contract, let alone signed it, and until I do, and until I've consulted with my attorney, and until I've spoken with my grandparents about this, I'm not meeting with you or Larry Schiller, whoever the hell he is. As far as I'm concerned, you're a bunch of money-grubbing ghouls who prey on tragedy and can't wait to pick the bones of my recently deceased parents."

"We think this is an important story that deserves to be told."

"You want to sensationalize their deaths and line your pockets," I said. "Besides, until the FBI investigation is complete, you don't have a story."

"We expect that to be wrapped up fairly quickly, and we want the backgrounds on your parents and all you children so we're ready to move when that time comes," he said.

"Barry, apparently I'm not communicating effectively. Until I have—"

"I get your point. I'll be in touch."

Two weeks later, at the office, I received a fat manila envelope with a Factor-Newland return address. As I read the contract, the words exploded in my mind like a squall-blown jib: Factor & Newland is granted "exclusive rights" to "any correspondence, diaries or written material" originated by me "during and in my lifetime."

Bullshit!

I tried calling Aileen and Bobbie, but neither of them answered. Why did that attorney advise them to sign this god-awful contract?

The original date on the contract, however, stopped me cold. It had been overwritten with a later date, but I could still make it out: March 21. The day *before* I left Tahiti. Gary had not said one word about it.

That's the act of a grief-stricken person?

I flung the packet across the office. When I retrieved it, my boss gave me a quizzical look. "Another house painter claiming to be Michelangelo?"

I pasted on an apologetic smile as I returned to my desk. "Something like that."

When I finally reached Aileen, she said our aunts and grandparents were outraged. But not with Gary. Aunt Vivian and Grandma Edwards had accused her, Kerry, and me of commercializing our parents' deaths. Gary, apparently, had told them that I had signed the contract first, and he had no choice but to go along to protect his interests. I wrote letters to Grandma Edwards and to Grandma and Grandpa Howatson explaining what had happened, and I included a photocopy of the page with the date. I also asked them for guidance in the matter. I never received a reply from any of them.

Thursday, June 8, 1978

Schiller phoned again and agreed to several changes, including the removal of the "exclusive rights" clause, but he insisted on a noncompete clause. I could not publish anything about my parents' deaths as long as the contract was valid. Farrell phoned immediately afterward, suggesting we meet that weekend.

"I have some tight deadlines, so I doubt I'll have the time," I said.

"I thought we had a deal."

"I only spoke with your buddy Schiller a few minutes ago, so until I see a revised contract, we have no deal."

"Shit!"

No longer Mr. Nice Guy, huh? You and Schiller can kiss my ass.

Nonetheless, I agreed to meet him on Saturday at five o'clock. He'd have a copy of the revised contract. But a half-hour before our meeting, I decided not to sign. Too late to call him, so I met him anyway.

"Son of a bitch," he said. "Now I have to make another fucking trip to San Diego."

I shrugged. I had no sympathy for him, what with the pressure he and Schiller were putting on me. He climbed into his green MGB, slammed the door, started the engine in a defiant roar, and lurched forward, tires squealing. Then he hit the brakes and leaned his head out the window. "How 'bout we go for a drink, just chat a little, off the record?"

I had him follow me to Fleas, a bar near the old ferry landing where I occasionally played darts. We ordered drinks, and he asked me about the grand jury hearings. I couldn't tell him much, since the jury divulged nothing unless it handed down an indictment. Kerry had told me she had testified to the same things she'd said earlier. Gary, still in Tahiti, had yet to testify.

Farrell wanted to know if I thought it possible that Kerry had felt pressured to come up with a "reasonable explanation" concerning her head injury. Could she possibly, subconsciously, be fabricating the assault and being smothered by a pillow?

"The problem with that theory," I said, "is that Gary told the FBI that he found her with a pillow over her head. What he didn't say, but Kerry did, was that the pillow was being pressed down on her face and she couldn't breathe. And don't forget, doctors in Papeete and Seattle said Kerry's skull fracture was no accident."

~

A week later, I flew to Seattle and visited Grandma Edwards and the Howatsons. They pleaded with me to stop the movie deal from going forward. I promised to do what I could, reminding Grandma Edwards that Gary had signed the contract two months before I knew anything about it.

From there I went to the National Old Time Fiddlers Contest in Weiser, Idaho. For a few days I forgot about the movie, my parents' deaths, work, the future. I lived for the moment, drinking and making music day and night . . . and more drinking.

AFTER I GOT back to San Diego, Schiller called me again. I passed along the misgivings of my grandparents and asked him to drop the book and movie deal.

He laughed. "I have signed contracts from your brother, your sisters, and Lori Oskam. We have a legal right to move forward, and we will do so, with or without you."

"I want the right to review. I don't want this based solely on the bullshit my brother's feeding you."

"It doesn't work that way. We've already made concessions to you that no one else got. Look, I can up the escrow amount to two-fifty, but that's it. Take it or leave it."

"I'll think about it."

The next day, I phoned the Howatsons twice but got no answer. I wrote them another letter, explaining the situation. Then I phoned Grandma Edwards and told her the news. "Like I said, if Gary hadn't signed the contract, we wouldn't be in this mess."

"He was under a lot of stress at the time," she said.

"Yeah, well, so was I, and I was still in Tahiti, but he never said one damn word about it. Now you expect me to fix it."

"It's not right. Something needs to be done."

"Then talk to Gary," I said and slammed down the receiver.

Saturday, July 15, 1978

Barry Farrell and I met in a motel room in Coronado. He'd brought the revised contract with him and I signed, figuring that it would be the only way to counter my brother's bullshit. But it prohibited me from writing about my own family, my own parents.

Farrell grabbed a pair of water glasses from the bathroom, poured me a generous dollop of Jack Daniels and handed me the glass. He poured himself a shot but never touched it.

We sat in chairs facing each other across the dingy room. The cloying smell of air freshener overlay the dank odor of mildew. I looked at him, eyebrows raised, and he began.

"Gary tells me that he excelled in everything he did, that he was far superior to you in every way, academically and athletically."

I laughed, thinking that Farrell might be stretching things to raise my ire, but I took his bait. "You have that tape recorder running?" He nodded and I began: "Gary was a C student in high school and maybe got an AA degree from Bellevue Community College. I was a B-plus student in high school, graduated from the University of Washington, and taught school for five years in Tacoma before quitting to go on the trip with my parents."

"He didn't mention that."

"I suspect there are a lot of things he failed to mention. Gary always had—still has, apparently—this fantasy world he lived in, a world where he was superior to everyone. He always took shortcuts. He never wanted to play fairly or to do the work required to succeed at something. Winning and dominating others were foremost in his mind. Like the time he cut down his slot car to make it lighter and faster than mine. Ditto for his short-lived tenure with the lumber company and the ignominious end to his army career. I don't suppose he told you about that, how he left the army?"

Barry shook his head.

"He got the boot for dealing dope. The charges, according to him, were trumped up. But our father didn't know about it until an FBI agent came by the house looking for Gary. Seems the army wanted its reenlistment bonus money back."

Barry frowned and jotted a note on his ruled pad. "What about sports?"

"Unfortunately for him, there were no shortcuts when we ran track. While I was up at five-thirty in the morning, running in the dark and rain and doing two-a-day workouts, he'd still be sawing logs. I guess he figured he was so good he didn't have to work at it."

"What about that one track meet . . ."

I chortled again. "The one time we met head-to-head, I was a senior at Lake Washington High School, he was a junior at Redmond. We were in the two-mile run and I lapped him, finishing well over a minute ahead of him."

Farrell glanced at the tape recorder's counter and made another note.

"Gary always fancied himself as being better than I in athletics, but it happened only in his dreams."

Farrell looked up, skepticism furrowing his brow.

"Don't take my word for it," I said. "I'll show you my high school yearbooks, my scrapbooks, the news clippings. More than likely, whatever he told you was total BS."

"OK, but . . ."

"Or in a fight," I added. "When we fought as boys—more like wrestling matches than fistfights—I always beat him, even though he was bigger than I. Apparently he can't accept that."

Barry's lips tightened as he weighed my words. "So, if Gary lied to me about that, maybe he lied about what happened on the boat."

"You tell me."

17

Friday, July 21, 1978

Movement across the office caught my eye. In the shadowy, backlit doorway, I could make out a wiry build, wispy beard, and shoulder-length hair.

For an instant, that silhouette became my brother. That's all the time my brain needed to register those features and begin rapid-firing synapses. Adrenaline dams burst; cortisol cramped my gut; twitching muscles poised for fight or flight. My heart shifted into overdrive.

Then the man spoke. Not my brother. I began breathing again—short, asthmatic gasps. I sat on my hands to stop the shaking. The intensity of the reaction shocked me. I had conned myself into believing that I was coping well, that I had returned to "normal." The scare left me skittish for the remainder of the day; I flinched every time someone stepped into the office.

A few days later, I wrote in my journal:

Had another nightmare about Gary. I was with Aileen, Kerry and Bobbie, standing behind an old-style bed with a metal frame. Gary walked through the door, his hair long and frizzy-like; wild-eyed; he was shocked to see me; his eyes bugged out, hate-filled.

Saturday, July 29, 1978

After being ordered by the probate court to either return the Spellbound to Seattle or release it to a professional crew, Gary sailed from Papeete. And promptly filled the bilge with water. He returned to Tahiti to make repairs, and one of his four crew members left. Gary set out a week later with the remaining three, figuring to be in Seattle by the end of September.

Meanwhile, I juggled relationships with women in two cities. When in Seattle in June, I had resumed my romantic dalliance with Sarah*, a woman I'd met during my teaching days in Tacoma, and she took me to Sea-Tac airport when I left. Alina* met me at the San Diego airport and I spent the night with her. Guilt over my two-timing tugged at my conscience, but not enough to stop. Lying naked with a woman and having sex anytime, anywhere, I felt free, with no constraints or cares. Like my parents, I could be dead in an instant. What hope did the future really offer?

TO BE NEARER my family while the issues with my parents were resolved, I decided to move back to Seattle, but first I'd have to sell my boat. Days later, through mutual friends, I met a woman, Emily*, who was visiting from Seattle. She played a classic A-model Gibson mandolin, and I took an immediate liking to her quick smile and soft laugh.

We went out a few times and, with both of us headed north, we agreed to rendezvous in southern Oregon at a fiddlers' campout. There we played house in my camper, which I'd bought to live in while waiting for my boat to sell. She offered to let me stay with her in Seattle until I found a place of my own. I then returned to San Diego to earn a bit more money before going north for good.

As for the other two women, I rationalized them away. We were all merely ports in life's storm.

Monday, September 25, 1978

Just after 9:00 A.M., an explosion shook the building where I worked in San Diego's North Park neighborhood. Everyone in the office felt the thumps on the roof, as if heavy objects had fallen from the sky. Several of us ran to the stair landing at the back of the building. Looking southeast, we saw two plumes of black smoke clawing upward into an otherwise pristine sky. Screaming sirens soon pierced the air around us. I learned, again, how tenuous life can be.

We tuned in news on a radio and heard that one of the worst airplane disasters in U.S. history had nearly engulfed us. Pacific Southwest Airlines Flight 182 had been struck mid-air by a Cessna 172. The airliner missed our building by just a few blocks and plowed through several homes. The thumps on the roof had been from pieces of the Cessna raining down.

For the rest of the day, the mood in the office remained dark, our usual banter subdued. I couldn't help but think about my parents' deaths and the anguish thrust upon the families of the crash victims.

That night, as if I needed yet another reminder of death, I went to the Garretts' home to watch the movie *Overboard*. One scene had a glimpse of Gary standing at the Spellbound's stern. His payback for signing the contract so quickly. The movie turned out to be melodramatic crap.

How badly will they butcher Mom and Dad's story?

The next day I drafted a letter to Factor-Newland, saying I hoped my parents' story would be more meaningful. I sent a copy to Larry Schiller as well. I never received a reply from either one.

Friday, October 6, 1978

The Spellbound arrived in San Francisco, and Gary told tales of thirty-five-foot waves, a broken bowsprit and mast, and a malfunctioning radio. He described the storm to Aunt Vivian as a tempest of biblical proportions, and in her eyes he again was the conquering hero. The Spellbound, the primary asset in our parents' estate, would have been lost without Gary's valiant efforts, she said.

"If my parents were still alive, the Spellbound never would have been in that storm," I said.

She only sighed in response.

Aileen called me, insisting that I immediately drive to Richmond, at the north end of San Francisco Bay where the Spellbound lay anchored near a boatyard, and take charge of the boat. "If you don't, Gary's going take all of Mom and Dad's stuff."

"No. I do not want to be aboard that boat," I said. The memories were still too vivid. Nor did I want to see my brother. "That's Vivian and Verney's problem."

Verney later told me that the dinghy ride to the boat with Gary was one of the scariest moments of her life. "He showed no emotion, just a deadly stare, and thinking of what happened to your parents, it sent shivers down my spine," she said. "I couldn't wait to get away from there."

Monday, October 9, 1978

I celebrated the sale of my boat—and my imminent departure from San Diego—with my pal, Ian Law, who played fiddle and banjo. On the day my father died, Ian had taken me to a hockey game. Screaming at the action on the ice had provided a needed relief valve.

On this night, he suggested we get some beer and sit under the Roscoe E. Hazard Memorial Bridge, which carried Adams Avenue over the 805 freeway. We muscled through the undergrowth beside the bridge, took seats on the bare dirt below the abutment, and popped our cans of Foster's. Below, cars and trucks growled up the steep grade as the streetlights blinked on and dusk settled in. The bridge thundered as vehicles passed overhead. Eau du car exhaust hung in the air.

"Larry, we've known each other less than a year, but we've become good friends. The Friday night trips to Aesop's Tables for gyros and beer, then to Bob's house in Crest to play fiddle tunes. I'm going to miss you."

I could only nod as I watched the traffic. We were silent for a moment, and I took a long pull at my beer. "I hope I'm doing the right thing," I said. "Everything's so fucked up. My parents' estate, the FBI, the family . . . I think I ought to be there."

"What about Emily?"

"Oh, well, that goes without saying. I'm horny as hell!"

We laughed and clinked our cans together, lustful grins creasing our faces. Then Ian's lips tightened as he put a hand on my arm. "If you need a shoulder, give me a call. And if you need to get away, I have a couch you can sleep on."

"Thanks, Ian."

Except that I'm afraid to sleep.

18

Monday, November 6, 1978, Seattle

Aileen called, agitation in her voice. Gary had shown up the day before, without warning, at the apartment she and Kerry shared in Redmond; Kerry had moved in with Aileen after splitting up with her boyfriend. Gary had stopped by to "say hello."

"So you let him in?" I said.

"What was I supposed to do? I was in shock."

"And you had tea and crumpets."

"Not funny. I asked him about the boat, but he changed the subject. He just wanted to brag about all of his girlfriends."

"What happened to what's-her-name?"

"He's through with her. On the sail from Hawaii, she slept on the settee."

"Where is he now?"

"He left this morning."

"He stayed at your place?"

"He slept on the couch."

"Why—"

"I was afraid of what he'd do if I told him no," Aileen said. "He was going to spend the night at some girl's place, but he came back a little after midnight. She'd kicked him out."

"He's gone now."

"Yeah, I just hope he doesn't come back."

"He will."

"Don't say that! I don't see why he doesn't go to Vivian's. She thinks he can do no wrong."

"Because the whole point is to continue his reign of terror over Kerry."

"But she doesn't seem afraid of him. I didn't sleep at all, but she slept just fine."

"Sure. As long as she keeps her mouth shut, no problem."

I hung up the phone and sighed. Emily eyed me, questioning.

"Maybe I should have stayed in San Diego," I said. "I'd be far away from this shit."

She stood and hugged me from behind, pressing her lips against my neck. "I'm glad you didn't."

Three weeks earlier, I'd arrived in Seattle, where Emily had rented a basement apartment in a house in the Wallingford District. I hadn't intended on making it my permanent abode, but after a few days the subject never came up again.

I wondered how I'd handle the coming winter after having spent a year in San Diego. It wasn't only the oppressive weather that affected me. I flinched at little noises around the house. And it being an older structure, it creaked a lot. Each night, I checked and rechecked the doors and windows to make sure they were locked. I told Emily about it, and the next time we heard an odd noise, I said, "It must be Gary!"

Her eyes spit venom. "You're scaring me."

Neither of us slept well that night.

The next Sunday, not long after going to bed, the phone woke me. I glanced at the clock's fluorescent hands. "One fucking A-M," I muttered. I lay there for a moment, willing the ringing to stop, figuring it was a wrong number. It didn't. I went to the front room and grabbed the receiver.

Aileen. Breathless. "Kerry just left. She slammed the front door three times on her way out."

I pictured our baby sister throwing a tantrum, methodically opening the door and slamming it shut. I rubbed the sleep from my eyes. "Is Gary back?"

"No, thank god. We were talking about the FBI."

"Hold that thought. I'm freezing my ass off and need to put some clothes on."

I returned to the bedroom and grabbed a pair of jeans, socks, and a sweatshirt. Rain pattered the street outside and I heard the shush of a passing vehicle. Clothes on, the shivering stopped and I picked up the handset.

Aileen said she and Kerry had been talking about the investigation.

While consuming copious quantities of booze, no doubt.

Sharon Wilder, the FBI agent, had phoned Aileen earlier in the week, trying to enlist her help in getting Kerry to be more forthcoming.

"She says the lie detector results show that Kerry is lying and that for her own good she should tell everything she knows. But Kerry denied it."

"And that's when she stormed out?"

"No. I also told her she has to be more responsible. Since she got a job, she's done nothing around the house, because she's 'tired.' She's a spoiled little brat. She just wants someone to take care of her."

"Don't we all."

Aileen went on to say that Kerry had threatened to quit her job because she couldn't handle the FBI's accusations of lying. Aileen had contacted the county mental health clinic and urged Kerry to get counseling. A therapist offered to talk with them both, but Kerry refused.

"She probably should get some help," I said. "But those quacks are crazier than we are and get paid a hundred bucks an hour to listen to us say 'woe is me.' "

"It won't cost her anything," Aileen said.

"What she needs to do is start telling the truth instead of all this bullshit about not knowing anything."

"She asked me why she has to grow up so soon."

"She's twenty-one years old!"

"Exactly. But she said she's tired of other people trying to control her life."

"And that's when she slammed the door."

"Yep."

Aileen speculated that Kerry might be just driving around. I told her to call me at a more civilized hour and went back to bed. I'd slept a few hours and finished my morning coffee by the time she called back. Kerry had returned but wouldn't say where she'd been.

Aileen and I urged Kerry to get psychotherapy. Aileen went; Kerry did not.

And me? I was the tough older brother. I was a MAN. I could handle it. I didn't need no stinkin' headshrinker to help me cope. I just popped another beer.

Later I talked to Bobbie.

"That lyin' little bitch!" Bobbie said.

"What do you mean?"

"I was at their place after Kerry took the lie detector test, and we were smoking pot and doing lines of coke with some of Kerry's friends, and she laughed about it. She bragged about how she'd blown the polygraph test. She said she'd lie on the witness stand, too."

EMILY AND I settled into "married" life. She worked as a substitute teacher; I worked on a novel while looking for a job. I could have substitute taught as well, but I had no desire to return to the classroom. After all, I was on track to become a best-selling author.

Emily introduced me to the books of Louis L'Amour, who'd written dozens of novels of the Old West. I don't recall the first title I read, but it wasn't long before I became addicted and a fan of the Sackett clan, especially the taciturn Tell Sackett. Would I have enjoyed the books as much had my parents not been killed? They were quick, easy reads, and we laughed over L'Amour's oft-used phrases—"somewhere a quail called" and "coffee strong enough to float a mule shoe." But the main attraction for me was that, in the end, the good guy took down the bad guy; good triumphed over evil; justice prevailed.

Just before Christmas, Sharon Wilder told my sisters and me that she'd spoken with Gary again, and, according to her, he said things that contradicted what he had told her colleagues earlier. "He won't give us a straight answer on anything; he's just flippant."

"That's his specialty," I said. "What's he saying now?"

"I'm not at liberty to say. But I can tell you that I asked him to take a polygraph test and he refused."

Friday, February 23, 1979

Aileen phoned. Gary was back in town. He'd driven north with a truckload of items from the boat and would meet Vivian and Verney at the storage locker where our parents' effects were being kept.

"The timing is no coincidence," I said. "Tomorrow is the anniversary of Mom and Dad's deaths. He wants to intimidate Kerry. If he tries to stay at your place again, call the cops."

I phoned Verney that afternoon.

"When I met him at the storage facility, I was very nervous," she said. "But I asked him about what happened on the boat, and he contradicted things he'd said before. He was telling out-and-out lies about the boat and what happened to your mom and dad. I told him I didn't believe a thing he said."

"Whoa! Good for you. What'd he say to that?"

"He just shrugged his shoulders and left."

"He didn't say anything specific?"

"Not today, but it's the things he's told reporters, like the pistol. He said he kept it among his things by his bunk. But he told you and the FBI it was hidden with the other guns."

"That's true."

"He also said your dad was hit by the boom, even though he'd said before that your dad lost his balance and fell."

"He probably can't remember what he's told to which people."

Verney said she and Vivian had argued after Gary left. Vivian believed Gary. "Even if my sister had wanted to kill herself, she wouldn't have used a gun," Verney said. "There were plenty of prescription painkillers on that boat."

"Yes, there were," I said. "Besides, women typically don't shoot themselves. And while steering the boat. Just a few feet from her critically injured daughter? Hard to believe."

~

I struggled financially. My novel languished with an agent, and I weighed my employment options. I applied to become a substitute teacher, but the bureaucratic paper shuffling dragged the process out, and I didn't pursue it. Five years in the classroom had left me disillusioned with the education system, and dealing with adolescent angst no longer interested me. I found a job working for a marine supply outfit in Ballard, the northwest region of Seattle.

BARRY FARRELL CAME from L.A. to see me and my sisters. He said Gary had quite a different perspective about Mom and Dad compared to us, but Barry refused to give us any details. He also said Gary told him that I was accusing him of killing our parents so I'd get a greater share of the inheritance, that it was only for the money.

"What do you expect him to say? That he did it?" I said.

"He seems sincere," Farrell said.

"Oh, puh-leeze. He's the prime suspect in a murder investigation."

"Point taken."

"Besides, it's the FBI who's accusing him of killing our parents, not me. Are they only doing it for the money?"

Barry looked at his notepad and said nothing.

"I hope they're wrong," I added, "but so far the evidence against him is pretty damning."

"The FBI says that about every suspect."

"My brother's comments say more about him than they say about me." My voice rose. "Don't forget that he signed the fucking contract with fucking Factor-Newland while I was still in Tahiti, and he never said a fucking word to me or anyone else in the family!"

He leaned back, a look of surprise on his face.

I lowered my voice and continued. "I only found out about the contract two months later, after my sisters and Lori were contacted by Larry Schiller. If that's not about the money, I don't know what is."

~

Friday, March 23, 1979

After three months of hearing nothing from the FBI, I got a call from Special Agent Pete Mercer*. Sharon Wilder had moved away; he'd been assigned to the case. He described himself as a polygraph expert.

"Polygraph tests don't make mistakes," Mercer said. "I'm going to try to get Kerry immunity from prosecution so she'll testify truthfully on the witness stand. I could use your help."

"I'm not sure what I can do."

"You can make a list of all the inconsistencies in Gary's statements that you can think of. And you could encourage Kerry to tell the truth."

"So, you want me to help you prosecute my brother for murder and convince my little sister to testify against him."

"I prefer to think of it as obtaining justice for your parents," he said.

I sighed. "OK, I'll go through my notes and get back to you."

That night I couldn't sleep and got up in the wee hours to go through my journal. I jotted down the contradictions in what I'd heard Gary say. When I finished, I slammed the book shut. *I'm wasting my damned time.*

The following week, Mercer called to thank me. "There will be more grand jury hearings and the case could be in court by June," he said. "I'm giving Kerry another polygraph test this week. We're going to nail that bastard."

Where have I heard that before?

I asked him about Kerry's behavior and her apparent lack of fear of Gary, even though she insisted she was afraid of him. Mercer said it could be the Stockholm syndrome, a paradoxical situation where trauma victims, such as those being held hostage or who have been kidnapped, actually come to like and sympathize with their captors.

"It's totally irrational," Mercer said, "but because she and Lori were stuck on the boat with Gary and the two bodies, all he had to do was look at them cross-eyed and the message was clear. He probably brainwashed them into believing that Kerry and your father were injured in accidents, and your mom killed herself. They may have come to see him as their protector, as the only person who could get them safely back to land."

"Sounds like psychobabble to me," I said.

"No, it's legit. The name comes from a bank robbery in Stockholm where the robbers took hostages and held them for about a week, but once the hostages were set free, they actually defended their captors. It sounds nuts, but it happens."

"And you think this might be the case with Kerry and Lori."

"It could be. Then again, it could be as simple as them, especially Kerry, thinking that as long as they don't implicate Gary, they're safe."

19

May 1979

Grandma Jane phoned me at work: Birth Woman . . . third-degree burns . . . intensive care . . . near death . . . no visitors allowed. Fire in her apartment . . . few details. I placed the handset in the cradle and stared at the desktop, then heard my supervisor call my name.

"Sorry, I wasn't trying to listen in, but . . . is everything OK?"

"My mother . . . my birth mother . . . she's in the hospital," I said, "but there's nothing I can do right now."

"Maybe you should take a break."

I nodded and left the store. The noise of the neighboring steel-rolling plant drowned out all other sounds in that industrial section of Ballard. I crossed the gravel parking lot and walked along the potholed access road, kicking the larger rocks.

I want her to die, to be gone, out of my life. She doesn't deserve to live. It's Dad who should be alive, not her.

I wasn't proud of my thoughts, but they were real. With her death, maybe the pain would subside—hers and mine.

She had abandoned us, according to my father's divorce papers, on the tenth of May, 1954, and she never came back—at least not to stay. I was four years old.

I couldn't recall that particular day. Unless it was the time Gary and I sat at the kitchen table, I on a stack of phone books, he in the high chair.

His wails compounded the din reverberating through the kitchen. I stared at my parents, my protectors, the adults who were supposed to keep my world safe and predictable, as that world shattered like the dinner plate my mother had hurled at the wall. She stood by the stove, arm raised, screaming at Dad, and he shouted back. Did I glimpse a saucepan in her hand, a glint of light reflecting off stainless steel?

Birth Woman charged to the door that led to the garage, jerked it open, and swept through the doorway in a swirl of yellow gingham. The door slammed shut with a finality that rattled the window. My three-year-old brother wailed even louder.

What happened afterward I gleaned from the stack of legal briefs documenting their divorce and the nearly two-year child-custody battle. I had discovered the documents in a box of Dad's personal items when he and Mom moved out of our home in Juanita. I wasn't being nosy. I was just picking through the contents, trying to figure out how to label the box correctly, and there they were, the answers to questions I'd been afraid to ask. Why Dad had saved that painful reminder I could only guess. Perhaps he had planned to tell me about it one day.

The box also contained their marriage certificate. Dad had muttered enough asides over the years that I suspected what had happened. He and Birth Woman were wed in August 1949. I popped into the world in November. I counted back on my fingers: She was five and half months pregnant on her wedding day. And though they lived in Seattle at the time, the ceremony took place at the county courthouse in Coeur d'Alene, Idaho. Dad twenty-one, Birth Woman two years his junior. The certificate didn't say whether any of the witnesses carried a shotgun.

I imagined Dad in the backseat of a car or in a sleazy motel. That moment of passion—and conception—setting in motion a string of events that culminated in a life of alcoholic stupor for one and the early death of the other.

I leafed through the divorce papers and pieced together the aftermath of their indiscretion. After four years of marriage, Dad had threatened her with divorce because she "openly seeks the company of other men." Yet, even with her marriage in peril, she "continued on her merry way and stayed out until the early morning hours and at times did not even come home." He filed the papers the day after she walked out for good, claiming she was "guilty of cruel conduct" and "inflicted upon him personal indignities, rendering his life burdensome and making it impossible" for him to live with her. The hellish image notwithstanding, I couldn't help but smile at the choice words. Legal boilerplate for the most part, but I could hear Dad say, "on her merry way."

When Birth Woman failed to appear at the hearing, his honor gaveled a default ruling in favor of Dad. But that didn't stop her from demanding custody of my brother and me, even though we had stayed with our father throughout the divorce proceeding.

Dad testified that she rarely visited us and showed up two weeks late to celebrate my fifth birthday. Then her attorney quit because she failed to pay his bills, and she moved around the state, leaving no forwarding address. The court tired of her antics and, after twenty-two months, granted Dad custody of my brother and me, as well as all of the communal property. A rare judgment in 1956.

Dad married Jody three months later. One incident from the first year of their marriage lay burned into memory. Birth Woman came by the house after dinner one night to take Gary and me out for an ice-cream soda. It may have been for our birthdays, which were just twelve days apart. But she arrived late, and Jody refused to let us go, saying it was our bedtime. I don't know where Dad had gone; he may have been working a side job, as he often did, or at night school. Birth Woman begged our new mom to let Gary and me go out, but Jody wouldn't budge. She accused Birth Woman of being drunk.

Still, she allowed Birth Woman to put Gary and me to bed. In the bedroom, the three of us sat on the floor, leaning against the lower bunk bed, Gary and I on either side of Birth Woman as she hugged us close, sobbing. Her tight skirt had slid up her thighs, exposing the tops of her stockings and garters. I felt embarrassed for her and knew I shouldn't be looking, but the mechanics of the garters fascinated me.

Later, she remarried and moved to Texas, then Tennessee. When she came to town, Gary and I visited her at Grandma Jane's house. For me, she was more of an eccentric aunt than a mother. Over the years, her visits became less frequent. My brother and I received sporadic letters that we read together in an attempt to decipher her nearly illegible scrawl. Years later it occurred to me that she probably wrote the letters while drunk.

She sent presents for our birthdays and at Christmas, but always identical gifts. Didn't she understand that we were two different people? I opened them reluctantly, especially at Christmas, when I had more presents than my sisters, and I didn't know what I'd done to deserve them. After all, wasn't I to blame for her leaving in the first place? I must have done something that left me unworthy of her love.

The screech of metal on metal at the steel-rolling mill brought me back to the present, and I stopped to watch the thunderous activity. I felt a kinship with the squealing pigs of glowing red steel that giant rollers spat out one end of the building—destined for a pedestrian role on life's poor stage.

I turned back toward the store, recalling my visit with Birth Woman three weeks earlier. She had returned to Seattle from Memphis after having a stroke and invited me to her apartment. I stood for a moment in the dim hallway outside her door. I hadn't seen her in more than a decade.

When she answered my knock, I recoiled from her shriveled, aging shell, a rat's nest of gray hair curdled atop her head, and the ravages of stroke evidenced by the cane that propped her up. She had just turned forty-nine. She was shorter than I remembered, probably because she wore slippers rather than her customary high heels.

She held me in a desperate embrace, longer than was comfortable. "It's so good to see you, Larry," she whispered.

I bit my lip and said, "It's good to see you, too."

She stepped back, appraising me with a glance. "I like your beard." She turned and limped into the kitchen, steadying herself with one hand on her four-pronged walking stick, the other on a wall. I followed, taking a quick look around. A cramped, one-bedroom apartment—government-subsidized housing in a forgotten neighborhood in Rainier Valley—stuffed with racks of clothing she would never wear again. It had the air of a thrift store.

In the living room, narrow aisles separated the multiple racks of clothing, leaving no room for a chair, let alone a couch. We were confined to a cramped kitchen that had a small table and two chairs, one stacked with phone books and unopened mail. She took the empty chair and I stood, leaning against a countertop cluttered with pots and plates and utensils glazed with the desiccated remains of several days' meals. She lit a cigarette and offered me a drink, but I didn't find a straight shot of vodka at noon all that appealing.

"Are you hungry?" she asked, tipping a glass to her lips. "I don't have much, but I could probably come up with something."

She had invited me to lunch, but I no longer had an appetite. "No, I'm fine. I had a big breakfast."

"Do you cook for yourself?"

"Mostly, yeah. But this morning I went out. There's a nice a little café in Ballard, not far from where I work."

"Where's that?"

"The café? Or where I work?"

"Your work," she said, a peevish tone to her voice.

"A boating supply store. The owners were friends of Dad's."

"It's too bad about Loren. I guess it's something he always wanted to do, sail off into the sunset. I could never do that. I like having solid ground under me."

Her glass empty, she stood and wavered as she reached for the bottle on the countertop. I stepped forward and steadied her while she poured a dollop of booze over shrinking ice cubes.

"Gary said it was pretty crazy out there. They were lost at sea and . . ." She shuddered and gulped from her glass. ". . . dead bodies on the boat."

So, he had been in touch. "The FBI says Gary was responsible for those dead bodies. They're going to nail his hide to the wall."

"I don't know how you can think that about your brother. Gary couldn't kill anybody, especially not his father."

I snorted. How could she know what Gary could or couldn't do, what he was capable of? She knew nothing about him—or me.

"Gary's kind and caring," she said.

"He testified against you when Howard divorced you."

She dismissed my retort with a shrug and drained her glass of its numbing potion. She couldn't indict Gary in Dad's death. To indict Gary meant indicting herself.

She slammed the glass on the table, startling me. "It's just all so unfair!"

I nodded, then realized she wasn't talking about Dad's death, or even the FBI investigation. "What do you mean?"

She took a long drag on her cigarette, then sneered as smoke shot from her nose like a cartoon dragon. She waved a hand to encompass the sphere of her wretched existence. "I deserve better than this. They're threatening to cut off my phone, but SSI won't give me enough money to live off of."

My stomach roiled. What did she know about life being unfair? She wasn't the victim, she was the perpetrator. She had brought it upon herself. I had wondered why her own mother refused to take her in. But as caring and forgiving as Grandma Jane was, I could see why even she couldn't bear to live with this, a daily remainder of what her daughter had become.

I had accepted Birth Woman's invitation hoping to get some answers. How had she met my father? Why did they split up? Did they ever love each other? Did she ever love me?

I also wanted to ask her about her first child, the one born before me. I'd always assumed I was her first, but one day while examining my birth certificate, I discovered a line in the lower right corner that I had not noticed before. It read: "Children previously born to this woman: How many OTHER children are now living?" and in the box was the number "1."

Was her first child a boy? A girl? What had been his or her fate? Most likely given up for adoption. But she hadn't even been a woman. A girl, really—probably sixteen, perhaps fifteen, when first knocked up. I had tried to get the information from the King County Office of Vital Statistics, but the record was sealed.

That girl-woman sat before me, the one who'd given me life, a woman I knew so little about other than she'd been born in Indiana in 1930, and I'd heard that her father was an alcoholic.

She drained her glass and looked at me. I'd seen that look before. The hollow-eyed plea of drunks I had encountered downtown while waiting for the bus during my freshman year in college, drunks dreading the onset of the DTs and begging for a dime to "call my wife" or "buy a pack of gum."

"Can you loan me some money?" she asked. "I'll pay you back when I get my next check."

I tensed from the rage scorching my mind. I'd been hoping for an apology, even a miniscule sign of regret. She'd lured me there with hope, saying she wanted to see me, that she missed me, that we had so much to talk about. But she only wanted money.

I felt sorry for the shrunken, paralytic body that sat before me. But I felt no pity for the person within it. I wanted to grab her, shake her, scream at her. You're my mother! Why did you abandon me, you thoughtless, selfish, pathetic bitch! Now my father's dead! It should be you!

But I said nothing. How could I dump a lifetime of pent-up rage on this hapless woman, wallowing so deeply in self-pity that she couldn't see beyond the rim of the glass in her hand?

Next time, I promised myself. I'll tell her next time.

I opened my wallet and tossed a handful of bills on the table, then said an obligatory good-bye.

But there was no next time.

Three weeks later, I got that phone call from Grandma Jane and went for the stroll past the steel-rolling mill. She asked me to go to Birth Woman's apartment with her son, my Uncle Bill, to see what we could salvage. The place reeked of burnt fabric and plastic, everything blackened by smoke. To look around, we had to rely on flashlights and what little light filtered through grimy windows.

The fire had started in the bed. Doubtless, she had passed out, drunk, with a cigarette burning between her fingers. With the out-of-fashion clothing that filled the bedroom and living room, the fire had spread quickly. Yet, Birth Woman had somehow survived and ended up in a convalescent home on Bainbridge Island.

I never visited her. I never spoke to her again.

I could not summon the compassion needed to stand at her bedside, to confront her scars—and mine. She would die two years later. Perhaps then she found some peace.

I found no peace. I had hoped that her death would cleanse me of the haunting memories. But that's not how it works. Bitter memories of the woman I had once called mommy plagued me. I still blamed myself for her leaving us. I couldn't forgive her without first forgiving myself.

I later visited her grave. The headstone read:

In loving memory
Phyllis Jean Schmidt
April 18, 1930 - Feb. 22, 1982

After Grandma Jane died, I visited the cemetery again. I could not find Birth Woman's headstone. When I went to the office and asked about it, the attendant insisted the grave was there and marked it on a map. I still couldn't find it. I counted the plots; I checked the numbers etched in the concrete slabs that housed the headstones of various members of my grandmother's family: her husband, sister, mother, and father—my Great-grandpa Funk, who had nurtured me during my first year of life.

It should have been where my grandmother was buried. I re-examined the plot numbers, kneeling by Grandma Jane's headstone and tugging at the grass, looking for any clue that Birth Woman lay there too. I found none.

Back at the office, the attendant checked the record again and pointed at the number on the reference card. "See? It has a 'Z' at the end. That means she's buried there, but there's no headstone." The woman looked up at me. "I'm sorry."

I considered calling her a stupid-fucking-moron for not explaining that to me in the first place. Instead, I offered her a wan smile and thanked her, then left the building. As an adult, I had never shed a tear for Birth Woman—until then.

20

Sunday, June 17, 1979

At midnight, Kenneth Brank and I made our grand entrance at the National Oldtime Fiddlers' Contest in Weiser, Idaho. Brank was a well driller by trade and about my father's age. He'd also built time in a federal penitentiary for making moonshine.

My muffler-challenged Chevy pickup signaled our arrival from a block away. When I got to the campground at the high school, I stopped and rolled down the window. A man with a clipboard said, "Where you guys been? The rumor goin' round is you got drunk and took the wrong turnoff."

"Nah, we just ran out of gas," I said. "But not whiskey."

He laughed and waved us in.

Brank and I set up a ramshackle camp that over the week and in subsequent years developed a reputation as "The Ghetto." People stopped by to gawk as well as make music. It might have been the free-flowing booze, eating peanut butter straight from the jar, or just the sheer fun we had in an environment rife with oh-so-serious tête-à-têtes about who'd win the contest or which judges could not be trusted.

I made the front page of the *Idaho Statesman*. Not for the quality of my fiddling. The photographer said he thought I looked like a "typical fiddler." I guess it was the instrument in one hand and a whiskey bottle in the other.

One night while returning to our camp from a jam session, Brank and I stopped to lie on the grass beside the school. Most people were asleep, although I could hear the faint sounds of swing tunes coming from what was known as "hippieville," where some of the best and often all-night jams took place.

As we gazed skyward, Brank said, "When I was a boy, my mother told me the stars are windows to Heaven and our dead relations watch over us from up yonder."

I stared at the brightest star, wondering if Mom and Dad were looking down at me.

Thursday, June 28, 1979

I met Pete Mercer for lunch at a café near the boating supply store where I worked. He filled me in on the status of the investigation, then whined about the "moron" at the U.S. attorney's office. For months, Mercer had been trying to schedule another interview with Kerry, but the prosecutor refused to grant her immunity.

"How am I supposed to get her to tell me anything?" he said. "It'd be a fuckin' waste of time."

I toyed with what remained of my sandwich. "What would he prosecute her for, conspiracy?"

Mercer shrugged. "Conspiracy for what? Without her testimony, he's got nothing." He leaned forward and continued in a low voice. "The guy's got his head up his ass."

"What about Lori?"

He snorted. "With her meteorite or space aliens, or whatever the hell she was saying, she'd be laughed out of court." Mercer shoved his chair back. "Gotta go."

We both stood and walked outside. "Sorry about the bad news," he said, "but right now my hands are tied. I'll keep pushing and let you know if anything comes up."

Afterward, I wanted to be alone, but I had to go back to work. Ditto for the home front. The realities of life would not allow me to withdraw. The following day a friend of Emily's invited us to dinner. I wanted to stay home, but Emily refused to go without me.

"We're a couple," she said, "and couples do things together."

We ended up going to see Woody Allen's *Manhattan*. It turned out to be an OK evening, although ultimately unsatisfying. I needed to silence the voices torturing me from within. After work on Saturday, a coworker and I went for beers. When I got home, I continued drinking and ate only popcorn for dinner.

Sunday morning, still woozy, I moped around the house, then left to have beers with a friend. When I got home, I made more popcorn and watched TV, capping it off with a movie that didn't end until after midnight. As I brushed my teeth, Emily criticized me for not helping her clean house, punctuating it with tears. Friends from San Diego were arriving the next day. In my inebriate fog, I'd forgotten about it.

"You could have said something earlier today," I said. "Now, at one-thirty in the fucking morning, I'm suddenly an inconsiderate bastard."

I went to bed and she stayed up to clean the kitchen. The next morning, I left for work without saying a word or kissing her good-bye.

On July 4, the band I played in with Roger and Janice Maddy performed at an Independence Day celebration, then I returned home, expecting fireworks from Emily. But she'd gone to Port Townsend with our friends.

She called and said she wanted me to join her for the weekend, but I went to Winlock to see Brank and perform at the Cheese Days festival in Toledo. With my dad dead, Brank had become more than a friend. For better or worse, he was the closest thing to a father I had. I also knew there'd be no shortage of alchy.

When I got home, Emily's withering look said more than any words she might have spoken. I knew I was being an asshole, that to make the relationship work I had to respect her wishes and spend more time with her.

But I didn't care.

Sunday, July 15, 1979

I met with Bobbie and Aileen to sort through family photos. The collection included pictures of Mom and Dad's bon voyage party two years earlier. Everyone smiling. No clue as to what lay ahead.

The following week, they asked me back to look at more pictures and go through some of our parents' things. I couldn't do it. I didn't give a shit. About anything or anyone. I told them I had car trouble and stayed home. Got drunk. Laughed at the irony. I had condemned Birth Woman for being a drunk. I didn't drink at work, but I made certain there was booze in the house, whether I intended to drink it or not. More often than not I did. Emily had left for the weekend, and I'd turned the house into a pigsty.

I just don't care.

Tuesday, July 24, 1979

News flash: A Florida jury convicted Ted Bundy, the charming serial killer, of first-degree murder. I shivered as I recalled his scrawled signature at the back of a gym locker at the school where I'd taught in Tacoma.

Will my parents' case ever go to trial?

IN AUGUST, EMILY went to San Diego and I had the house to myself for a couple of weeks. I enjoyed the solitude, yet I missed her companionship. And drank less.

When she returned, we were happy to be reunited, but four days later we were back in our rut. We were friends who lived together, slept together, occasionally had sex, but did little else.

I moved into my camper, which I parked at the store. I only had to walk fifty feet to get to work. Good deal for my boss, too, because I provided nighttime security.

In late September, my father's aunt and uncle celebrated their fiftieth wedding anniversary. Gary showed up. The first time I'd seen him since I left Tahiti.

He approached me, smiling, and extended his hand in greeting, as if there were no ongoing murder investigation, as if nothing had happened. Part of me wanted to pummel that grin from his face. Part of me wanted to patronize him in hopes of getting him to say something incriminating, or at least offer a hint of remorse or regret. I clung to the belief that he'd eventually be locked behind bars.

I shook his hand and spoke in a civil tone. He said he was still working at the boatyard in Richmond, California. He didn't ask what'd I'd been up to. Then he flashed his classic smirk, as if he'd just scored a point. I'd been played for the fool. As he walked away, I muttered, "It's just a matter of time."

November 1979

Still no measurable progress with the FBI investigation. My job had become intolerable. I had a well-meaning, well-intentioned boss, but he was not a great businessman or manager. With little or no advance notice, he'd order his employees to work on their days off. Never mind that we'd made other plans; in my case, commitments to play music gigs. I had words with him, as did the others, and he made promises, but nothing changed. I wanted to quit, but I needed the money.

I'm no different than a whore.

One night I returned to my camper after playing darts at the Lockspot Tavern. My hands shook from the cold as I tried to start the heater. I picked up a flashlight, but it wouldn't light up. I rummaged around in the half-light for a match to ignite the propane lamp.

Shit! Out of propane.

I reached across the table for another flashlight. It didn't work either. I'd only bought them a few weeks earlier. I stepped out of the camper and slammed the flashlight to the ground. It didn't break, so I kicked it and kicked it and kicked it across the gravel parking lot, screaming, "You motherfucking-cocksucking-sonofabitch!" until the hapless device shattered into more than a dozen pieces. I leaned over, hands on my knees, chest heaving, and sucked air. After a moment, I calmed down enough to pick up the larger pieces, return to the camper, and crawl into bed, my body shaking.

What's happening to me?

The following week, three of my coworkers resigned. I quit shortly afterward, a few days before Thanksgiving. I didn't know what I'd do for money. I just knew I couldn't work there any longer.

Aileen invited me to dinner for the holiday. She had rented an apartment in Redmond and wanted a family get-together—for the remnants of our family: me, Aileen, and Bobbie, and their preschool daughters.

I preferred to spend the day alone but felt obligated to go. I hadn't been to her new place, which was in a big apartment complex with multiple buildings and dozens of units. I had trouble finding hers. If I'd made the effort, I could have located it, but the difficulty gave me the excuse I needed. Besides, what did I have to be thankful for?

I popped the clutch, squealed the tires, and drove back to Seattle, where I spent Thanksgiving Day alone in my camper, listening to a football game and thinking about doing laundry, warmed by my CAT heater and the half-gallon of wine I'd bought that morning at an outrageous price.

I'm back where I was right after Mom & Dad died. Dinner is a six-pack.

I drove to the Olympic Mountains for three days of solitude.

Saturday, December 22, 1979

I had apologized to Aileen for my Thanksgiving antics and she invited me over for Christmas. I told her no. The holiday meant nothing but aggravation to me.

"Don't get me a present," I said. "And you should not be buying anything for your friends. You're broke, like me. It's all commercial hype anyway."

"I know, Mr. Scrooge, but I'll feel guilty if I don't."

I felt no guilt and the next day returned to Boulder Creek, where I'd spent Thanksgiving weekend. Heavy rains had washed out the road, which meant a four-mile tramp through the snow to reach the hot springs.

It also meant I had the place to myself, my only companions the towering fir, spruce, hemlock, and cedar trees. An occasional shush of a zephyr rustled the branches overhead, and the creek burbled in the canyon below. Snowflakes melted on my face.

On the hike back, darkness descended and I tensed in fear. I thought of the sasquatch tracks Emily and I had seen the year before. Where would a sasquatch likely hang out in winter? At hot springs. Like the elk in Yellowstone. Same for bears. I quickened my step and hiked like who flung the chunk.

Then I stopped and laughed, took a couple of deep breaths.

If the sasquatch wanted the hot spring, he would've tossed your sorry ass into the canyon an hour ago. The bears are hibernating.

Overhead, I could see a few stars between breaks in the clouds. Were Mom and Dad watching?

Back in the camper, I fixed a cup of pre-Christmas cheer—eggnog and nutmeg, no booze. I hadn't had a drink since Saturday.

I returned to the hot springs on Christmas Eve. As I hiked up the road, the clouds rolled off the mountain and a light mist hung suspended in the canyon. At my favorite spring, I alternately lay in the soothing water or stood in the rain, naked, eating tangerines.

A ghost of Christmas past drifted into my thoughts—the time I broke the Eleventh Commandment: Thou shalt not tell your little sisters there is no Santa Claus. They had burst into tears, thinking Santa had died and wouldn't be bringing them any presents.

"Go to your room," Mom said. The hiss of her voice through clenched teeth heightened the intensity of portending doom should I fail to obey.

I shuffled toward the stairs that led to the basement and my bedroom. "He's not real," I muttered.

"What did you say?" Mom asked.

"Nothing."

"It had better be nothing, young man. Now go!"

I clip-clopped down the stairs, secretly pleased with the uproar I'd caused. But I knew there would be consequences.

In the basement, I wound my way through the rec room and past Dad's workshop to the bedroom I shared with Gary. I took a deep breath, the cool air laden with the scent of sawn wood from one of Dad's projects.

In my room, I gazed through the window at the sullen sky,

wondering what would happen next. Mom was mad. Madder even than the time I'd told Aileen how bad the needle would hurt when we went to the doctor's for our tetanus shots. When Aileen's turn came, she'd sprinted across the examining room, the nurse chasing her.

I lost TV privileges for a week.

I vowed to keep my mouth shut in the future. But sometimes I couldn't help myself. This time when I dropped my little bomb, Mom was dressing my sisters for the annual trek to the Northgate Mall in Seattle, where we'd get our picture taken with Santa.

I just blurted it out. As soon as I said it, I knew I'd made a mistake. That look of horror on Mom's face said it all. But if she hadn't told us Santa wouldn't be bringing us any presents unless we behaved, like that stupid song about being naughty or nice, I never would have said it in the first place.

So it was her fault. Like the needle not hurting. She shouldn't lie about those things. I sat on my bed, arms crossed on my chest. Heavy footsteps descending the stairs signaled Dad's imminent arrival. I flinched as he stepped through the bedroom door, anticipating the flat of his hand on my backside. But he just sat next to me on the bed.

"Don't you want to go see Santa?" he asked.

"No!"

He sighed and stared across the room. I wished him away, but he didn't budge. Finally, he spoke in a low, slow cadence. "Your brother and sisters want to see Santa. He'll give you a candy cane."

"I don't want a candy cane. I don't want to see Santa."

"You've always wanted to see Santa before, sit on his lap, tell him what you want for Christmas."

"He's not real."

"Of course he's real," Dad said. "Who do you think brings you all those presents?"

"You do. And Grandma and Grandpa. You just made Santa Claus up so we'd be good."

"Larry, come on. The others are waiting. They don't want to go without you."

"I'm not going. You lied to us."

Dad put an arm across my shoulders. "It's just a game we play . . . for the younger kids."

I cinched my arms together. "You always said it's wrong to tell a lie."

"You know how you and Gary like to play Robin Hood and cowboys and Indians in the woods?"

I nodded.

"It's like that. A game of pretend."

"But they were real."

"So was Santa Claus. You know the story. They called him Saint Nicholas, Ol' Saint Nick. He would hand out presents to all the children in the village. When he died, other people pretended to be him so the children would still get presents."

I felt my resolve cracking.

"Your sisters will be disappointed if you don't go," Dad said. "You don't want to spoil Christmas for them, do you?"

"I don't care."

Dad sighed again, and I sensed his patience eroding. He grabbed my chin and twisted my head, forcing me to look at him. A greasy smudge blackened an unshaven cheek. He'd been changing the oil in his truck when Mom delivered the news. His hard eyes locked onto mine, and when he spoke again, his voice had risen a notch.

"You're nine years old. It's time you start acting like it."

I didn't respond.

"What you did was wrong. Didn't you see how upset you made Aileen and Bobbie?"

I dropped my chin to my chest. The time for repenting had arrived. But I couldn't admit I'd done anything wrong.

Dad continued. "You don't have to believe in Santa Claus, but don't upset the girls. They're too young to understand."

I thought about it.

"Just pretend. It'll be our little secret, OK?" He pulled me close and patted my arm as I nestled against his chest. I could feel his heart pounding, and his grungy T-shirt smelled of day-old sweat. The odor comforted me—my dad was close. While I believed I was right, his approval meant more to me.

"Let's go," he said.

I went.

When I reached the top of the stairs, I spotted Mom standing in the living room, hands on hips. Her glare defied the holiday mood set by the colorful scarf draped around her neck. I offered an apologetic smile as I stepped toward Aileen and Bobbie, who sat on the couch in their best dresses and patent-leather Mary Janes. They eyed me warily as I knelt in front of them.

"I was just teasing," I said. "Santa's real. You're going to get lots of presents. I promise. You still want to get your picture taken with him, don't you?"

Their faces brightened, and their heads bobbed in renewed excitement.

"Then what are you sitting here for? Come on, get your coats on!"

As I stood, Dad ruffled my hair. I looked up at him and raised a finger to my lips. "Our little secret."

Mom glanced at him with questioning eyes.

"We could write a book," he said.

THE HEAT OF the hot spring forced me out, and I stood, tears mixing with the sweat dripping from my brow. They could have written a book. But now they're dead, and all the pretending in the world won't bring them back.

I moved down the mountain to the Elwha River, where Christmas dawned sunny, dappling the forest glen. Thick moss carpeted the ground in the adjacent maple grove, which nature had accented with sword ferns. Fallen trees lay strewn about in an asymmetric jumble, as if tossed there by a giant playing pick-up sticks. I spent the day reading and writing, more relaxed than I'd felt in months.

January 1980

Relishing my aloneness proved short-lived. My thoughts turned to Emily—and a warm bed, as the thermometer inside the camper registered twenty-eight degrees. The mercury rose to seventy-five at eye-level, but the condensation from the propane stove turned to frost on the lower half of the walls. My toes were numb.

Seattle experienced one of its heaviest snowfalls ever. Upwards of eight inches in twenty-four hours, which brought the city to a standstill. Fine with me. I didn't have anywhere to go—except the Lockspot to play darts and get drunk. I had my journal to pour my heart into and my CAT heater to keep me warm. Until I ran out of propane.

Then I ran out of money. My unemployment had been hung up in the bureaucratic maze, delaying it for weeks. Adding to my economic woes, I still had not been reimbursed for the expense of my parents' memorial service almost two years earlier. The roadblock, I found out, was Gary. My aunts had insisted that all the heirs agree to distributions of funds from the estate so there would be no questions of favoritism. My sisters had signed off on the reimbursement, but Gary had not. The fucker.

The novelty of living alone in the camper having worn thin, Emily and I returned to domesticity in an apartment in Ballard. I found a job at another marine supply store. With the snow gone and spring on the horizon, life no longer seemed so bleak.

Except that I hadn't heard squat from the FBI in nearly eight months.

21

Sunday, February 24, 1980

The second anniversary of Mom's and Dad's deaths. I recalled Linda phoning with the news and how it didn't seem real until I began to tell my boss and coworkers. The tears, the lump in my throat, the choking sensation. The emotions had overwhelmed me.

It's happening again. Maybe it always will.

That afternoon, I met Pete Mercer at his office downtown. Our footsteps echoed as we walked through the building's vacant halls. He was manipulating me, scheduling a meet on that emotion-laden day, but I played along, grateful for a progress report. He motioned me to a chair, then sat at his desk.

"I feel bad that this investigation has dragged out so long," he said. "I know you're frustrated, and I'm equally so."

"What's the hang-up?" I asked. "Kerry?"

He nodded and said he'd gone to see her in San Diego, where she was staying with the Garretts. "I shouldn't be telling you this, but you have a right to know. It's going to come out anyway."

I stared at him, fearful of what he might say.

"Your brother is the one who hit Kerry, and when your folks intervened, well, you can figure out the rest."

I sighed, as much in dismay as relief. I didn't like the image of my brother's whacking Kerry, but it was preferable to it having been Dad or Mom. "But why?" I asked.

"She's coming to Seattle next month. While she's here, she'll tell you and Aileen and Bobbie what she told me. And she's going to testify, this time telling the truth."

"Why didn't she say this before, instead of feeding us bullshit?"

Mercer shook his head. "It's been a battle with her. Browbeating doesn't work. I've had to befriend her, to be like a caring uncle she can confide in."

The outcome of the case, he explained, depended on how tough Kerry could be when testifying before the grand jury again and, if necessary, at Gary's trial.

"Talking to you and your sisters will be a dry run of sorts," he said. "She needs to know you support her. Don't yell at her or berate her. If you do, she's just going to clam up again."

I leaned on an elbow and looked at the floor, pondering his words. I didn't like the idea of coddling my sister after what she'd put us through, but I agreed.

"Then we're going to meet with Lori and confront her with what Kerry tells you," he said, adding that a family friend would be called to testify as a character witness, and I would testify as well. "I hope to have a grand jury indictment by June and go to trial in six months."

"You were saying that a year ago."

"I know, but we can make this happen. My biggest worry is Lori."

Saturday, March 22, 1980

I met Aileen, Bobbie, and Aunt Verney at Mercer's office. He took us to an interview room, where Kerry was already seated. We sat in a circle. Mercer nodded at Kerry.

"I don't know where to start," she said, her head down.

Mercer sighed. "You were asleep . . ."

She nodded but didn't look up. "I was on the settee, sleeping, and he . . ." she said, then paused.

"He did what?" I said.

"He attacked me . . . and got in bed with me." She paused again, as if she were through.

"Then what?" Aileen asked, her voice laced with annoyance.

"He . . . he had sex with me."

"Did you try to stop him?"

"I was unconscious!"

Aileen, Bobbie, and I glanced at one another. We had suspected it, but there it was, splayed out like an ugly wound. Kerry's halting statements, however, sounded more like a toddler explaining a mishap to her parents.

She's fucking this up. She'll never be a credible witness.

On further prompting, she said Dad, then Mom came to her aid. They were killed, first one, then the other, although she said she didn't actually witness the deaths.

I looked at Mercer. "If she didn't witness the deaths, then what good is her testimony? He'll just say she made it up."

"We have plenty of other evidence that leads us to reasonably conclude that he killed your parents," he said.

I turned back to Kerry. "What about the bodies?"

"Gary told me that we were lost and it might be a week before we reached land. That Mom and Dad should be buried at sea."

"A week?" I said. "That's ridiculous."

Kerry glared at me. "That's what he said, a week."

"The trip from the Marquesas to Tahiti was supposed to take five days and you were over halfway there. There had to have been an island nearby."

"He'd already bashed my head in, and I was afraid of what he might do," she said. "I had no choice but to go along. He dumped the bodies right after Mom was shot."

"Which means his claim about the bodies decomposing is bogus," I said.

Mercer shot me a look of reprimand, then turned to Kerry. "Don't you have a little more to say?"

Despite the scrutiny, Kerry seemed to enjoy being the center of attention and displayed a smirk not unlike Gary's. "No, I've told you everything."

"What about the reason Gary attacked you?" Mercer asked.

She shook her head. "I have no idea why he did that, other than to have sex with me."

"Kerry, you failed two polygraph tests. Why don't you at least tell your family the truth?"

Kerry began to cry. "You're badgering me, saying I should know more when I don't."

Mercer rolled his eyes as if to say, I tried.

I wanted to yell at her, but per Mercer's instructions, I kept my voice low. "Kerry, right now you're not a credible witness. You don't sound like someone whose parents have been murdered and wants justice. You sound like some kid giving a book report on a story you never read."

She didn't reply and I went on. "If you want to see that son of a bitch brought to trial, which you say you do, then you have to sound convincing."

She dabbed at her tears but said nothing. Meeting over. Aileen, Bobbie, Verney, and I walked out, leaving Mercer with Kerry.

As we went to our cars, Aileen said, "I don't believe her. Gary didn't hit her for nothing."

"Did you see her face?" Bobbie said. "I wanted to slap that little bitch."

"Me, too," I replied. "But I don't want to alienate her."

Aileen offered to talk to Kerry that night. "Maybe I can get somewhere with her."

"I hope so," I said. "Pete's counting on having enough support from her and Lori that Gary will plead guilty. But I'm not holding my breath. Not after what we saw today."

We met with Lori two days later. Waste of time. If Lori had spoken with a German accent, she would've been a perfect impersonation of Sgt. Schultz in *Hogan's Heroes*: "I know nuh-thing."

She showed up with an attorney and claimed to have slept through the incidents involving Kerry and Dad, and to have been in the galley when Mom was shot. "I only know what Gary told me, that Kerry fell, Loren was hit by the boom, and Jody shot herself," she said.

Mercer suggested that she must have been a very sound sleeper. Lori whimpered, complaining that she'd told us all of this before. "Why doesn't anyone believe me?"

"Because, Lori, you're well aware of what happened," Kerry said.

Mercer looked at Lori. "What about it?"

"I was asleep," she said. "I didn't see or hear anything until Gary woke me up and told me to steer the boat."

I interrupted. "In Tahiti, you told me that Gary said my father lost his balance and fell. You and Kerry both said that Dad couldn't have been hit by the boom because the boat was under power, which meant the boom was lashed down."

Lori shook her head. "No, I've always said I thought he was hit by the boom."

You lyin' sack of shit.

22

August 1980

Verney contacted me to say the Spellbound had finally sold and the probate hearing would be sometime in November or December. If all went according to plan, the judge would rubber-stamp the proposed settlement of my parents' estate.

"Which means Gary and Kerry will each get an equal share," I said.

"Yes."

"How much?"

"In terms of cash, you will each get about twenty thousand dollars, plus there will be some income from the real estate contracts. But there are expenses. So, until those have been paid and we get the lawyer's bill, we won't know the exact amount."

Looking back, $20,000 doesn't seem like a lot of money, but adjusted for inflation to the year 2012, it would be equivalent to nearly $58,000.

"Can't we delay the hearing until the FBI is done with the investigation?" I asked.

"Your sisters, especially Aileen and Kerry, are putting pressure on me and Vivian to wrap this up."

"You know as well I do that Gary shouldn't get a penny," I said. "And Aileen says Kerry talks about nothing but how she's going to spend her share."

"Vivian wants to be done with it," Verney said. "Frankly, I do, too. It's dragged out two and a half years already. But I'd hate to see Gary get anything from it."

The next day I contacted Pete Mercer. He'd been on the case for a year and a half and still no grand jury indictment. He agreed to meet me at a fish-and-chips shop in Ballard. We ordered, and I told him about the probate hearing.

"There's nothing I can do," he said. "Until we've completed the investigation and sent the report to the U.S. attorney's office, there will be no criminal prosecution." He said the FBI was preparing a visual investigative analysis chart, or VIA, to illustrate that Gary had lied about the movements and positions of the Spellbound following my father's death.

"Even then there's no guarantee Gary will be prosecuted," Mercer said. "That's up to the U.S. attorney's office. And the case is circum-stantial. Still, I think a jury will see through his bullshit. I know I told you it would be over by now and Gary'd be on his way to prison. But without Kerry's truthful testimony, we're in a bind. Still, I think we can be in court early next year."

Our food arrived and I sprinkled vinegar on the fish filets, then dabbed ketchup on the fries. I stared out the window as I ate, watching the traffic on Shilshole Way, feeling the anger swell within.

I looked back at the agent. "Gary and Kerry will get an early Christmas present of twenty grand apiece. So much for justice."

Mercer reached inside his suit coat and pulled out a sheet of folded paper. He opened it and handed it to me. A photocopy of a newspaper article. I glanced at the headline and read the first few paragraphs. An Issaquah man had been found responsible for the death of his wife, and the court denied him any inheritance from her estate. A lawsuit had been brought against the man by the woman's children from a previous marriage. The man had claimed that his wife slipped and fell down a steep slope while hiking in the mountains near Snoqualmie Pass. The children claimed he pushed her to her death so he could get his hands on her money. The jury agreed with the children.

"We could sue my brother?"

Mercer nodded. "It's filed in civil court, not criminal court. If the defendant is found responsible for the death, like this guy, he can't inherit. Period."

"But how could we prove Gary's responsible for the deaths of our parents if your investigation is not complete?"

He explained that in civil court the burden of proof is lower than in criminal court, where the prosecution must convince a jury that the defendant is guilty beyond a reasonable doubt. In civil court, the plaintiff only has to show that a preponderance of the evidence—greater than 50 percent—supports the claim. In other words, show that it is more likely than not that the defendant is responsible for the death.

This type of lawsuit gained notoriety when the Brown and Goldman families sued O.J. Simpson following the not-guilty verdict in Simpson's criminal trial. But that happened seventeen years later. For me, sitting in the fish-and-chips shop with the FBI agent, the concept came as a revelation.

"So we might get some justice out of this," I said.

He shrugged. "I can't give you legal advice. You found that article on the floor."

"Understood. Now I need a lawyer."

He nodded at the photocopy in my hand. At the bottom were the name and phone number of an attorney.

In the parking lot, Mercer apologized for the investigation taking so long, saying he had other cases with higher priority.

"What could be higher priority than a double murder, and an assault and rape?"

He sighed. "Look, this case is two and a half years old. The prosecutor . . ."

I waved his words away. "Pete, I'm sure you're doing everything you can. I'm just pissed off over this whole god-damned mess."

"So am I, but I'm not giving up," he said. "I intend to make a case against Gary. We have that VIA I told you about, which will prove he lied. The biggest roadblock is Kerry. She's not cooperating."

I nodded. "The only thing she's interested in right now is that money. Aileen and I tried appealing to her conscience, but she didn't blink an eye."

"The people I routinely deal with wrestle with many things," he said, "but their conscience generally is not one of them."

BACK AT MY desk, I called the attorney. He said that under Washington's probate law there was a slayer statute—a person found responsible for the death of another cannot benefit from that death. He also said it could cost as much as $10,000, and it could drag out for years.

Yikes! I had just committed to backing Roger and Janice Maddy's second recording, to the tune of $3,000. We hoped to release it before Christmas. The band had already started recording at a studio in Tacoma, so I couldn't back out. Where would I get the money for the attorney?

That night I called Aileen, then Bobbie. They liked the idea, but they balked at the cost. Aileen, claiming financial hardship, had already contacted the estate attorney, trying to get an advance on her inheritance. But he told her he couldn't release any funds without court authorization and, in all likelihood, the court would deny the request.

"Look at it this way," I told her. "If we win, and I think we will, Gary won't get any money, so we pay the lawyer out of his share of the estate. The lawyer will bill the estate, so we don't pay anything up front." Besides, I added, all we really needed to do was delay the division of the estate until the criminal case was over, and Mercer thought that could be another six months or so.

Aileen replied: "He said that last March, but we aren't any closer now than we were then, thanks to Kerry."

"Yes, but if we sue her along with Gary, it could force her hand."

"What if we lose?"

"That's the risk we take. I really don't care. I'll gladly spend half of my inheritance to get some semblance of justice for Mom and Dad. Isn't that, ultimately, what we want? Justice? And, if nothing else, our conscience will be clear."

"How long would it take?"

"It depends on what Gary does," I said. "But we have three or four months until the probate hearing and, with any luck, the FBI case might be resolved by then."

When Aileen didn't say anything, I continued. "And here's the best part. Any evidence that comes out in civil court can be used in criminal court. We can present all of Gary's contradictions and improbabilities, and put an end to his bullshit forever."

"I like that," she said.

Still, we wrestled with the decision. We knew that Dad's side of the family would not be pleased. And what if it did end up costing us ten grand? But we wanted our parents to have their day in court, to set the record straight. We wanted to know why our parents died.

Bobbie said she'd go along with whatever Aileen and I decided, so the two of us met with the attorney a few days later. The initial draft of our objection to the dispersal of the estate named Gary and Kerry. We figured that Kerry would be dismissed, but we wanted that leverage against her so she'd testify truthfully. Besides, Aileen, Bobbie, and I were pissed off about Kerry's uncooperative attitude and her vow to lie in court. And for all we knew, she might have had a hand in our parents' deaths. She, Gary, and Lori could have cooked up the entire scenario they had fed us, although Mercer told me he believed, fundamentally, that Kerry was telling him the truth, even if she had lied or misled us about some of the details. I didn't expect a confession from Gary, but I believed enough facts would come out during the probate hearing to show that Gary was responsible for our parents' deaths.

On September 15, we notified the estate attorney of our intentions. Predictably, Grandma Edwards, Vivian, and others howled in protest. But Verney, along with Grandma and Grandpa Howatson, supported us. Kerry had returned from California and moved in with Aileen again, which complicated matters, but we plowed ahead.

In early October, our attorney met separately with Kerry and explained her options. Afterward, he said he got nowhere with her. The same old story—tears, I don't know why they're doing this to me, I've told them everything I know. He believed her and said we ought to leave her out of it; otherwise, we'd look bad. We followed his advice, and Kerry agreed to testify on our behalf in return for being dropped from the petition. She and I gave sworn statements, known as affidavits, to be filed in King County Superior Court in support of the allegation that

Gary was the "slayer" of our parents and he should "not be allowed to profit by his own wrong."

In my affidavit, I laid out what I believed to have happened aboard the Spellbound, based on my talks with the FBI, Kerry, Gary, and boaters in French Polynesia. Moreover, it would become part of the public record, a rebuttal to what Gary had told the news media.

The affidavit read, in part:

> [O]n February 24, 1978, in the early morning
> . . . Gary Edwards . . . commenced assaulting
> Kerry and was apparently discovered in the process
> by the decedent Loren Edwards. In the course of
> the assault, Kerry suffered two severe blows to
> the head, causing extensive bleeding, a fractured
> skull, and was raped. The following day a
> [C]rescent wrench was found in the couch where
> Kerry had been sleeping prior to the assault.
>
> Upon being discovered in the course of the
> assault, Gary went on deck, and then a few
> minutes later called his father, Loren Edwards,
> on deck, stating he thought he had seen an
> island. The weather was calm, clear, and warm,
> and the vessel under power with sails down. The
> next thing anybody heard was a crash, and Gary
> stating that his father has "fallen down." At
> later times Gary variously stated that his father
> had been struck on his head by the boom
> (virtually impossible) or fallen against the
> spokes of the wheel of the vessel (extremely
> unlikely). No one witnessed the fatal injury to
> Loren Edwards except Gary. In the cockpit area of
> the vessel where the death of Loren Edwards
> occurred, there are a number of heavy metal
> instruments with sharp edges, especially winch
> handles.

Loren Edwards died within an hour of the injury, and his body was placed by Gary in a sleeping bag which was placed on the stern of the vessel.

While Loren Edwards lay dying, and after his death, Joanne Edwards reassured the family that everything would be OK and that "they would make it alright."

[Later] Gary Edwards and Joanne Edwards were alone on the deck of the vessel which was under power in calm seas. Kerry Edwards and Lori Oskam were below, Kerry was in the main cabin of the vessel very near the entrance to the cockpit. Joanne Edwards was sitting in the cockpit, and Gary Edwards was on deck. A gunshot was heard, Joanne Edwards was fatally shot in the head, apparently from the rear.

Gary Edwards reported that his mother had committed suicide with a pistol (Gary Edwards himself had purchased the pistol a few days before he departed from Seattle to join the boat in San Diego, though both Loren and Joanne Edwards had asked him not to bring the gun aboard), which he kept hidden in his belongings. Joanne Edwards was not familiar with guns, and did not have a predisposition or expressed desire for suicide, and, as indicated, had earlier asserted that everything would be OK following the death of her husband. Gary Edwards did not allow Kerry or Lori to look at the body of Joanne Edwards, but placed the body in a sleeping bag on the stern of the vessel.

These deaths occurred within 24 hours or less running time to the island of Rangiroa, French Polynesia. At one point, notwithstanding superior navigating training and experience, Gary reported

on the radio that he was "hopelessly lost." Using
this as justification, claiming that it would
take them a week or more to get to port (which
obviously was not true), Gary stated that he was
going to dispose of the bodies of Loren and
Joanne Edwards over the side, and did so. Gary
also refused medical assistance for Kerry, even
though it was known to him that there was a
vessel with an American doctor on board.

While making my statement, my hands trembled and my throat went dry. But I'd done it. I had publicly accused my brother of murdering our parents.

However, Kerry's affidavit, given on October 7, provided the most damning testimony.

23

Tuesday, October 7, 1980

I called Kerry to reassure her. "Everything will be fine. All you have to do is tell—"

"I don't want to do this," she said. "It's all your fault."

"It's not my fault Mom and Dad are dead."

"It's not my fault either."

"Do you want me to say you conspired with Gary to cover up the facts?"

Silence.

"Then tell us, on the record, what happened. It'll take less than an hour."

I heard her sniffling, then the line went dead.

Too fucking bad. They're your parents, too.

I worried that she might not keep the appointment with the attorney, but she went. Her sworn statement read, in part:

```
I remember waking up with an awful headache
and trying to sit up and couldn't, because my
head hurt too bad. Then someone pushed me back
down and tried to strangle me and was putting a
pillow over my face so I couldn't breathe. I was
trying to get away but couldn't. Dad walked up
```

from his cabin and said "What's going on?" Gary said "She flipped out or something," and went outside. Mom came up then and wanted to know what was going on; Dad said he wasn't sure.

I believe in the time while I was unconscious Gary had sexual intercourse with me without my knowledge or consent. I believe that because my underwear was wet and it was sticky. And I think when I woke, his leg was over my stomach, like he was sitting on top of me.

They were working on fixing the cut over my eye when Gary called Dad outside because he said he saw land. So Dad went outside to see what he wanted. Mom had just gotten the band-aid over my eye when there was a loud crash outside. Mom asked Gary what happened. He said "Dad fell down." Mom went outside and said "Oh my God! Gary, help me." They brought Dad inside and Mom was trying to revive him and Gary was standing there doing nothing. Mom asked him to help; then he gave him [Dad] mouth to mouth, which didn't work. It seemed like Gary was almost smiling, like he thought it was funny.

Dad died about then. When Dad died, the seas were calm and not a lot of wind.

Mom had awakened Lori in the meantime to steer the boat. When [Dad] died, they wrapped him up in a blanket and left him on the floor in the main salon. Gary called Mayday to all ham radio operators. Mom gave me something for pain and we talked for a few minutes. I asked her what was going to happen to us; she said not to worry, that everything was going to be alright, and we would make it.

Then I went to sleep for awhile — I don't

know how long. When I woke up, Mom took my
temperature and pulse. She never said how I was
doing. I think I went back to sleep then. In the
time I was awake, I didn't get out of bed for any
reason at all. I don't remember any conversation
between Gary and I except him asking me how I
was. I think that is when we talked to that other
boat. I'm not sure, though.

When I awoke, I asked Mom how soon we would
hit land; she asked Gary, and he said about six
to eight hours. I said "We will be in by dark
then" and Mom said, "For sure." Somehow we got
off course, and it would be the next morning. I
slept a lot that day.

Mom, Gary and Lori shared running the boat. I
think Gary and Lori did more than Mom did. . . .
[W]hen we were supposed to have seen land, Mom was
on watch [in the cockpit, steering the boat] and
Gary was doing something out on deck; Lori was
coming up from the kitchen. There was a gunshot and
I jumped to a kneeling position and saw Mom all
slumped over, covered with blood and someone was
standing very close behind her. Then Lori pushed me
back down on the couch. Gary stuck his head inside
the door and told us not to go outside. He came
back in a few minutes. Lori and I asked what had
happened and he said "Mom's with Dad, right where
she wants to be." A few hours later, he and Lori
came to talk to me. Gary said he was wrong and we
wouldn't hit land for a few days and they thought
it best if we buried the bodies at sea, because
they would smell and be gross when we got to shore.
So I said "Yes, go ahead."

When I saw my mother, she was sitting down,
her head was slumped over to her chest and she

was very bloody. I could not see her hands because I think they were under the blanket she had on her lap. All I remember is seeing her from the chest up. I saw no gun near or around her that she could have been holding. It appeared to me that my mother's face was the most injured, like she was shot from behind.

He sent Lori and I down to the settee while he buried the bodies. He used no chain, like he said [he did], because we would have heard it.

Gary then tried to give me something that would put me to sleep. There was a pill and some white powder in water which was not dissolved all the way. I took the pill, but would not take [the] powder. I did taste it; it was very bitter.

I went to sleep for awhile. When I woke up, Lori and I talked for awhile. I asked her what was happening; she said not to worry, Gary would get us out of this. Later that day, we were powering along and the engine stopped, and Gary didn't know what was wrong. He checked around for awhile and said we were out of fuel, so we would have to wait for someone to find us. A little while longer, a boat saw us and was going to help us when all of a sudden Gary found a full fuel tank and started the engine, and we were heading in. An airplane [had] flown over looking for us. Some people from Rangirora [sic] came out in a cabin cruiser; they had a doctor with them and he came and stayed with me until we got to shore where they put me in the hospital. Between the time when I got off the boat in Rangirora [sic] and before the police got on the boat, Gary had the boat cleaned up. My pillow and bedding were washed and everything cleaned up. Earlier he had

```
thrown one nightgown I had on overboard because
it had a lot of blood on it and he said it
wouldn't come clean.
```

Kerry, for the first time, had stated for the record that Gary had assaulted and raped her, countering Gary's claim that she had injured herself in an accident. She didn't actually say that Gary killed Mom and Dad, but she made it clear that Gary was the only other person on deck at the time of their deaths.

Kerry's testimony also contradicted Gary's account of Mom's death. She stated that immediately after hearing the gunshot, she looked out the cabin window and saw "someone" behind Mom. Since Lori was with Kerry, the only other "someone" on the boat was Gary.

Gary had told the FBI he was at the bow of the boat and ran to the cockpit after hearing the gunshot. But for Kerry to have seen him behind Mom immediately after hearing the gunshot, he would have had to cover an obstacle course of thirty feet or more in the time it took Kerry to sit up and look out the window. Under that scenario, apparently Gary was the superman my father's family believed him to be—he could run faster than a speeding bullet.

Kerry also said Mom appeared to have been shot from behind, in effect saying Mom did not shoot herself. And Kerry said Mom died the same day as Dad, refuting Gary's claim that Mom had died the next morning.

Missing from Kerry's statement was Gary's motive for assaulting her. When I asked her about it, she again insisted she didn't know, but her expression and change in tone of voice told a different story. I wrote in my journal: *Why does Kerry get that smirk and blush when confronted about not telling us everything she knows?*

In cases like my parents', where the evidence is circumstantial, a criminal prosecutor prefers to have the defendant's motive to convince a jury of his guilt. But in the civil case, to prove "unlawful killing," motive wasn't as critical. With Kerry's sworn testimony, Aileen, Bobbie, and I believed we would prevail. We also hoped Kerry would finally explain why Gary attacked her and that testimony would be used in the criminal case.

We didn't bother asking Lori to testify. Not after her absurd meteorite comment and her insistence that she had seen nothing.

Our attorney filed the petition and my affidavit on Friday, October 22, and the court scheduled a hearing for two weeks later. However, our attorney did not immediately file Kerry's affidavit. Nor did he submit comments from Tal Sturdivant, who had offered assistance but which Gary had declined, or the comments of the surgeon who had operated on Kerry.

The news media didn't discover our action until the following week, when, on Halloween, my parents' story returned to the front pages of the *Seattle Post-Intelligencer*—"Murder Alleged on Deaths on Yacht"—and *The Seattle Times*—"Son Accuses Brother of Killing Parents." Regional papers, radio, and TV subsequently picked up the story.

However, the coverage introduced new errors pertaining to my parents' deaths, including yet another version of how my father died and that the original Mayday call was made on February 25, when in fact Gary had made that call twenty-four hours earlier. Some of these errors were repeated later in published accounts of my parents' deaths, including true-crime writer Ann Rule's book, *But I Trusted You.*

Gary, of course, disputed my claim. In a legal brief filed by his attorney, Gary argued that because Kerry was not named as one of the petitioners, and because I was not aboard the Spellbound at the time of the deaths, my accusations were invalid. He also claimed that I had "bragged" about being able to get Aileen and Bobbie to sign anything. He told *The Seattle Times*: "I have no plans to show up. They will have a hell of a time holding a hearing without me."

Aunt Vivian phoned to ask me how I could do such a thing. My hands trembled and I struggled to remain calm, barely able to control my rage. "Gary will be held responsible for their deaths."

My sisters and I prepared for the anticipated court battle, compiling what evidence we could on the movements of the Spellbound on February 24 and 25, 1978. We intended to show that Gary's explanation not only contradicted the facts, it defied the laws of physics.

Saturday, November 1, 1980

Pete Mercer led the way down the dock. Aileen, Kerry, and I trailed close behind. Our attorney and an FBI photographer completed the entourage. The Spellbound's familiar lines and yellow hull took shape as we approached. When we reached the boat, adrenaline toyed with my nerves and my body quivered in anticipation of going aboard.

The new owner emerged from the cabin and welcomed us aboard. As we spread out on the aft deck, the man said, "You must be Larry," and offered me his hand. As we shook, he added, "I'm not going to change a thing. I'm going to leave it just the way your parents had it."

I jerked my hand away and turned toward Kerry. She had a glazed look, as if she had entered a fantasy world.

Mercer had arranged for the visit. He'd never seen the boat and wanted me to explain the layout to him. And he hoped that Kerry, from the shock of being back aboard the boat, would be jarred into testifying more truthfully.

Aileen, Kerry, and I—Aileen as Mom, myself as Gary—reenacted Kerry's version of the story. Aileen sat in the cockpit, hand on the wheel, pretending to steer the boat, and I squatted behind her. As I pointed a finger like a gun at her head, I broke into a sweat and my body began trembling anew.

When we finished, my head was swimming, and I nearly lost my balance. I sat on the edge of the cockpit, breathing heavily. But it had been worth it. The reenactment steeled Mercer's resolve to see the thing through.

As we walked along the dock toward shore, Mercer said, "I hope to finish my report and get it to Frank Diskin, the U.S. attorney, sometime in December, and he can take it to the grand jury in January or February."

I'd heard it before, but I had to believe him.

We lunched at a McDonald's and discussed the case. Mercer spoke to Kerry about going to trial and testifying.

"That's going to take a lot of time," she said, her voice whiny. "How am I supposed to support myself?"

"How are we supposed to get justice for Mom and Dad if you don't?" I said. "You're coming into a big chunk of money. That will see you through this and then some."

Kerry, her eyes narrowed to slits, fanged a snarl at me.

On the way home, Aileen and Kerry argued. When I couldn't stand it any longer, I shouted, "Shut up, both of you!" Then I leaned forward from the back seat and, in a gentler tone, said, "Kerry, we're on your side. We're only trying to help you. But try to understand our frustration. The way you respond makes it sound as though you're unsure of yourself, as if you don't believe it."

"But it's true!"

"I know it's true. But you need to practice testifying to be ready to answer questions on the witness stand. In the affidavit, you did great. It's a clear, concise account of what happened." She nodded and smiled at my praise. "You just need to be able to repeat that in court."

Her smile faded, and none of us spoke for the remainder of the drive.

THE COURT POSTPONED the unlawful killing hearing and combined it with the probate hearing on December 11. We were disappointed, but the delay gave us more time to prepare. As the day approached, I grew confident we'd finally get the matter resolved. Gary would be held accountable for our parents' deaths and enough evidence would come out to indict him for murder.

On November 25, in a prehearing conference, the attorneys met with the probate judge. Afterward, my attorney phoned. "It's over," he said. "Gary will not contest it. The probate hearing will be a formality."

Gary and his lawyer had rolled over when shown our hole cards: Kerry's affidavit and the statements from Tal Sturdivant and the surgeon. But it was a hollow victory. Gary had denied our parents their day in court. My sisters and I never got to present our case. And we still didn't know for certain how or why our parents died. I reassured myself, thinking that's OK. It will all come out in the criminal trial.

Gary's lawyer gave the outcome a textbook PR spin in a statement issued to the press on my brother's behalf: "I am innocent" . . . "nothing to gain" . . . "tragedy must be put behind us" ... "to needlessly prolong this serves the interest of no one." Some of the comments appeared in news reports the following day, including: "I will not be part of the ghoulish rehashing of details for the sake of blood money."

It's blood money all right. Like the blood money you got from Factor-Newland when you signed the movie deal in Tahiti.

I never spoke to the press. Emotionally, I was tapped out. I also thought it might jeopardize the criminal investigation.

In hindsight, however, I realized my mistake. A mistake made before I learned how easily the press can be manipulated, especially TV reporters and scribes with tight deadlines. By not speaking to the newshounds, I'd given Gary sole possession of the public arena—again. He said whatever he wanted without rebuttal. Were I to do it over, I'd call a press conference, read a statement, hand out copies of the affidavits, and repeat my talking points ad nauseam, in print and over the airwaves. I would leave no room for doubt as to our intent and why we had taken such action.

That might have influenced some family members as well. Then again, it may not have made any difference. Facts and logic rarely sway strongly held beliefs.

Grandma and Grandpa Howatson thanked me for doing it, as did Verney. But it upset Aunt Vivian, Grandma Edwards, and others on my father's side of the family. I spoke with Vivian by phone, and again she insisted that a son does not kill his father. Never mind that in the real world sons do kill their fathers. It was even in her Holy Bible. Again, I pointed out the contradictions and improbabilities in Gary's story.

Vivian sighed. "Gary wouldn't lie about such things. What Kerry said sounds like the fevered ravings of someone suffering from a severe head injury."

"The FBI has doctors' sworn statements saying that Kerry's fractured skull was no accident."

"The doctors could be wrong," Vivian said. "Kerry should be thankful Gary got the boat to that island when he did. He saved her life."

"Whatever," I replied and hung up.

With the exception of Vivian's daughter Linda, no one from Dad's side of the family would even consider my point of view, let alone change their minds. Grandma Edwards' sister summed up their sentiment in a letter she mailed on December 26. Just three sentences long, it read: "Please do not send me any more of your letters. I do not want to hear from you anymore after what you did to your brother. You are about as low as they come."

Merry Christmas, Larry.

24

May 1981

Pete Mercer's assurances notwithstanding, another year and a half had passed without any definitive news about the investigation; more than three years of being in limbo, without justice for my parents. When he called, I got my hopes up, but his tone of voice effected resignation. He refused to give me any details over the phone.

"Come downtown and I'll go over it with you and your sisters," he said.

On a Saturday morning, we met at the FBI's cloistered office complex. Kerry wouldn't look me in the eye. I greeted her cordially but not warmly. Mercer, grim-faced, led us to a soulless meeting room of bare walls. We sat in a circle on stackable, institutional chairs. He held a cardboard box on his lap.

"Let me begin by saying I'm sorry," he said. "We gave it our best shot. We still believe we have a solid albeit circumstantial case against your brother—"

I stopped him. "Are you saying it's over? You told us—"

Mercer shot me a Fibbie glare. "I don't have to do this, you know."

I apologized and he continued. "We gave our prosecutive report to the U.S. attorney's office in February, and we sent a second request for prosecution in April. They agreed we had a case. But we have no bodies." He paused and looked at Kerry. "And she is not a reliable witness.

Without her truthful testimony, the odds are simply not good enough. They do not want to incur jeopardy with a not-guilty verdict."

I stared at him, stunned. "You mean they don't want a blemish on their record."

He did not react.

"They could at least nail him for rape and attempted murder," I said.

"Her word against his."

"Son of a bitch!"

Mercer extended his hands, palms up. "Were it up to me, we'd prosecute. But unless Kerry's willing to step up to the plate, it ain't happenin'. At this point, we will not enforce the subpoena for Gary to appear before the grand jury. There will be no indictment, no trial."

I looked at Kerry with as much hostility as I could muster. Bobbie and Aileen did the same. Kerry gazed down at her clasped hands and said nothing.

"Kerry," Mercer said, "this is your chance to tell them the whole story, leaving nothing out."

She continued to stare into her lap. "Like I said before, I've told you everything. There's nothing else to say."

"Bullshit!" I said. "We have a right to know why Mom and Dad died."

Without looking up, Kerry said, "You don't want to know."

I froze. Gary had said the same thing to me in Tahiti: "You don't want to know." Three years of the same evasive crap. *Fuck you, you little bitch!* I turned to Mercer. "You said you have some things to return to us?"

He reached into the box and pulled out three spiral-bound note-books—the journals kept by my parents and Kerry. He handed one to Kerry and offered me the other two, one with a yellow cover, the other green. I handed the yellow one to Aileen, and I opened the green one. I recognized Dad's handwriting and noted the paper clips marking some pages. I wanted to begin reading immediately, but that would have to wait. I set it on the floor by my feet.

Mercer next handed me three hardbound books—a pair of red daily diaries, and the Spellbound's beige, untitled logbook. I leafed through them, then set them on top of the journal. Next he handed over a packet of letters bound by a thick rubber band, and I added them to the stack.

Mercer hesitated before going on. "These next items are what we believe were the weapons used. If you don't want them, we can dispose of them." He extracted a large adjustable wrench, which Kerry had said she found under the cushion of the settee after she'd been attacked and raped. Mercer offered it to her, but she winced and shook her head. Aileen took it, examined it, then handed it to me. I turned it over in my hands, saw no obvious signs of blood, and set it on the carpet, next to Dad's journal.

Next came the stainless steel winch handle. "This is what we believe was used to kill your father," Mercer said, and handed it to me.

I felt its heft in my hands. I had not held it or its twin for more than three years, but the memories were as clear as if I'd just stepped off the boat. I inspected its shiny surface, shape, and length. One end had a cube-like pawl that protruded from the handle at a right angle and fit into a slot in the top of the winch. If the handle were swung with sufficient force, the sharp corners could easily rip through a person's skin and penetrate bone. I shuddered at the thought and dropped it to the floor, too hot to hold.

I knew what came next, what Mercer had saved for last. From the box, he withdrew the handgun, a Walther PPK semiautomatic, and offered it to Kerry, who cringed and looked away. Aileen took it, glanced at it, then held it out to Bobbie, who shook her head. Aileen handed it to me as if it had singed her fingers.

I realized later what Mercer was up to. By making a show of giving us the weapons, he had hoped to get a reaction from Kerry, to break her down, to get her to finally tell us the truth. But it didn't register at the time. I was still in shock from his announcement that, as a practical matter, the case against my brother had hit a wall.

No! It can't end like this.

As I held the pistol, the gun that had killed my mother, I remembered it as being larger. With a barrel just over three inches in length, it looked almost toy-like. It had an unassuming innocence, as if I could point it and pull the trigger, and say, "Bang, you're dead!" and my victim would fall down, act out the throes of agony, then a few seconds later get up laughing.

I turned the pistol over, my fingertips sensing the rough surface of the cross-hatched grip. For a moment I considered keeping it, then handed it back to Mercer.

"You want me to get rid of it?" he asked.

"Please," I said.

He assured us it would be destroyed so it could never be used to kill again. Then, still holding the gun, he turned to Kerry and invited her once more to tell us everything that had happened aboard the Spellbound.

She shook her head and tears shined at the corners of her eyes. Tight-lipped, I surveyed the room. Bobbie shot Kerry a toxic glance. Kerry assumed a defiant expression and said nothing. Mercer looked at me and shrugged.

For an instant, I thought, leave me alone with her for a couple of hours and I'll get it out of her. Then just as quickly I knew that if three years of coddling and appealing to her conscience hadn't gotten us anywhere, I wouldn't break her stony silence that day.

I gathered up the items on my lap and at my feet and headed for the door. In the hallway, Bobbie stepped up beside me and said, "I just want to slap the little bitch."

"You'll get your chance on the way home," I replied, then stopped to wait for Mercer. When he caught up to me, I asked him about the statute of limitations.

He shook his head. "There is no statute of limitations for murder."

I felt a moment of relief. It wasn't really over. There was still a chance, however slim that might be. Only later did it sink in that he hadn't told me the whole truth either. With the evidence returned and the gun to be destroyed, the FBI, like the U.S. attorney's office, had thrown in the towel.

THAT EVENING, I pored over the Spellbound's logbook and my parents' journals looking for answers. The paper clips left by the FBI helped me zero in on key entries, the times my parents had mentioned dissension aboard the boat, and Dad's alleged problem with his equilibrium. But as I read the scrawled entries, more questions came to mind.

Even without answers, the journals and letters gave Bobbie, Aileen, and me a look at life aboard the Spellbound. Mom and Dad made friends easily and had enjoyed the camaraderie of others. Mom expressed excitement about Bobbie's pending wedding, yet disappointment that she could not attend.

On the flip side, I found references to Gary and Kerry bickering, as well as the battle of the sexes. Dad wrote that Mom and Kerry had complained about never being given enough responsibility, such as driving the boat in and out of port, and not being involved in the decision making. Instead, the "girls" were expected to perform the menial work of cooking, laundry, hauling in the anchor, and raising the sails.

When I was on the boat, Dad's captaincy manifested itself as appeasement. He wanted everyone happy. Never wanted to upset anyone. His version of giving orders amounted to, "Well, shall we . . .?" But that approach had the opposite effect.

I wrote in my journal at the time: "We need a skipper on this boat!" I suggested to Dad that we have a week-long training session at sea, but he refused, saying Mom and Kerry would never go for it. Dad was no Captain Bligh; he was Caspar Milquetoast.

In his journal, I found brief and somewhat veiled references to infighting on the boat in the weeks prior to his and Mom's deaths. On January 17, he wrote that they "got into the argument about the crew again," and on January 20 he wrote, "the gals . . . made peace with Gary."

That peace didn't last, however. On January 23, Dad wrote that they had a "crew meeting to iron out bad feelings" because "Jody's feelings were hurt. She thinks she has lost out."

That must have been when Mom threatened to leave the boat "because of Gary," as Lori had told me in Tahiti and which the Browers later confirmed.

Dad had been forced to choose between his wife and his son.

But I found no specifics as to what any of them had said or done to instigate a violent rampage. Surely my parents weren't killed simply because they were sending Gary, and maybe Kerry and Lori, home.

The final entry in Dad's journal described Gary's wrist injury, which Gary had mentioned in Tahiti. Then it struck me: How did Gary even know what was in Dad's private journal? Why would Gary be reading Dad's journal when he was supposedly lost at sea? When the bodies of his dead parents lay decomposing on the aft deck, and he was trying to get his injured sister to safety? Unless he needed to make sure the story about his wrist was corroborated.

I examined the page again. Was that truly Dad's handwriting?

I flipped through Dad's *Daily Reminder—1976*. I doubted it would contain anything relevant to his death, but I was curious. I wanted inside his head. It documented the year before they left, and it gave me a glimpse of my parents' lives that I hadn't witnessed firsthand. In it Dad had recorded, almost ledger style, the weather and what he did on any given day: worked on this project or that; went to the hardware store; had drinks and dinner with so and so. If he and Mom took the boat out, he noted the details of the trip. Only on rare occasions did he confide his feelings about any of these things.

As I turned the pages, a folded slip of paper fluttered to the floor. I cursed, certain that I'd never figure out what day it belonged to. I retrieved the paper and, as I spread open the first fold, then the second, flattening it on the table top, I recognized the handwriting as Mom's, not Dad's.

What have we here?

I examined the tattered paper and its unrefined cursive, and began smiling, yet not ready to shout my joy. It could be a grocery list Mom had given Dad.

No. I'd found one of Mom's poems. Over the years, she had written a lot of poetry. Well, we called it poetry because it rhymed and had a certain rhythm to it, if at times forced.

"She's a poet and don't know it," Dad had said.

Academics would have dismissed her efforts as doggerel. But we delighted in the triumphant readings of her verse, written for any occasion. They often accompanied a gift to a friend or relative, telling a story about that person. I recalled a day when Mom stood in her customary spot over the heat register, back to the window, reigning over her brood seated at the kitchen table, as she read one of her commemorative paeans.

She gave all of her poems away. In the days before photocopiers and scanners, she kept no duplicates. I'd given up on ever seeing one of them again. Yet there I held one in my hand. Faded blue ink on yellowing, unlined stationery, torn at the edges and dog-eared at the corners. Short, untitled, and undated verse—a mere twelve lines that spoke volumes:

> *These socks for you I have finished at last,*
> *Even though five years have past.*
> *I'm sure that you won't give a darn,*
> *If I couldn't match the dark brown yarn.*
> *I looked and looked in every store*
> *But just couldn't find any more.*
> *Please keep on your shoes when wearing these,*
> *Because our friends will be sure to tease.*
> *Happy Valentine's Day to you, my dear,*
> *Even though it is not quite here.*
> *I hope that we will never part,*
> *Cause I love you with all my heart.*
> *Love and kisses from the Mrs.*

I read Mr. Romantic's entry for February 14, as well as the days immediately preceding and following it, but he made no mention of the poem or the socks. On the day dedicated to lovers, he merely described their departure from Yarrow Bay Marina and the subsequent outing on Puget Sound. Yet, he had saved Mom's missive. I returned the poem to the safety of the diary.

The next day, I took the books to Aileen's place. We cracked a jug of gin and mixed drinks. I showed her the most revealing entries and Mom's poem. She got out the tissue.

We then reviewed the sequence of events aboard the Spellbound as told by the survivors. "I don't believe them," she said. "I think Mom died right after Dad, or even before Dad. If she were still alive when Gary made the Mayday call, she would have talked to that doctor, and she would have talked to her parents to tell them she was OK."

"And if that's the case," I said, "then everything that happened from then on was staged, including being lost and out of fuel."

We thumbed through the journals again and reread their letters, but we found no mention of Dad having trouble with his equilibrium and falling down, other than one or two times he'd been to parties, had a bit too much drink, and struggled to keep his balance while getting into a wobbly dinghy.

"And look at this," I said, pointing to the last entry in the Spellbound's logbook, dated February 23, 6:25 A.M. "That was twenty-four hours before Dad died—if Gary can be believed."

"Which he can't," Aileen said.

Gary was supposed to have been the expert navigator, yet, beginning a full day before Dad was said to have died, and for a span covering two and a half days, the logbook did not contain a single entry. Why?

Dad hadn't always updated the logbook right away. He jotted course and sail changes on a notepad, then wrote them in the logbook later on so the entries would be neat and precise. But it seemed unlikely that he would have let it go for twenty-four hours, if he had been able to do it.

I shook my head in disgust. Aileen picked up our glasses and began mixing another round of drinks. She threw ice cubes into the glasses with more force than necessary and said, "This just makes me madder and madder."

"The irony," I said, "is that our family had been coming together, if for no other reason than we'd all grown up, matured, and become more accepting of each other's failings."

Aileen handed me the drink and sat down. "Me and Dad had become friends. We were doing things together as father and daughter."

"But he . . . they . . . never got to see you turn your life around and become a computer geek working for Boeing."

She snatched another tissue from the box, then handed one to me. We looked at each other across the table, fresh tears glistening our eyes.

I lifted my glass in a salute. Aileen clinked it with hers, and I said, "As Dad used to say, 'Down the hatch.' "

25

August 1981

Emily and I crammed a U-Haul truck with our worldly possessions and left Seattle for San Diego. I got my old job back at Action Resumé, and she landed a job with the county. We moved into her childhood home, a three-bedroom ranch. We talked of marriage. I reconnected with musician and sailing friends, joined a darts team.

Neither of us had wanted to spend another winter in the Pacific Northwest. For me, it wasn't just the dreary winters, but the cold shoulder I'd been getting from my father's family. And Kerry. I hoped to put it all behind me.

But I couldn't outrun the memories. Most nights I awoke after a dream had shaped a garish fantasy that left me shaking from a cold sweat. Sometimes my parents welcomed me back into their lives. More often I was with my brother in an unfamiliar house, lying in bunk beds as we did as boys, and at times Dad appeared. Little, if anything, was said, but the torment left me afraid of sleep, afraid of going to bed.

Even when awake, my mind conjured up images of my parents, triggered by a stranger's laugh, the shape or color of someone's hair, a body type in a crosswalk, a waft of sea breeze, or the slap of a wind-whipped halyard on a sailboat's mast.

Alcohol numbed the sting but concerned Emily. Making several gallons of moonshine in the garage didn't help matters. One day she handed me an AA brochure. I agreed to cut back but still used any excuse to drink—darts, a music session, holidays, a car breaking down.

I bought a small sailboat for tooling around San Diego Bay. Emily and I discussed buying a larger sailboat and living aboard, then going cruising. Lying in bed one night, as I read about a couple who had cruised around the world, Emily said, "You're not going to sail off without me, are you?"

"Of course not. I want us to do this together."

"I'm not as enthusiastic as you are."

Nonetheless, I figured she'd come around eventually. After all, we'd had a grand time gunkholing through the San Juan Islands the previous spring.

Hadn't we?

Friday, February 24, 1984

I arrived home to a quiet house. I'd worked ten days straight, some mornings leaving for work at six or six-thirty and not returning home for twelve hours. Emily and I had postponed celebrating Valentine's Day, and I looked forward to a romantic weekend, to doing something fun to blot out the fact that it was the sixth anniversary of my parents' deaths.

I mixed a drink, then settled into a stack of unread newspapers. When Emily got home, I hugged her and tried to kiss her, but she stiffened and turned her head away.

"What's wrong?" I asked.

She glanced at me, fear in her eyes. "I need a drink," said the woman who rarely drank. She pulled a bottle of brandy from a cupboard, poured herself a generous dollop and sat at the kitchen table.

I joined her. "It's your mother, isn't it? What'd she say this time?"

Her parents criticized every decision, from her career to her clothing to her choice in men. They tolerated me but never warmed up. I wasn't thrilled about the prospect of having a former judge—whose opinions were not to be questioned and whose decisions were final—for a father-in-law. But, for better or worse, Emily and I loved each other.

Didn't we?

"Umm . . . this is hard," she said and chugged more brandy.

I waited.

Tears moistened her eyes. "It's over. You, me."

I stared at her for a long moment, then said, "I guess this means we're not having sex tonight."

She laughed, then turned serious. "You can stay here until you find a place, but you have to sleep in the guest room."

"Just like that? After five years?"

"I met someone else."

"But I thought . . ."

"Larry, I like you. You're a good person. You work hard; you work too much. But we never do anything together. You go off and play music or darts or whatever, and I'm afraid that one day you're going to sail away. That's your dream, not mine."

"Do I know this guy?"

She blushed and bit her lower lip. "Dan*. We have a date tonight."

"Son of a bitch! I practically introduced you."

She went out.

I got drunk.

I MOVED INTO a nearby mobile home park, which sat on a frontage road adjacent to the I-8 freeway. I soon adjusted to the incessant hum of the traffic, which had a sound not unlike a river—except when big rigs hit the Jake brakes.

The memories moved with me. One night I half awoke and saw Gary at the bedroom door. I couldn't move, immobilized by sleep paralysis. Panic gripped me as my semiconscious mind willed my body to defend itself, but my muscles failed to respond. After a moment, the vision evaporated and I gradually regained control of my limbs. I lay there, struggling to breathe, and pulled the covers tight under my chin. I slept fitfully the rest of the night.

Then I quit my job, unable to look at one more SF-171 civil service application, and began working part-time at the *San Diego Reader*. I drank to combat loneliness and the sleep demons. In September, Labor Day weekend, Ian Law invited me to a party at the Cape May Cultural Center—the name ascribed to the tiny duplex he rented in Ocean Beach. It had become a hangout for his fellow musicians.

Friends introduced me to a woman, Janis, who reminded me that I'd actually met her months earlier at a party at the same place, shortly after I'd been dumped by what's-her-name. Janis was one of Ian's fiddle students, and I vaguely recalled sitting in a corner of the kitchen, drinking from a bottle of whiskey (I'd thrown away the cap), and playing guitar. But I didn't remember her.

She invited me and mutual friends back to her place for a swim. After the friends left, Janis and I sat up talking until 2:00 A.M. She taught sixth grade. My being a former schoolteacher gave us some common ground, along with the fiddling.

We started seeing each other regularly. Sunday evenings we made popcorn and watched Murder, She Wrote. But Janis had no clue as to what she was getting into. Not at first. At some point, I told her about my parents.

After two years, we bought a condo together—easier than getting married—and officially tied the knot a year after that. We gathered at Presidio Park in San Diego's Old Town on a sunny August morning. Janis glowed in a Laura Ashley gown, with her sisters Lynn and Suzanne as bridesmaids. Ian Law and Kenneth Brank stood beside me as Rich Goben, destined to become the captain of the tall ship Star of India, pronounced us husband and wife. At the reception, Brank gave the toast, saying to me, "I never met a better." A coterie of fiddlers provided music for contra dancing as we ate, drank and made merry.

Kerry and Bobbie came to the wedding. We found out later that Kerry went home pregnant. I had stayed in touch with Kerry, hoping a guilty conscience would eventually compel her to reveal what instigated the violence aboard the Spellbound. Aileen and I had again urged her to get counseling, but she refused. She became involved with a drug dealer, and I heard from her infrequently. When I did hear from her, she asked for money. I refused to give her any, but I maintained contact through holiday greetings and birthday cards.

One year Grandma Edwards and her sister—the one who had said she never wanted to hear from me again—came to San Diego for the winter months. We reestablished ties, although any discussion of Gary and the deaths of my parents was *verboten*.

Over the ensuing years, I periodically traveled to Seattle to visit friends and family. Grandma Edwards had moved into an assisted living facility; osteoporosis had left her slumped in a wheelchair. During a visit, as I sat holding her hand, she said, "I'm disappointed that you and Janis don't want children. It will be the end of the Edwards line through Loren."

"Kerry has a son," I said.

"Yes, but he's not a real Edwards."

I thought that maybe if Grandma met the boy, she'd have a change of heart. But, as with Grandma Howatson, Kerry never went to see her. I didn't have to ask why.

December 1996

Janis handed me an envelope with what appeared to be a Christmas card inside. "From Kerry," she said.

We hadn't heard from Kerry in more than four years. When I opened it, I found a letter and a photo of her son. As I read the letter, I began muttering, then cursed.

"Larry, can't you just this once relax and enjoy the holiday season?"

"Listen to this," I said and began to read aloud:

> *Dear Larry,*
>
> *How are you? I haven't heard from you for a long time. I wonder if I will ever hear from my big brother and my sisters again. I'm a single mother, living alone, and they ignore me. I am sick of trying to explain to my son why you never acknowledge his presence. He needs a male figure in his life.*

"She's got a lot of nerve," Janis said. "We sent her a gift when her son was born and never got one word of thanks until you called her to find out if she received it."

"There's more," I said. "After that woe-is-me, I'm-the-victim bullshit, she now wants me to track down her son's father."

"The guy that she . . ."

I nodded. "It'd be nice, for once, to get a letter from her with no strings attached."

I began drafting a response, but I took my time for fear of what I might say—and how I'd say it. With the holidays, the start of a new year, and work, the days stretched into weeks, then months.

I flew to Seattle in March for a friend's fiftieth birthday and stayed with Aileen. Still angry with Kerry, I did not contact her. I did, however, visit Grandma Edwards, who had been moved to a convalescent home. When I said hello, she pointed toward the window and said, "I have a lamb. It's right out there. Mommy says I have to take real good care of it."

I took her hand and patted it, then glanced at Aunt Vivian. Anguish lined my aunt's face and she shook her head. I turned back to Grandma and squeaked a response. "I'm sure you will." My grandmother no longer recognized me, and she had only a glimmer of recognition of her daughter. At Christmastime, she'd turned ninety-six; I doubted she'd see ninety-seven.

Afterward, I went to Vivian's. But the visit turned into a love fest about my brother. I never asked about him, but she and Uncle Keith insisted on parroting Gary's grandiose tales of how he'd become the greatest computer programmer on the planet and Levi Strauss & Company's global empire would collapse without him. They gushed on about him more than their own children, although they acknowledged that he was divorced, no children.

I boiled inside, wanting to scream at Vivian: *The FBI believes he killed your brother!* But what was the use? I made a quick exit.

Kerry got wind of my visit, and the following Monday, back home in San Diego, I received a terse email:

Will I hear from you if I write this way? Please send a birthday card to my son. I do not understand why he is forgotten in your eyes. He thinks there is something wrong with him because none of his family wants to know him. A lot for a nine-year-old to understand. If we don't hear from you this year, forget we are alive.

I did feel guilty for not having replied to her Christmas letter, but I dreaded the task. I wrote a draft and sent it to Aileen. She judged it as harsh, so I toned it down a bit and said, in part:

> You made the choice to distance yourself from Aileen, Bobbie, me, and the rest of the family; you made the choice to not visit Grandma Howatson; you made the choice to not visit Grandma Edwards. I've tried to keep in contact with you, hoping you might eventually mature enough to realize that relationships, even family relationships, are two-way streets.
>
> Did you ever ask us to try to comprehend what you went through and what your fears are? No. You simply said it was none of our business and refused to discuss it with us. We are entitled to an explanation of how and why our parents died. Particularly, why they died.
>
> We know you lied to us and to the authorities. You said so yourself. All we want is the truth. But if you're unwilling to discuss that, then our relationship will be strained, and the lack of contact with you and your son is likely to continue. Aileen and I would like to meet and talk to you, but not on a superficial level. Nor do we want more of this guilt trip laid on us.

Kerry replied with a degree of humility, although she claimed she never lied, she just hadn't provided all the details—ignoring the pesky fact that she had failed at least two lie-detector tests. I agreed to visit her the next time I was in the Seattle area. That came five months later.

26

Saturday, August 30, 1997

As I exited the car, I spotted Kerry coming around the corner of the house. A shack, really, but all she could afford. Weather-worn siding slanted toward a corner in need of jacking up; the swaybacked roof sported a thick coat of moss that glowed green in the sunlight streaking through the tall firs surrounding the structure.

"It's about time," Kerry said, making no effort to veil her sarcasm.

I hadn't seen her since my wedding—nearly ten years—and that's how she greets me? Not, "Hi, how are you?" Or "I'm glad you came, it's so nice to see you." I thought my letter the previous March would have made a difference. But Kerry had had a sense of entitlement since she was young. Daddy's little princess. And when Aileen, Bobbie, and I needed her most to get justice for our parents, she had turned her back on us. Yet, in her time of need, she expected me to be there for her. I almost turned around and left.

Still, she had agreed to see me, to talk to me, although she refused to go to Grandma Edwards' memorial, saying Gary would be there. Aileen and Bobbie had also declined to attend, still harboring animosity toward not only Gary but those on the Edwards side of the family as well.

I didn't want to see Gary, either, but I felt a sense of duty, of duty to my father, who couldn't be there to pay his last respects to his mother.

"Good to see you," I said to Kerry, and we hugged in a stiff, obligatory fashion. When we separated, I got a peek at her before she turned and led me to the front of her home. She'd turned forty. Faint crow's feet crept from eyes that no longer held that impish twinkle, but she had retained a youthful figure. Blond hair fell past narrow shoulders that seemed weighed down by . . . what? Motherhood? Life? Guilt?

We sat on a picnic table outside the house. The morning air lay cool, at least for a no-longer-acclimated visitor from Southern California. She had on a T-shirt, but I kept my coat on until the sun warmed me.

"Hungry?" I asked. When we'd spoken a few days earlier, I'd offered to take her out to breakfast.

"Yeah, but I want you to meet your nephew first," she said and called to her son. He stepped out of the house, head down, looking at me through raised but hesitant eyes. I stood and shook his hand, and we exchanged a few words before Kerry said he could return to his video game.

"He's shy," I said.

"Well, what do you expect? He's never met you."

I gave her a hard look. "Don't start."

She went to the door and told her son we wouldn't be gone long.

"You're leaving him alone?" I said.

"He'll be all right."

I flicked my eyebrows but said nothing more. At a nearby restaurant, while waiting for our food, Kerry delayed the inevitable with chitchat about the weather, the Mariners, her new job, her son's progress in school. It continued through the meal, but when we finished, I asked for more coffee and switched gears.

"I want to know what you told Pete Mercer."

Kerry looked at me with an almost pleading expression, as if begging me not to make her go there. I recognized that it pained her, but it pained me, too.

"I don't know what I can say that I haven't told you already," she said.

"When we went to the FBI office that final time, Mercer asked you to tell us what you had told him, but you refused. That's all I'm asking now."

She looked away.

"Mom and Dad's deaths didn't happen in a vacuum," I said. "Something precipitated the violence. There was an argument, a fight about something. Dad even mentioned it in his journal, so it had to have been significant."

"You always say that, but there wasn't anything. Just the little arguments you'd expect, family stuff."

"Then what was it?"

"Nothing. I don't know why he did it."

"You mean why Gary killed Mom and Dad?"

"I mean why he hit me, why he . . ." She stopped and dabbed at her eyes with a napkin. "Gary was antisocial. In the islands, he either stayed on the boat reading or went ashore and took long walks by himself. I don't know why he'd want to . . . to attack me."

As she spoke, she directed her gaze across the restaurant. Her eyes had a vacant quality, as did her voice, as if reciting a practiced litany whose underlying meaning had been long forgotten. Short of torture, I wouldn't get any more out of her, and I doubted even that would work. She'd led a tortured life. What kind of pain could I inflict that would compel her to tell the truth . . . the whole truth?

"But you believe he killed Mom and Dad. He must've had a reason."

She looked at her watch. "I should go."

On the short ride back to her house, we didn't speak, but when we arrived, she invited me in. It had one bedroom, taken over by her son. She slept in a small living room stuffed with her life's harvest. She moved sheets and blankets to make room for me on the lumpy couch.

We paged through two photo albums. One of them Dad had made of his high school and army days; in the other, Kerry had assembled pictures from the trip aboard the Spellbound. She said I could take the albums and copy the photos.

Before I left, I said, "Have you given any more thought to Grandma's service?"

"I told you, I'm not going. Not with him there."

THE THOUGHT OF seeing my brother twisted my gut like a rope walk. The drive from Kerry's house to Vivian and Keith's was only a couple of miles, so I delayed the inevitable, driving past old haunts. The

Merriman farm where my family had lived that spring while Dad began building the house in Juanita. I chuckled at the memory of trying to ride the Merrimans' goats. We spent more time with our butts in the manure and mud than on their backs.

I drove on to Grandma and Grandpa Edwards' old place. I hadn't seen it in years. With her dead, I didn't know if I'd ever see it again. Or if I'd want to.

I slowed to a stop opposite the long driveway that led to the one-story, ranch-style house. Ghostly silhouettes moved behind drawn curtains. I recalled the warm floor, heated in winter by hot water flowing through pipes embedded in the concrete slab. I'd always loved Grandpa Edwards' den. He had one wall shelved floor to ceiling with books.

Up the slope behind the house, the rows of raspberries that had lined the field were gone, probably plowed under. There'd been times I wanted to plow them under, after sweating in the hot July sun, picking the red berries for ten cents a box. After the berries were picked, my cousins and I cooled off on the broad porch beside the house. Shaded by a grape arbor, it still looked inviting that summer day. Too nice of a day for a funeral.

I turned the car around and drove to my aunt and uncle's house, about a mile away. When I stopped in the driveway, people poured out. The clan had gathered to lay to rest the family matriarch. Grandma had outlived Grandpa, and her youngest son, by nearly twenty years.

I stared at the grinning faces as they came down the steps to greet me. I didn't understand their apparent excitement. Were they pleased to see me? Or anticipating a confrontation between me and my brother? Then there he was, one of the stragglers. Why had he bothered to come out at all? As the others gathered in front of the car, Gary remained at the back, a questioning look on his face. Did he genuinely want to see me? Or would he take sadistic pleasure in needling me?

When I got out of the car, Uncle Keith stepped forward and gripped my hand, then drew me close. "Now, you go over there and shake hands with your brother."

I probed his eyes, wondering if he was as serious as he sounded or whether he'd break into a smile and say, "Just kidding."

He wasn't kidding. Apparently I was supposed to admit that I had done something wrong and should be asking for forgiveness, not the other way around.

"You know I can't do that," I said and jerked my hand away.

I glanced at Gary. I hadn't seen him in nearly two decades. Our eyes met fractionally before he looked away. He still wore his longish hair pulled into a ponytail, now streaked with gray, and he struggled to cultivate a mustache beyond the wispish bit of fluff it had always been. A T-shirt hung loosely, as if a size too large, and he'd stuffed his hands in the pockets of his blue jeans. He seemed thin, weathered, and weary, a bit like Kerry's house, as if life had been hard on him. I hoped it had.

Images of the Spellbound flashed through my mind—shouting, arms flailing, pools of blood. I wished I had kept that pistol.

I went to Vivian and greeted her cordially, then the many cousins. I saved Linda, her eyes as inviting and prankish as always, for last. As we hugged, I whispered, "Got any booze handy?"

She laughed and said, "Later."

We all went into the house and made small talk before going to the service. If my brother drew near me, I moved the opposite direction. At the cemetery, Vivian sat in a chair, looking so alone, even though surrounded by family. A burial urn containing Grandma's ashes sat on a small black pedestal. It would go into the ground above Grandpa's coffin.

I prayed for a short ceremony and got my wish. A little bit of Jesus goes a long way. I stood behind and apart from my brother so he'd be faceless. But as we crowded in to lay roses beside the urn, I ended up at his back.

I leaned in close and said, "You don't belong here, you lyin' sack of shit." He flinched but said nothing and moved forward past our grandmother's remains. I'd said it low enough that none of the others appeared to have heard me. Later, I wondered why I hadn't said it louder, but I hadn't wanted to cause a scene. Not there.

But if not there, where? And when?

After the ceremony ended, Linda and I visited my parents' headstone near the cemetery entrance. No coffins or urns buried there. Just undisturbed dirt.

The others drove past and waved, then seemed perplexed, as if wondering why Linda and I were dallying. Perhaps they had forgotten about the headstone. Or maybe I never told them. I saw Gary in one of the cars. He'd never hear about the headstone from me.

The marker depicted the Spellbound on a placid sea, the sun's rays beaming down, a reminder of happier days. Black moss had begun to fill in the grooves etched in the granite, blurring the detail. Even stone didn't mean forever.

I found a twig on the grass and used it to pry out chunks of moss. I'd remind Aileen to give it a scrub now and again.

Linda and I recrossed the broad lawn to the car. Workers were taking down the awning at our grandmother's grave site. Rose petals fluttered over the grass.

At the house, mourners filled the backyard, piling cold cuts, bread, and marshmallowed Jell-O onto paper plates. I drifted among the folks, shaking hands and wishing them well, while distancing myself from Gary. We were like two magnets in a boyhood science experiment, one pushing the other away. As he spoke to others, his grins and laughter heaped salt on my unhealed wounds, and those nagging questions surfaced yet again: Was he innocent? Or was he simply without conscience?

Linda and I ladled food onto our plates and took seats at a table separate from Gary. We immediately attacked the wine. I had hoped for red but found only white. Oh, well. Any port in a storm. When we finished eating, I brought out the photo albums Kerry had loaned me and showed them to Vivian. Paging through Dad's collection, she put some names to faces, dates to places.

When we'd finished, she asked, "Why didn't Kerry come?"

As with her husband earlier, I stared at her for a moment, taken aback by her thickheaded, if not cruel, question. "You know why," I said, and looked toward my brother, who stood not far off, talking to a cousin.

Vivian seemed genuinely puzzled, then followed my eyes. Did I see a flicker of comprehension? Or just more denial?

I picked up the albums and left.

27

Friday, August 9, 2002

The twenty-fifth anniversary of my parents' deaths was just months away. A quarter century. A generation of grandchildren had reached adulthood. My grandparents had all died. I'd lived in New Zealand for six months while covering the America's Cup yacht race; Aileen had spent a year in Benin, Africa, with the Peace Corps. I had passed my father's age at the time of his death: fifty.

Rarely did a day go by that I didn't think of my parents, but the nightmares had pretty much stopped. What with work, music, and marriage filling most waking hours, I no longer dwelled on their deaths, other than on the actual anniversary date, or when Aileen and I got together for our ritual drink-fests.

Even so, the "why" of their deaths still haunted me and Aileen. Seeking an answer, we tracked an FBI agent willing to talk to us about the case. The man had retired and taken a job in the private sector.

On the way to his office, I stopped at a vending machine and got coffee. Not exactly Peets, but it gave me something to hang on to, something to divert my attention during spikes of stress.

In his office, the agent motioned Aileen and me to chairs, then slumped into the one behind his desk. "I feel guilty about Gary never being prosecuted," he said. "The FBI, the Department of Justice . . . we failed your family."

"Kerry failed our family, not you," I said, surprising myself with the bitterness of the tone. "I harbor no ill feelings toward you or the agency."

"It's Kerry we're mad at . . . and the U.S. attorney's office," Aileen said.

His eyebrows shot up. "Not your brother?"

"Mad doesn't even begin to describe how we feel about him," I replied. "But thanks to Kerry, we never got justice for our parents."

He pursed his lips, then said, "I don't know what I can tell you that I haven't already. Gary is guilty as hell, but unless Kerry comes forward, there's nothing anyone can do, and I don't see how I can tell you anything you don't already know."

"Kerry still hasn't told us what triggered the violence," I replied.

"Yeah, Gary didn't attack her for nothing," Aileen said.

"It's all in the report," he said, a trace of defensiveness creeping into his voice.

"We've never seen the report," I said.

He frowned. "You didn't get it under the Freedom of Information Act?"

"I figured that until the case was closed, we weren't allowed to."

He shrugged. "For some reason, I thought you'd seen it."

I shook my head and continued, my voice almost a plea. "We just want some answers, that's all. But we don't know where else to turn. Kerry clams up any time we ask her."

I reached for the coffee, my hand trembling, and put the cup to my mouth, then jerked it away as the liquid scalded my lower lip. The brown liquid spilled on my shirt, and I set the cup down.

The retired agent scooted his chair forward and offered me a tissue, then he picked up a slip of paper and read aloud. "Case number four five dash five six six. I wish I could get you a copy, but I'm prohibited by law. You'll have to contact the folks in Washington, D.C."

"Can't you just tell us what's in it?" Aileen asked.

He exhaled heavily, then spoke as if thinking aloud. "I'm not supposed to do this, but it is in the report . . . and of all the cases, this one bothers me the most." He paused and looked at Aileen, then me, then across the room, as if asking permission—or forgiveness—from a higher authority. Finally, he said, "You deserve to know what happened."

I glanced at Aileen. Her lips tightened. She offered me a wan smile.

He drew a deep breath. "Kerry told me that she and Gary had been having sex," he said. "It probably began before they left San Diego. Possibly even earlier than that, when Gary returned from the army."

"She . . . I . . . Oh, god damn it!" Aileen said and slammed a fist on an arm of her chair.

I crunched my teeth until they hurt. "That explains it," I said. He and Aileen looked at me, and I went on. "I hadn't thought about it until now. When I was still on the Spellbound in San Diego, Kerry, Lori, and Gary were in the cockpit, passing around a joint. I was sitting in the main cabin, just a few feet away, but they couldn't see me, and I heard Kerry's voice: "You know what they say, 'Incest is best.' They all laughed and I dismissed it as a ribald joke. Apparently it wasn't."

"She said that at Bobbie's one time, too, remember?" Aileen said. "Her and a bunch of friends were drinking and getting high, and she said that, 'Incest is best.' "

I dropped my head into my hands and stared at the floor.

"Kerry was like a dog in heat," Aileen added.

The retired agent continued. After the Spellbound reached the Marquesas Islands, Kerry called it quits with Gary when she started fooling around with men on other boats.

"Did she say why she'd slept with him?" I asked.

He answered with a flippant tone to his voice, as if mimicking Kerry. "Yeah. She said, 'He was only my half-brother, after all, and I hadn't seen him in a long time.' "

"Motherfuck—" I mumbled and stood.

"That little bitch," Aileen said.

I left the office and walked to the end of the hall, hands clenched at my sides. I never understood what women saw in Gary. And his own sister? He and Kerry had spent a lot of time together before the boat left San Diego, drawn together, in part, by their mutual disdain for me, their judgmental older brother. Like the day they caught a bus to Disneyland. Or so they said.

Doubtless, Gary had flattered her, and for twenty-year-old Kerry, who swayed her hips and offered coy looks to any young man who happened by, having casual sex was as natural as breathing. One time a guy from Seattle visited her before the Spellbound left San Diego. Not the ne'r-do-well boyfriend she had promised to marry then left behind, but someone else. Mom and Dad were at the Garretts, and the guy ended up staying the night on the boat. He and Kerry had sex just a few feet from where I was attempting to sleep. When they walked past me the next morning, Kerry shot me a haughty look, as if to say, "See? I'm not a little girl anymore."

I returned to the office and sat down. "Sorry," I said.

"Do you want to hear the rest of it?" the retired agent asked.

I nodded and he continued: "Kerry was on watch, steering the boat. It was late at night, and everyone else was sleeping. Gary came out of the cabin."

"She told us she was on the settee, asleep, when Gary went after her," I said.

He flicked his eyebrows as if to say, hello, she lied to you, then he went on. "She told him to forget it, that she wasn't going to put up with his bullshit anymore."

"What'd she mean by that?" Aileen asked.

He lifted a shoulder. "She probably had sex with him a few times as a lark, but he expected it to be a regular thing and pressured her. She was vague about that."

Aileen snorted. "I bet she was."

"When she told Gary to buzz off, he lost it," he said.

An image filled my mind: Gary standing over Kerry, a pernicious grin creasing his face and hawkish eyes intent on their prey. "But that doesn't make sense," I said. "At sea, any change in the motion or the sound of the boat is a cause for alarm. If he'd gone on deck expecting to have sex, there would have been no one to steer the boat. It would have wandered off course, causing it to roll, and if they cut the engine to let it drift, the noise level would have dropped instantly. Either way, Dad would have woken up and investigated."

"Maybe he just wanted a blowjob," Aileen said.

I laughed but said, "Get serious."

"Well, it's possible."

He cleared his throat, and we turned our attention back to him. "The next thing Kerry remembered," he said, "was Gary straddling her as she regained consciousness. She said her thigh was wet. I asked her if it was sperm, and she said, 'What do you think?' "

As his words sank in, I stared at the bookshelves lining the wall behind his desk, then turned to Aileen, shook my head in resignation. I felt numb.

As the man continued, his voice sounded distant, tinged with a faint echo, as if speaking in a dense fog. He said the probable scenario was that Gary not only resented Kerry spurning him, but blamed her for the likelihood that he would be sent home once the boat reached Tahiti. In a moment of blind rage, he attacked and raped her. When Kerry regained consciousness, she cried out. Gary attempted to silence her with a pillow over her face, and that's when Dad got there. "The feeling of betrayal, after all your father had done for his son, must have been overwhelming," he added.

I pictured Dad checking on his little princess, finding her injured, calling to Mom. Mom uses compresses to halt the flow of slick blood oozing from wounds over Kerry's eye and at her left temple. Kerry moans and jerks in spasms of pain as Mom dabs raw flesh with disinfectant. Dad trails Gary outside and confronts him. It's dark. Voices rise like a sudden squall materializing in moist, tropical air. Pushing. Shoving . . .

My hands trembled and my face contorted as I tried to quell the sobs being lobbed like mortars from deep within my gut.

"You OK?" the agent asked.

I gazed at him through unfocused eyes, his face featureless, one of the supporting cast framing the drama that played out on my mind's stage. I sucked in a deep breath and nodded, then reached for my coffee. I sipped the now-cold brew, not out of desire but from the need to grasp anything and satisfy that oral craving that chaperoned distress.

The man eyed me for a moment, then went on. "According to Kerry, your mother told Gary he 'won't get away with this,' but Gary said he wasn't going to be punished for 'giving the little bitch what she deserved.' Your mom displayed a great deal of courage in her race against time. Her husband was dead, and her daughter was bleeding from two head wounds, and she was stuck on that boat with your brother."

The action resumed in my mind's eye: Gary skulks about the boat, retrieving his pistol and ammunition, biding his time as the day breaks. Mom sits at the helm, hand on the wheel, eyes darting to the low light of the compass, intent on reaching port, the closest port, as quickly as possible. Gary, under the guise of attending to the boat, maneuvers behind her in the early light of dawn . . .

I stared at the retired agent, feeling as dazed as I had that day aboard the Spellbound, listening to Gary's implausible tale of the events that led to our parents' deaths.

I reached toward Aileen and squeezed her hand, the tears that moistened her eyes matching my own. We knew the rest of the story. Gary said he got "lost," which gave him a rationale for dumping the bodies over the side. But the retired agent said Kerry had supplied more details about that, too.

"She said that after Gary told her they were lost, he was on the radio to a ham operator saying the boat was under sail. But a boater broke in to say the Spellbound was in sight and there were no sails up. Then, in just a few minutes, Gary started the engine and the Spellbound got under way."

"Probably the Sturdivants," I said. "They wrote about it in a newspaper article."

The retired agent nodded and went on. "I tried to play the nice guy with Kerry, acting concerned, like I was her friend, but I never could warm up to her. She had no interest in seeing justice done. She was only interested in what was best for her in the short term. She refused to testify against Gary, saying that he'd be out in seven years and find her and kill her. She said, 'Where will you be then?' I told her he'd be put away for life. But she wouldn't have any of it."

Aileen looked at me, shaking her head. "Mom and Dad died because Kerry decided to fuck Gary."

"Mom and Dad died because—"

"But it never would have happened if Kerry hadn't slept with him."

"She was the catalyst, and she helped cover it up," I said, "but don't ever lose sight of what actually happened."

I turned to the retired agent. "Is that it?"

"Like I said, it's all in the report."

Thinking about it afterward, I acknowledged that the sex only scratched the surface. The deeper issue concerned dominance and control. That had been Gary's motivation for anything he did. Did it stem from feelings of low self-worth that developed in early childhood? The factors that guide us, even drive us, often have their roots in subconscious memories buried so deep we no longer recognize them. Nonetheless, we must be held responsible for our actions.

TWO DAYS LATER, Aileen and I attended the annual picnic of Mom's family, the Howatsons, at Denny Creek Campground in the foothills east of Seattle. She parked amid the thick growth of cedar, fir, and spruce trees that cast broad shadows on a cool morning. We found our aunts, uncles, and cousins huddled around a campfire, palms to the flames. Smoke fogged the air, and the nearby creek gurgled over a stony bottom.

Verney offered us coffee, and we joined the others at the fire. Aileen mentioned our meeting with the FBI, but they said nothing as they skittered glances at one another. Even Verney, after a moment, busied herself with setting out the food. I stepped away and glared at them over the top of my coffee mug. How could they not want to know why their beloved sister, their aunt, had died? How could they just shrug it off and go on as if it had never happened? Yes, everyone deals with grief and loss in their own way. Nothing could change the fact that they'd never see her again. But how could they not be outraged at the injustice?

Later, Verney apologized for not being more supportive. She said none of them were ready to hear about it. "It's still a very uncomfortable subject with most members of our family."

I had brought along my fiddle and played a few tunes, including a new melody I had composed a few weeks earlier while watching the debut of *Monk*, a TV series about a former police detective. The opening scene had the character Adrian Monk playing a clarinet at his wife's grave.

I played along with the emphatic phrasing, then the scene ended abruptly, cutting off the music. I memorized the few bars he'd played and toyed with it until I had a full thirty-two-bar melody in three-four time. As tears streaked my cheeks, I dubbed it "Spellbound Waltz" in honor of Mom and Dad, whose bodies had been dumped without ceremony into an unmarked grave in the middle of the Pacific Ocean.

28

December 2003

The hefty package arrived.

Finally.

I had submitted my request to the Department of Justice under the Freedom of Information Act in October 2002. Fourteen months of letters and phone calls later, the report emerged from the FBI's byzantine filing system.

I ripped open the package as I carried it to my office and plopped into a chair. The title page read:

FEDERAL BUREAU OF INVESTIGATION
PROSECUTIVE REPORT OF INVESTIGATION CONCERNING
[GARY LEE EDWARDS]
CRIME ON THE HIGH SEAS

Next came interdepartmental correspondence related to the case. The report had been sent to the U.S. attorney's office in Seattle on February 23, 1981. The cover letter accompanying the report—attention Francis J. Diskin, assistant U.S. attorney—consisted of a single sentence: "Dear Sir: For your information, I am enclosing communications which may be of interest to you." The letter was signed by Allen P. Whitaker, Official in Charge.

That's it? These guys need a lesson in marketing.

On March 26, Assistant U.S. Attorney Michael P. Ruark replied, declining to prosecute, and on April 7 Whitaker wrote to Ruark's boss, U.S. Attorney John Merkel, saying: "We will continue to investigate this case . . . and intend to have a Visual Investigative Analysis (VIA) chart prepared to assist in demonstrating the facts in this case which we feel will support a decision to prosecute."

I flipped through the pages of the report, a bittersweet blend of excitement and dread playing tug-of-war with my mind. The report began with a narrative summary of the case and a list of witnesses recommended for testifying at the trial.

Seeing my name on the witness list startled me, and a tingling of realization swept through fingers, hands, arms, and up into my shoulders, neck, and face. *Those calculating bastards!* I thought back to the day I stood on the deck of the Spellbound, an observer to the FBI agents' further questioning of Gary as he walked them through the bloody events that had taken place there. The FBI had orchestrated my presence so I'd have to testify against my own brother.

Yet, shouldn't I be grateful? I was the only person outside of law enforcement to hear my brother's statements to the investigators.

The other witnesses included Kerry, the neurosurgeon who treated Kerry's skull fracture, an agent from the FBI's Behavioral Science Unit, and the attorney who handled the "slayer" motion. The final witness was a family friend who would testify as to Gary's behavioral patterns during his "formative years" as well as to Mom's emotional stability following the death of her first husband.

Why not Lori? I wondered. Then I recalled her "meteorite" theory regarding Dad's death.

I turned to the evidence form. When I read the final word in the description, I shivered as if the temperature had just dropped:

Title and Character of the Case:
UNSUBS: Loren Edwards (Deceased)
        Joanne Hazel Edwards (Deceased)
        CHS - Murder

I learned later that "UNSUBS" stood for unknown subjects of the investigation; the "CHS" referred back to the title page: Crime on the High Seas. I needed no explanation of the word "murder."

The evidence list included a blood-stained deck plate, a blood-stained strip of wood, a Crescent wrench, a stainless steel winch handle, two glass slides, and one Walther PPK 9mm semiautomatic pistol (along with a report stating that the gun had been tested and it "exhibited no defects which would produce an accidental discharge"). A paltry assemblage, but the boat had been cleaned by hotel workers.

Additional items included my parents' journals, my father's diary, the Spellbound's logbook, and a tape recording of radio communications from the Spellbound on February 24 and 25, 1978, and "notes regarding same." I found reports from forensic examinations of the gun, hair, and fiber collected from the boat. However, the evidence that would reveal how my parents had died—forensic reports on the bodies—did not exist.

The case file contained reports from the Bureau of Alcohol, Tobacco, and Firearms regarding Gary's purchase of the pistol, confirming what an FBI agent had told me: that Gary had lied about where he got the PPK—a pistol also known as the "James Bond gun."

In its report on the condition of the Spellbound, the FBI wrote that a visual examination of the outside wheel disclosed "no apparent damage" to any of the six-inch wheel spokes. "No evidence of any tissue, hair, or blood-like stains were [sic] observed on the wheel spokes, the wheel itself, or on the nut in the center of the wheel," which Gary had suggested might have caused Dad's severe injury.

The agents had found evidence of "blood-like spots" and "hair or fibrous material" in and around the cockpit and inside the cabin. "Inside the salon, a blood-like stain was located under the seat cushion of the couch located against the aft cabin wall. . . . The stain was 12 ¾ inches in length . . . a heavy four-inch-long, half-inch-wide coagulated section of that stain . . . was lifted. These stains . . . also show reddish stains appearing on the cushioned back of the couch over the seat. Additionally, reddish stains appearing on the back edge of the seat cushion can also be observed." A number of these samples were identified as human blood, head hair, and head-hair fragments.

Another report in the file stated that a friend of my parents, upon hearing of my father's death, had contacted the U.S. Coast Guard in Seattle "to assist her in warning Jody Edwards of the danger she was in." The woman said "she wanted Jody 'to lock [Gary] up in one of the rooms' aboard the vessel until help arrived." But the woman never spoke with Mom.

I also found a letter from Factor-Newland, sent to the FBI in 1985, saying the movie production had been dropped. *The fuckers. Couldn't be bothered to inform me. At least now I can write about my parents' deaths.*

The final page described a phone call received by the FBI on October 26, 1993. The female caller claimed that "Loren and Joanne Edwards were murdered while aboard their sailboat, the 'Spellbound,' . . . and advised this has been bothering her and she didn't know if it would do any good at this point to report it but was willing to take polygraph . . ." The name of the caller had been redacted, as had specific details given during the call. Was it Lori wrangling with a guilty conscience? I had no way of knowing, and if the agency followed up on the call, I found no evidence of it.

I flipped back to the interview transcripts, which comprised the bulk of the report. The interviews of Gary, Kerry, and Lori were heavily redacted. I hadn't expected to find much new information there anyway.

I found an interview of a boater who said that my father, while still in the Marquesas Islands, had told him the trip had been "no bed of roses." And a radio operator who had regularly patched calls from the Spellbound to family members back home stated that at no time did he "hear that Loren Edwards was suffering from any type of balance problem or inner ear infection."

The report included a transcription of the Mayday call and the descriptions of radio communications from the Spellbound following my parents' deaths. It also contained statements of boaters in the vicinity who had communicated with Gary by radio, along with a firsthand account of the so-called rescue operation.

This information clarified much of what had happened aboard the Spellbound during the thirty-six hours following the report of Dad's death. Even more important, it illuminated the hours following the report of Mom's death.

Gary had said that after Mom died he had no communication with other boaters or people ashore, that he became "hopelessly lost." That justified his decision to dispose of the bodies at sea. But the FBI's official account of the radio calls told a different story. Gary had communicated with the U.S. Coast Guard, French officials, and other boaters throughout those two days, reporting his positions.

A prickling sensation shot up my spine.

With these missing pieces, I could track the movements of the Spellbound leading up to and during the two fateful days and maybe set aside those persistent doubts about my brother's guilt that had plagued me for a quarter of a century.

I grabbed a pen and paper to create a timeline, beginning with the entries in the logbook. I would develop my own visual investigative analysis chart, like the one the FBI never got to present in court.

On February 20, the Spellbound took on fuel, food, and water at Hiva Oa in the Marquesas Islands and departed Atuona Bay on a beeline for Tahiti. The trip of roughly 550 miles would take about five days, maybe less if the weather cooperated.

For three days, the Spellbound maintained a southwesterly 230-degree course across the open ocean. The heading would take them through the heart of the Tuamotu Islands. Most vessels going from the Marquesas Islands to Tahiti skirted the northern end of the island group, but that added another day or two to the trip.

The highest wind speed recorded aboard the Spellbound was ten knots, and at times light breezes required the use of the engine to maintain a reasonable speed on the urgent passage to Papeete. There Dad would catch a flight home to see his dying father.

Then, in the early hours of February 23, Dad had sat at the boat's navigation table and, unbeknownst to him, jotted down his final written words:

en route to Papeete
0205—speed down to 3+ K. c.c. 230°
0540—doused main—block on main sheet lost pin.
       changed blocks
0625—untangled jib & got it set. 4 K.

Having no further logbook entries, I extrapolated the relevant information from the Spellbound's radio transmissions as reported by amateur radio operators (known as "hams"), the U.S. Coast Guard, and other boaters.

On the evening of February 23, a ham in a Seattle suburb patched through a call from my father to his sister, Vivian, at 5:12 P.M. in French Polynesia, 7:12 P.M. in Seattle. That was the last time anyone who was not on the boat spoke to my father. Vivian had told me they talked about airplane reservations, the position of the Spellbound, and Grandpa Edwards' deteriorating condition.

The next morning, on Friday, February 24, at 6:45 A.M. (Tahiti Time), Gary interrupted a shortwave radio transmission between a boater and Ron Carpenter, a ham living in La Puente, California. Carpenter operated the Marine Mobile 3 network for boaters cruising the Pacific Ocean. He and a ham in Hawaii recorded the call, which the FBI later transcribed.

"Mayday, Mayday, Mayday! This is W-B-7-S-W-T . . . whiskey bravo seven sierra whiskey tango . . . the sailing vessel Spellbound . . ."

Carpenter responded and asked Gary for details. That's when Gary first told his story of Dad and Kerry being struck by the boat's boom. An assertion he later changed.

Static garbled portions of the transmission, and the ham asked for confirmation of what he'd heard.

Carpenter: "I understand that Kerry has severe head injuries and your father is dead."

Gary: "Affirmative."

At times, when direct communication was lost, an unidentified boater relayed information between the Spellbound and the ham.

Boater: "Can you read me?"

Carpenter: "Yeah, roger, I am barely reading Gary . . . I'm not sure if the southerly coordinate is thirteen or another number."

Boater: "I have fourteen degrees south, one four five three zero left. Do you copy?"

Carpenter: Roger . . . give us the name of the vessel and your father's last name."

Boater: "I have full copy on him. We know the vessel very, very well . . . Gary says his father is dead. The name is Loren Edwards."

"Give us the name of the vessel."

"The vessel is Spellbound."

A chill spread across my shoulders and into my chest. Unable to read further, I went to the kitchen and made coffee.

Clutching the mug, I stood at a window as twilight settled in, melding the shadows into a general darkness like the shroud descending over me. After a long moment, I returned to the transcript, fearful of reading on, yet drawn by a fascination for more details.

Boater: "The course is two hundred thirty degrees true. The vessel is OK. Do you copy?"

Carpenter: "Roger, roger."

At that point, Carpenter contacted the U.S. Coast Guard in Long Beach, California. "About fourteen minutes ago I received a Mayday call from a vessel called the Spellbound," he said. "The owner's name is Loren Edwards. The man at the mike is a son. He reports that they are sixty miles northeast of Ahe and one hundred eighty miles northeast of Rangiroa in the Tuamotu group."

The Coast Guard acknowledged and contacted the Spellbound directly: "Gary, if you're copying me, would you please give us a report. Can you navigate the vessel to a harbor?"

"Yes, I can navigate the vessel," Gary said.

Then a Coast Guard radio operator in Hawaii broke in. "We will have medical information coming from the public health service hospital in Honolulu shortly."

Gary repeated what he had told Ron Carpenter, and the Coast Guard set up an hourly schedule for Gary to update officials as to the Spellbound's position and Kerry's condition. Gary said nothing about his injured wrist or inability to use a sextant, as he later claimed.

When the doctor in Honolulu got on the radio, he asked Gary to report regularly on Kerry's condition, including her temperature, ability to talk and function, size of pupils, and her mental state, and to keep a written record of these conditions. (That written record, if kept, was never found.) He also recommended that Gary discourage her from eating and give her some medication from the stock of prescription painkillers and antibiotics Mom had stowed aboard the Spellbound.

Another boat in the area, the Samarang, had a medical doctor on board. The doctor suggested a rendezvous with the Spellbound so he could examine and treat Kerry. He estimated it would take about six hours for the boats to come together. Gary declined, saying that even though he couldn't get to Rangiroa until late the following day, he wanted to go there because it had a medical facility and an airport.

Where's Mom? Why isn't she talking to these doctors? She would have insisted that they meet up with the Samarang. If she were still alive.

To make sense of the numbers whirling through my head, I plotted the course of the Spellbound from Hiva Oa on a navigation chart for French Polynesia. Then I added the position at the time of the Mayday call, followed by the boat's subsequent movements. But rather than clarifying, it amplified the confusion.

Gary had given his position as 14 degrees south, 145 degrees, 30 minutes west. That would put the Spellbound about thirty miles north-east of the island of Mahini, which lay between the Spellbound and Rangiroa. It also confirmed what Kerry said Mom had told her after Dad died: They would make landfall before dark. (See Chart 1.)

Boaters familiar with the region recommended that Gary go to Mahini or Ahe, an island just west of Mahini. Both islands had medical clinics and airfields. Gary again refused, saying it would be dark by the time he got to either one, and the narrow passages into the lagoons were too dangerous at night.

But his reasoning didn't add up.

Based on the Spellbound's average cruising speed of roughly five knots, it would take thirty-six hours to reach Rangiroa, and by then it would be dark. Traversing that channel would be equally risky.

A little while later, Gary reported seeing an island, which logically would have been Mahini, although it's unlikely he could have been in sight of the island so soon. Later that morning, Gary again reported seeing an island. However, he identified it as "probably Takaroa."

Huh? How could that be?

I reexamined the figures and the lines I'd drawn on the chart,

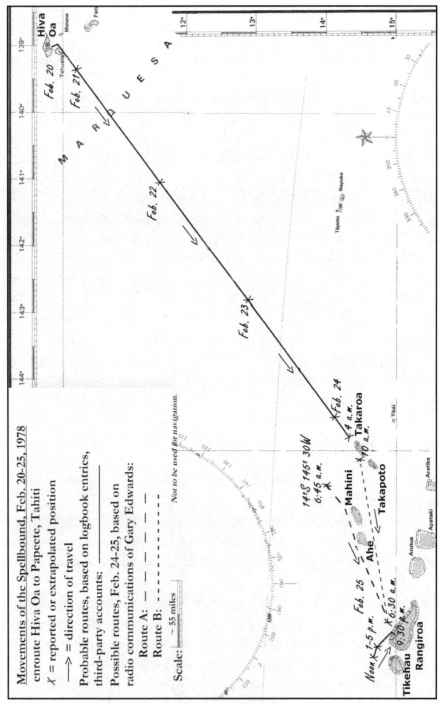

Chart 1

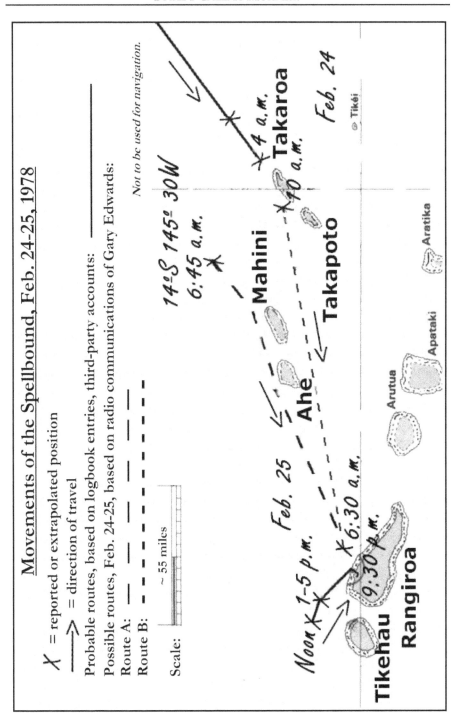

Movements of the Spellbound, Feb. 24-25, 1978

X = reported or extrapolated position

⟶ = direction of travel

Probable routes, based on logbook entries, third-party accounts: ⎯⎯⎯

Possible routes, Feb. 24-25, based on radio communications of Gary Edwards:

Route A: — — —

Route B: —·—·—

Scale: ~ 55 miles

Not to be used for navigation.

14°S 145° 30W

6:45 a.m.

4 a.m.

Takaroa

Feb. 24

10 a.m.

Mahini

Ahe

Takapoto

Arutua

Apataki

Aratika

Tikéi

Feb. 25

1-5 p.m.

Noon

6:30 a.m.

9:30 p.m.

Tikehau

Rangiroa

Chart 2

vectors that led to the Spellbound anchoring in the Rangiroa lagoon thirty-nine hours after the Mayday call. Based on the position Gary had given initially, he should have been at least forty miles northwest of Takaroa and headed away from it, not toward it.

I read the transcript again. *According to Gary's reports, the Spellbound was in two places at once.*

Had he made a huge navigational error when he said they were northeast of Mahini? Or had he lied about seeing Takaroa? I showed the chart to a friend, an experienced ocean navigator. He shook his head, saying, "This is crazy."

Based on the heading from Hiva Oa, the Spellbound should have been in the vicinity of Takaroa, which lay southeast of Mahini. Seeing Takaroa made sense. So how did the Spellbound get to the north side of Mahini, as Gary first reported? Even taking drift into account, the boat should not have been anywhere near that island, unless . . .

Kerry had said that Mom told Gary, "You're not going to get away with this." I pictured Mom taking the helm, changing course, and heading straight for Mahini—and safety—at the fastest speed possible. Gary would have glanced at the compass, then gone to the nav table, where he peered at the chart. The outcome would have been as obvious to him as to me. And even before the Spellbound reached Mahini, Mom would radio the gendarmes.

Gary couldn't let that happen.

But afterward, Gary would have realized that having reported his precise location, anyone looking at a nautical chart would see that he could put in at Mahini before nightfall. I could only conclude that he misled the Coast Guard and other boaters by later claiming to be near Takaroa. That way, he could justify not being able to reach a safe harbor before dark.

The hourly calls continued until noon, then stopped. *Is that when he disposed of the bodies?*

Gary reestablished contact late in the afternoon. French officials at Tahiti told him to put in at Takapoto, an island west of Takaroa, or at Mahini, but he refused. Again, no indication that Mom had been involved in any of the radio transmissions. Yet, Gary had said she didn't die until the next day.

If she were alive, wouldn't she have talked to the doctors? Wouldn't she have wanted to contact her frantic parents? Her children? Let them know she was OK?

There were no additional calls reported until the following morning, on Saturday, February 25, when Gary again contacted Ron Carpenter.

Why didn't he contact the Coast Guard in Honolulu?

"My mother, Jody Edwards, died during the night," Gary said. But he refused to discuss the details of her death.

Carpenter: "What's your position?"

Gary: "About ten miles north of Rangiroa."

You fucker.

Gary had told the FBI, in my presence, that the Spellbound had "drifted all night," that he hadn't kept track of their heading, that he didn't know where they were. That he was lost. But in his radio transmission, he said they were ten miles, or about two hours, from Rangiroa —an island that, at thirty-two miles in length and the second-largest atoll on Earth, would have been hard to miss.

I read on. Later that morning, Gary told a boater he was twenty miles northwest of Rangiroa, saying he'd gone farther north than he originally thought. Gary reversed his course, and at approximately 1 P.M. he reported that he had motored southeast, back-tracking toward Rangiroa. He said he was seventeen and a half miles from the island, at which point, according to Gary, the Spellbound ran out of fuel. The boater said nothing about Gary's being "lost." (See Chart 2.)

Son . . . of . . . a . . . bitch!

My hands shook as I reviewed my notes and triple-checked the figures. Then I called Bobbie.

"What's going on?" she asked, sounding groggy and annoyed.

"We got an early Christmas present from the FBI," I said.

"The only present I want is sleep. I worked a double shift yesterday."

"I can call you back."

"I'll nap later. What's up?"

"I've been reading the FBI report. It proves Gary lied about what happened after Dad died and especially after he reported that Mom was dead."

I told her what I had learned.

"My head is spinning," Bobbie said. "You know I was never that good with numbers."

I took a deep breath. "It means that on Saturday, February 25, the Spellbound was never more than thirty miles from Rangiroa and more like twenty, not the sixty miles he later claimed and was reported in the newspapers. Besides, if Gary had been lost, how could he have known how far he was from the island, let alone the precise distance of seventeen and a half miles?"

"He couldn't," she said. "And Kerry and Lori both said that Gary told them it could be a week before they reached land, and in that tropical heat, the bodies would decompose and had to be buried at sea."

"Yep," I said, "but throughout that morning, French officials and boaters at Rangiroa monitored the Spellbound's progress and expected them at the island before noon. When the boat didn't show up, the Tahiti Rescue Coordination Center ordered an Air Tahiti aircraft aloft to search for it."

I summarized what happened next. As the sun began to set, the air crew spotted the Spellbound "maneuvering erratically" and radioed the boat's position ashore. A crew of volunteers scrambled aboard the sportfisher Tarvana and departed Rangiroa at roughly 5:00 P.M. The air crew then contacted the sailboat Little Revenge, owned by Tal and Lee Sturdivant, who altered course to intercept the distressed vessel.

"They wrote about it in an article published in *The San Diego Union*," I said and read from the article. " 'We said we would come alongside and stand by to help. We had extra fuel aboard we could give them. . . . We could see the boat quite plainly. . . . Bright yellow hull. Two-masted. . . . No sign of life on deck. Spooky.' "

"I remember that," Bobbie said.

"But Gary told them he had just found fuel and he no longer needed their assistance. The Sturdivants said the Spellbound then 'motored away.' "

"So they offered Gary help and he turned it down."

"And a little over an hour later the crew aboard the Tarvana located the Spellbound 'heading for Rangiroa under power,' according to one of the guys aboard the Tarvana."

"If Gary was lost, how did he know which direction to go?" Bobbie asked.

"You tell me."

I then laid out the rest of it for her. When the two boats came together, a male nurse went aboard the Spellbound and tended to Kerry's wounds. Another man from the Tarvana also went aboard the Spellbound to guide the boat into port. The Spellbound anchored near the Kia Ora Hotel in the Rangiroa lagoon at roughly 9:30 P.M.

The return trip to Rangiroa had taken about three hours at a speed of six and a half to seven knots, according to an American marine biologist aboard the Tarvana. That meant the Spellbound was no more than twenty miles—not sixty—from Rangiroa when the Tarvana arrived.

"That's the linchpin," I said. "The sixty-mile figure was not only inaccurate, it was impossible—unless the Spellbound had been equipped with a jet engine. Even a fifth-grader could calculate that at sixty miles it would take ten to twelve hours to get to the island, not the three hours it actually took."

"So this means that Gary didn't have to bury Mom and Dad at sea," Bobbie said.

"Not unless he wanted to keep a medical examiner from determining the cause of death."

"That bastard," she said. "I'd love to talk more, but I have to go. Merry Christmas."

"Yeah, Merry Fucking Christmas." I hung up and slammed a fist on my desk, bouncing pens and pencils to the floor. I had wanted the truth. But it didn't comfort me.

Maybe Bobbie had it right. Just live with the fantasy that our parents were on an extended vacation and one day they'd return.

But I couldn't. Mom and Dad deserved to have their truth known.

I looked down at the stack of pages from the FBI report. The details refuted my brother's statements and called into question his entire explanation for what had transpired aboard the Spellbound on February 24 and 25, 1978. It proved that Gary had lied—to me, my family, the FBI. To everyone.

I picked up the chart and again scrutinized the headings and positions I had penciled in. Gary had known precisely where he was. Based on what I had learned, I figured he must have sailed in circles or let the boat drift, buying time to cover his ass, all the while hoping no one spotted the Spellbound until another day or two had gone by. Then he could waltz into port with a credible tale of having been lost. What he hadn't reckoned on was the search-and-rescue aircraft spotting him so quickly and the chance meeting with the Sturdivants, which exposed his charade.

I tossed the chart onto the desk, again cursing the U.S. attorney's office. I had reached the same conclusion as the FBI, which had stated in its letter: "Gary Edwards' account of the events aboard the 'Spellbound' could not have happened the way he said they [sic] did."

How was that not sufficient evidence to prosecute?

29

Friday, October 1, 2004

I sucked in a deep breath and exhaled, then punched the numbers on the telephone keypad. A man answered. I identified myself and asked to speak to Kerry. The man said, in a muted voice as if he'd turned away from the phone, "Hey, Kerry, do you have a brother named Larry?"

Has she not told this guy anything about her family?

A moment later Kerry came on the line. My hands were shaking, so I aimed for nonchalance. "I'm calling to find out if I should vote for you or not."

She chuckled. "This is unexpected."

"I heard you mentioned on NPR the other day in relation to the presidential election, as one of several 'Kerry Edwards' around the country. Were you contacted?"

"No, but you're not the first to say that. Not when I'm working for a bunch of rich Republican farmers."

Curiously, her first question to me was "Do you know how to get to Aunt Mary and Uncle Bob's old farmhouse?" A defensive maneuver if there ever was one. I told Kerry how to find it and inquired as to her health and welfare. She'd moved away from the Seattle area, bought a double-wide, and had just installed air conditioning after two weeks of 110-degree heat.

I detected a near tremolo in her voice, a quaver of fear.

"Are you working?" I asked.

"For the farm co-op," she said, adding that her son, a junior in high school, had asthma but was doing much better in the dry climate, also doing better in school.

She didn't ask me what I was up to or even why I had called. I heard the sounds of a cigarette being pulled from its pack and a lighter sparking. My cue.

"I'm writing a book about Mom and Dad, and I want you to be involved," I said.

Silence, except for her inhales and exhales as she puffed on the cigarette.

"I have a literary agent. She thinks she can sell a two-book deal. My book and your book."

"This is pretty sudden," she said.

"You don't have to make a decision today. I just wanted to let you know what's going on. We can talk about it after you've had a chance to give it some thought."

She agreed to that, and I went on. "There could be some serious money in it for you," I said. "A New York publisher is interested in it."

More puffs on the ciggie.

"It means coming forward, telling the whole story about what happened on the boat."

"Like I said, I'll think about it."

"I got a copy of the FBI report," I said.

She didn't respond, and I started to tell her that I knew about her relationship with Gary, but my chest constricted and my voice cracked. I faked a cough. Once I had relaxed enough to speak, I told her my agent would contact her by email and explain the project in more detail.

Afterward, I phoned Aileen and Bobbie to fill them in. Both were excited at the prospect of the book being published but unhappy about Kerry making any money from it.

On Monday, my agent sent Kerry an email outlining the project. Kerry's book would focus on how Gary took advantage of a vulnerable girl who looked up to her older brother, and that led to her parents' deaths.

Kerry didn't reply to the email, so I called her the following weekend. She hadn't read it; she'd been busy, she said. I didn't believe her but didn't see any value in calling her a liar. She agreed to read it and we'd talk again.

Saturday, October 30, 2004

Four weeks and my agent still had not heard from Kerry. When I phoned again, Kerry apologized and said, "I'm giving it serious thought, but my biggest concern is my son. He's sixteen and may not take it well. I'm worried about a bunch of reporters harassing him."

"He'll probably be out of high school before this breaks. He'll be an adult."

"I'm thinking about it."

"Kerry, these are our parents, Mom and Dad," I said, struggling to keep from shouting at her. "It's the right thing to do. We'll see that justice is done. You'll get enough money to send your son to the college of his choice."

I paused, and when she didn't say anything, added, "You've said yourself that Gary belongs behind bars."

"That would be too good for him," she replied.

But a week later neither I nor my agent had heard from Kerry. Another phone call. When she answered, she seemed annoyed, as if I were a pesky housefly. To warm her up, I asked her to recall what Gary was like before the incident, if he'd been acting strange.

"You mean stranger than usual?" she said.

"Did he do anything out of the ordinary?"

"He always acted superior . . ."

"That's a good start."

She was silent for a beat, then said, "When the Polynesians were aboard, he'd purposely put the boat in irons, then walk away from the helm wearing that smirk of his and leave Dad to sort out the mess."

I pictured Gary moving the wheel slightly, turning the Spellbound into the wind—the equivalent of slamming on the brakes—and leaving the boat wallowing in the swells. The poor Polynesians would be leaning over the lifelines, puking, as Gary stood to the side, congratulating himself.

"Anything else?"

"Not really."

"Then tell me what happened from the time you left the Marquesas and were heading for Tahiti." I figured that by getting her to talk, she'd see that it would be cathartic. I also thought I'd finally get the truthful version. But it was pretty much what she'd said before. Except for one comment that sparked my gray cells.

"Mom died that morning, not long after Dad," she said.

"What do you mean?"

"Before Gary got on the radio. She was already dead."

My gut recoiled and a tremor swept through me. Aileen and I had suspected that to be the case, but for the first time Kerry had acknowledged it to be true. It was the closest she'd ever come to saying outright that Gary killed our parents. For me, it confirmed what I'd come to believe, that Mom's alleged suicide had been contrived to cover up what actually happened aboard the Spellbound. And possibly, as the French police suspected from the outset, that there had been a "melee." That it all happened quickly, perhaps in a matter of minutes.

"Then why did you say Mom died later on?" I asked.

"That's what I was told to say."

"By whom?"

"Who do you think?"

"Why did he do it?"

Kerry hesitated before answering, then said, "I've told you, I don't know. Gary was always a little crazy."

"What about your having sex with him?"

"That's bullshit!"

"Why would the FBI put that in their report then, if you didn't say it?"

"I have no idea."

"Their entire case depended on your testimony. They weren't going to knowingly sabotage it."

She didn't respond.

"You were the one making the jokes, saying, 'Incest is best.'"

"I never said that."

"I heard you say it, and so did Bobbie."

She puffed on her cigarette, then said, "Friends of mine offered to kill him for me. But I said no. I'd be the first person the cops came looking for."

"So you told your friends what you have refused to tell your own family?"

"I have to get dinner ready."

The line went dead, and I slammed the handset into its cradle.

Sunday, November 14, 2004

I phoned Kerry. She again denied having consensual sex with Gary.

"I would never do that," she said in an odd tone of voice, almost pleading, like a child talking to a parent, as if begging for the transgression to be forgotten, if not forgiven, never to be mentioned again.

"What about the book deal?"

"I'm not going through all that again. The nightmares finally stopped. And how am I going to explain this to my son? He doesn't know anything about it, other than his grandparents are dead."

"Don't you think he should know?"

"I don't know how to tell him."

"He's going to find out eventually. He should hear it from you first."

She didn't respond.

"Look," I said, "we need to get this behind us so we can be a family again. At least with what's left of it. You said that's what you wanted for your son. We owe it to Mom and Dad not to have it end this way. You and I both believe Gary belongs in prison."

"He'd get out after a few years and come and kill me."

"If he goes to prison, he's never getting out."

"What if he's not convicted?"

I sighed. "At least think about it."

"I have thought about it, and I won't do it."

"I'm still going forward with my book."

Silence.

I had to muster every bit of self-control to keep from screaming at her. I wanted to reach down the wires, grab her, shake her, slap her.

Instead, I spoke in a measured tone. "Kerry, I don't want it to end this way, with our family ripped apart."

"I don't either, but I'm not gonna do this."

"Good-bye then."

"Good-bye," she said in an almost sing-song manner.

I clutched the handset, ready to slam it down, then caught myself and returned it to the cradle in a slow, deliberate motion, as if lowering a coffin into a grave.

30

Saturday, April 29, 2007

Another funeral, this time for Uncle Keith, Vivian's husband. Aileen wanted to go with me, to see Gary.

"I don't want to talk to him," she said. "I just want to know what he looks like so if he comes around here, I'll recognize him. And I'm taking my camera. I want my daughter to know what he looks like, too. Ruth* hasn't seen him since she was four."

We drove to the church in Woodinville, windshield wipers working overtime. In the parking lot, we sat in the car for a moment and looked at each other. I took a deep breath and said, "You ready?"

"I need a drink first."

I scanned the parking lot. Not seeing anyone, I reached behind the seat and grabbed a bottle of rum, unscrewed the cap and handed the bottle to her. She took a swig, then I did the same. As I recapped the bottle, a door in the van next to us opened and a woman got out.

We both giggled. "The windows are foggy," Aileen said. "I doubt she saw anything."

We opened the doors, popped our umbrellas and crossed the parking lot, careful to step around the larger puddles. The air smelled of cedar. Living in San Diego, I missed that. But I didn't miss the interminable dank weather.

Inside the church, at least a hundred people were already seated in the sanctuary. Some heads turned and I spotted a few of my cousins. I nodded a silent greeting, then Aileen and I slid into a pew near the back.

"Do you see him?" she whispered.

"He's sitting near Vivian."

When the service ended, Aileen and I waited in the foyer as people filed out. Cousin Linda saw me and walked over.

"I'm so glad you're here," she said. "You're coming to the house, aren't you?"

"Of course."

Vivian emerged from the sanctuary taking slow, deliberate steps, assisted by a son at each arm. We exchanged greetings; I said we'd talk at the house. I saw Gary out of the corner of one eye but didn't look directly at him. If he saw me, he didn't react. He followed Vivian outside, then took her elbow while one of her sons went for the car. Gary had graying hair gathered into a ponytail that reached halfway down his back.

"He's gaunt. He looks older than you," Aileen said. "I wonder if there's something wrong with him."

"I hope so."

At Vivian's, Aileen and I took another nip from the bottle before going inside. When I walked in, I found Gary seated in a chair next to the door. He turned to see who had entered and gave me an almost imperceptible nod, as if he'd mistaken me for a long-lost friend, then realized his error and caught himself. Or was he merely testing the waters, gauging my reaction?

I stared at him for a moment, the living reminder of my dead parents and the injustice that taunted me still. I wished again I had kept that pistol.

Could I actually pull the trigger?

I had to say something to him. Not like last time. Something everyone would hear. But what? And when?

I moved on, Aileen right behind me. I said hello to Joe, Vivian's youngest son, then went on to Vivian, who sat in a rocking chair near the fireplace. She smiled, took my hand, and thanked me for coming. I offered my condolences, and she asked if I was still working as a writer.

"I left journalism and am now with a public relations firm," I said. "Janis and I will celebrate our twentieth wedding anniversary this summer. Hard to believe it's been that long."

"Keith and I celebrated our sixtieth last year," she said, then chuckled. "Sometimes I wonder how we did it."

I smiled and squeezed her hand.

"How's Kerry doing?" she asked. "I haven't seen her since I ran into her at the polls . . . three or four years ago."

"She moved. I haven't talked to her for a while," I said.

Mourners crowded around us, waiting to talk to Vivian, so I went in search of Linda. I found her in the kitchen with a group of friends. She handed me a glass of wine and got out childhood pictures, which gave us a few laughs. The assemblage had the tenor of a high school reunion. Aileen joined us, and at one point, Gary stuck his head through the doorway, a forced grin creasing his face. Did he think we'd invite him in? Linda noticed him, too. She glanced at me and rolled her eyes. Gary disappeared.

After a few more yucks, Aileen and I went to the living room. Gary stood talking to a pair of cousins. He chuckled in response to one of their comments, then replied. I couldn't hear what he said, but his demeanor set me off.

You son of a fucking bitch, carrying on as if you don't have a care in the world.

He wore a khaki duster that draped past his knees. The house had become so warm the doors had been opened. Yet he continued to wear that heavy coat. He also wore western-style boots and blue jeans. I'd heard he had moved to Texas.

I leaned toward Aileen and said, "Where's your Stetson, cowboy?"

She laughed and pulled her camera from her purse. She snapped a picture of Gary, the flash lighting up the entire room. Gary turned toward her, and she took another.

"Is there a reason for that?" he asked.

"As a matter of fact, there is," she said and stared him down.

He returned to his conversation with the cousins, and I went back to the kitchen for another glass of wine. People began leaving, and Aileen suggested we go, too. I went to Vivian, knelt beside her rocker, and took her hand in mine. I again offered my condolences, then stood and said good-bye to Joe and all the others in the room, purposely ignoring my brother.

Gary, sitting in a chair near the side door, eyed me with an expectant look, as if hoping I'd say something or at least acknowledge his presence. When I'd finished my rounds, I stepped up, towering over him, and locked eyes.

"I have nothing to say to a murderer," I said, emphasizing the final word and turning the r's into a snarl. I spoke loud enough that everyone could hear me. The room hushed.

He looked down and mumbled, "You can think whatever you want."

I almost laughed aloud. *I just called you a murderer and that's all you have to say? Where's the indignation? The outrage? The denial?*

I left the house and strode to the car, Aileen at my heels. As I reached for the door handle, a voice called out. A tremor of anticipation ran through me. I looked back, expecting to see my brother, but saw Joe quick-stepping across the driveway. I sighed in relief, but the adrenaline rush left me quivering.

When Joe reached me, he said, "What was that all about?"

"You don't know?"

He shook his head. From his expression, he seemed truly puzzled.

"Do you want the answer right now?" I asked.

He nodded, and I looked at Aileen, who shrugged as if to say, why not?

I laid it out for him in a few short sentences. Shock registered on his face. He glanced at Aileen, and she, tight-lipped, nodded.

"Wow," he said. "I've never heard that before."

"Never?"

He lifted a shoulder. "I was in high school then. I only heard what my mom said about it."

"Your mother is in denial. Has been for thirty years. I just can't imagine what goes through his head when he comes here."

Joe stared at me for a moment, as if balancing my words against those of his mother. "The Bible says, 'Murder will out,'" he replied.

That may be, but I don't want to wait for Judgment Day to find out.

I knew I'd left myself open to a charge of slander by my brother. In fact, I wished he would sue me, because then he'd have to defend his actions in public, which he declined to do when I filed the "slayer" petition in probate court. But I never heard another peep from him.

WHEN AILEEN AND I got back to her place, she mixed stiff drinks and we sat on her couch. I raised my glass and clinked hers. "We did it," I said. "We stuffed it in Gary's face. I feel liberated, giddy, as if I just won a fight."

"Me, too," she said and set down her drink. She connected her camera to a laptop and downloaded the photos. The cowboy wannabe in his duster.

"They're great," I said.

"I was so scared, I was shaking. I'm surprised they're in focus."

"A side view and front view. You can create a wanted poster."

We clinked our glasses again.

Aileen then got serious. "Thank you for saying that to him. No one else in that family will."

"I'm just happy the others heard it."

But I paid a price. Back in San Diego, I became listless. I couldn't even be bothered to glance at the morning newspaper. Luckily, I worked from home. I went through the motions, counting down the minutes to cocktail hour.

Later on, I talked to Joe and Linda. Joe said that when he returned to the house, no one uttered a word. "They just went on as if nothing had happened."

I wished I could go on like that, pretending as if nothing had happened; nothing that night, nothing three decades earlier.

31

November 2007

An unexpected phone call. From Connie Saindon, a marriage and family therapist. She needed an editor for her book, which dealt with grief associated with violent death. She said it was for those who'd endured the murder of a loved one.

Emotion skulked out of hiding and reached up from my belly, grabbing my throat. I couldn't speak.

"Who have you lost?" Connie asked.

When I could squeak out a few words, I told her about my parents.

"It sounds like you're the right person for the job," she said.

At our first meeting, Connie told me about her work as the founder of the Survivors of Violent Loss Program in San Diego and the book she had written, *The Journey: Ten Steps to Learning to Live With Violent Death.* Again, memories of my parents roiled up like a massive storm front. I hadn't realized how vulnerable seeing Gary and confronting him at the funeral had left me, even months later.

Connie offered me a tissue. "Just being who I am triggers responses like yours," she said. "We're members of a club we never wanted to join."

Years earlier, her seventeen-year-old sister had been murdered, and that led her to form the program to help other survivors of violent loss deal with their unique manifestation of grief. She knew what I was going through.

"People with experiences like yours often suffer from post-traumatic stress," she said. "It never goes away, not even after thirty years. But by talking to people who have suffered a similar loss, it diminishes the pain." She urged me to get into the Survivors ten-week group session.

"I'll think about it," I said.

Meanwhile, I also had deadlines at my day job and the pending holidays to deal with. Thanksgiving was just days away, followed by Christmas, which had added stress to my relationship with Janis from the outset. I didn't like the holiday; she did. I wanted to be alone or with just her. She wanted to spend it with her family.

I suggested that we rent a cabin at Mount Laguna and spend Christmas there, just the two of us. My fondest memories of the holiday were the times I spent in the Olympic Mountains, where I saluted the change of the seasons and the beginning of a new year. A ritual predating Christmas by thousands of years.

But Janis's mother had died in September; it would be the first Christmas without her. And to accommodate health and travel issues, her family would celebrate it twice. To accommodate my needs, I surprised Janis with a solstice dinner that included our favorite cheese—Stilton— on stone-ground wheat crackers, with cashews, a pot of potato soup, and a tasting of three pinot noir wines. I built a Yule fire in the fireplace and lit candles.

But I still needed time alone. Being particularly sensitive to piercing sounds, shrill voices, and shouting—all related to PTSD, I had learned from Connie—I had to get away, fearful of how I might act around Janis's family if I didn't.

After painting on a smile and doing the Christmas *thang* on the twenty-third, I spent Christmas Eve day alone at Mount Laguna, away from shoppers, jingling bells, and decked halls. I hiked on the Pacific Crest Trail, crunching through patches of snow. Just the prescription I needed.

Saturday, December 29, 2007

Linda phoned to tell me her mother had died. Aunt Vivian had been the last of my father's immediate family. The funeral would be the following week, Linda said, then added, "Gary's on his way."

The words chilled me. I wanted to support her and her siblings, but I couldn't go. Not with him there. I told her I'd have a busy week at work, and the short notice was problematic. I learned afterward that Gary didn't stay for the service.

Sunday, February 24, 2008

The thirtieth anniversary of my parents' deaths. I returned to my refuge at Mount Laguna. A late winter storm shook the truck with such force I could have been back aboard the Spellbound, pounding through a riptide outside of Campbell River, British Columbia. Had I released the brake, the wind would have pushed the truck over the side of the mountain and into the Anza-Borrego Desert lying two thousand feet below. Yet, I felt alive with Nature in all her fury, wind howling over the mountain while I sat snug in my truck with hot coffee, ham sandwich, and mp3 player, listening to fiddle tunes.

Even so, I could not clear my mind of thoughts of my parents. Had they died on such a day, the victims of a weather-related accident, I could have made sense of it. But under the conditions at the time—little wind and the boat under power—the only explanation I could conceive comprised a hurricane of human emotion.

Saturday, December 13, 2008

A year passed before I followed Connie's advice and got involved in the Survivors of Violent Loss Program. I started with the annual holiday memorial, where Connie introduced me to a number of people, including those profiled in her book.

The level of cheerfulness surprised me. However, the mood darkened when survivors began speaking of their loved ones, most of them murder victims. I realized later that the initial levity stemmed from these survivors being among their peers, people who truly understood them and the internal battles they fought.

Connie urged me to speak. I had never told my parents' story in public, and just the thought of addressing the group unnerved me. As others told of their losses, I marveled at how some of them spoke with such eloquence and courage. A ten-year-old boy told us how much he missed his mother, who had been shot and killed by her boyfriend. A woman described how her grandmother had stopped at a store on her way home from church and was killed by gangbangers during a robbery. Another described how she and her best friend had been kidnapped and raped, and her friend murdered, while the man, although identified, had never been prosecuted. I sure as hell could relate to that.

I didn't have to speak, but I thought it would be good for me, for my psyche. When a lull occurred, a number of us glanced around to see who'd be brave enough to go next. Connie looked my way. I hesitated for a second, then took my place next to the Christmas tree, its dozens of ornaments consisting entirely of memorials to loved ones who had died violent deaths. I glanced at the others seated in a semicircle before me. They waited with a patience born of understanding.

I choked up several times, but I managed to croak out the basics. I heard murmurs of dismay, and I tried to wrestle down another sob, but my body convulsed again. I had fashioned a crude ornament from a picture of the Spellbound, and as I gazed down at it, I felt the fool. I hung it on the tree, vowing to make a better one the following year.

Monday, January 19, 2009

I began the ten-week group therapy program. The sessions helped me identify the emotions that troubled me and deal with them more effectively.

The Survivors program distinguished natural death from sudden violent death, for which there is no time for good-byes, no time to adjust or make preparations, no time for coming to grips with the intense emotions that result from the unnatural way a loved one has died. The emotions comprise not only grief, sorrow, and depression, but also intense anger. Compounding the tempest within are dealings with police, the news media, and the criminal justice system. The process can drag on for years and, in cases like mine, the trauma is heightened by family members blaming one another.

Claire*, the group facilitator, explained that our volcanic emotions were a normal response to an abnormal event. The program would foster resilience and help us prevail over our debilitating emotions. We would learn coping strategies and how to compartmentalize our feelings, because in traumatic bereavement there is no closure. Survivors of violent loss live with the trauma forever. It's particularly intense in cases where the crime remains unsolved, when there is no justice.

Associating with others who'd experienced losses similar to my own offered an odd sense of companionship I had never felt before. I was no longer alone. After three decades, I had met and could talk openly with people who understood what I'd been through, and what I continued to experience.

Even so, listening to their stories left a lump the size of a cantaloupe in my gut. As at the memorial, I dreaded the moment I'd be called to speak. I feared most the loss of control, my emotions getting the better of me, and appearing as a blubbering fool. When my turn came, I struggled but got through it, shredding a couple of tissues in the process.

On February 23, the day before the thirty-first anniversary of my parents' deaths, I made a commemorative presentation to the group. For that segment, participants were to bring symbols, photographs, and mementoes of their loved ones. We would recall the memorable times, not the deaths.

Janis, the master scrapbooker, helped me construct a three-panel display using photos of my parents at happy moments—their wedding, family gatherings, Mom's christening the Spellbound, the bon voyage party, the boat under sail. I included a transcript of the tune I had composed in their honor, the Spellbound Waltz, and played a recording of it in the background while I made my presentation.

I told the story of my first sail aboard the Spellbound and how the unruly jib nearly dragged me over the side because lifelines had not been installed. I had shouted at Dad, who stood at the helm: "Get me some help—or grab a camera!"

Back home, I set up the commemorative display in the family room as a reminder of the good times my parents had enjoyed, and as an aid for refocusing and compartmentalizing my mental images.

Two weeks later, I had to make another presentation, but it consisted of death imagery. Claire had instructed us to depict how our loved ones died. The process, though painful, would help us purge our minds of the horrific mental images, to blow out the associated emotions in a safe environment, then return to the happier, commemorative images, to focus on our loved ones' lives rather than their deaths.

On a poster-sized sheet of paper, I drew panels illustrating my conception of the violence aboard the Spellbound. I didn't think I had the ability to draw, but I surprised myself and created realistic scenes, like a storyboard: Kerry being attacked with a large wrench; Dad being struck with a winch handle; Mom being shot with a pistol.

As I showed the scenes to the group and explained their meaning, three decades of suppressed grief and anger poured out. I sobbed; I cried; my voice rose to falsetto. When I finished, I collapsed into my chair. Yet, I felt lighter, as if a burden had been lifted.

It also left me overwhelmed. Before driving home, I sat in my truck for several minutes and listened to soothing melodies while my heightened emotions settled down.

The sense of relief didn't last, however. The sessions had opened the old wounds. I had difficulty concentrating on my work; my productivity decreased; I cursed at the slightest inconvenience, which in turn upset Janis. The intense feelings lasted for nearly a month, then began to lighten up as the program drew to a close.

For the next-to-last session, the friends-and-family night, we met in Balboa Park. To anyone passing by, it would have looked no different than a family or office gathering—except for the boxes of Kleenex strewn about the lawn. For the occasion, I baked a pecan pie, Dad's favorite.

Janis came with me. She had become a part of the healing process. Each night when I returned home from a session, she and I talked for a couple of hours. She learned more about me during those moments than she had in twenty years of marriage.

At the final session, each group member handed out mementoes to fellow survivors. One woman had wine glasses containing blue marbles, another lavender candles. A man and his wife gave us Christmas ornaments wrapped in green cellophane. I gave everyone a seashell, saving two for myself. When I got home, I placed shells on the fireplace mantel, one for Mom, one for Dad.

In the days and weeks that followed, I fell asleep more quickly and slept more soundly. I awoke feeling more refreshed than I had in decades. I had learned how to move beyond the emotions, to live more productively in what's known among survivors of violent loss as the "new normal"—life with grief and the at-times overwhelming sense of loss. I put the images of my parents' final, gruesome moments of life in a "compartment" and slammed the door. Their lives I placed in a separate compartment but left that door open to draw upon their smiles and memories of the fun times we had enjoyed: summer dinners on the sundeck and playing badminton in the backyard below; waterskiing at Aunt Betty's beach; weekends at the cabin at Trail's End Lake.

Participating in the Survivors program also motivated me to return to work on my book. I reminded myself that I was telling Mom and Dad's story because they couldn't. But it meant opening that other compartment.

IN APRIL, JANIS'S ninety-five-year-old father died. We visited him the night before his death. He had the TV on, and we laughed over a rerun of the Andy Griffith Show. We watched a bit of the Speed channel.

"Can you believe that?" he said, shaking his head at a Formula 1 race car.

Janis glanced at him and smiled. "You've always liked your cars."

He grinned back at her. His first car had been a Model T Ford. "Man, the technology they have today for making those things go faster and faster."

I excused myself and went to the bathroom to dry my eyes. I hadn't been able to say good-bye to my father. Not like that.

July 2009

Janis and I flew to Seattle to see Aileen and her daughter, Ruth, who'd become a surrogate daughter to me. That first night, Aileen and I performed our years-old ritual: mixing gin-and-tonics and voicing our outrage at the lack of justice for our parents. I told her about my involvement in the Survivors program.

The next day, Ruth gave us a tour of the house she and her husband had built, in part with money Janis and I had loaned them. We were to have been repaid before then, but the real estate market in Seattle, like the rest of the country, had tanked. Ruth spoke of bankruptcy, doubtful that she'd realize a profit from the sale. Still, she told Janis and me not to worry.

"I have it all worked out," she said. "You'll get your money back."

I trusted her.

Janis and I entertained Ruth's three young sons with our fiddling, and one afternoon Janis, Aileen, and I took the two older boys on a hike in the Cascade Mountains. We hunted for crystals and the boys splashed in the chilly waters of Denny Creek.

Another afternoon I visited my parents' headstone. I couldn't call it a grave, not without any bodies buried there. I took my fiddle from its case and played the Spellbound Waltz. The marble etching of the Spellbound bobbed on my tears.

AS SUMMER EASED into autumn, or at least what passes for autumn in San Diego, I looked toward the coming holidays with less apprehension than I'd experienced in years. Did it have to do with my participation in the Survivors program? I thought so. I had reached a better place in terms of my parents' deaths, and I hoped to reunite, at the SVLP memorial, with some of the people I'd met during the group program.

Then, in early December, Aileen called.

32

Thursday, December 11, 2009

I answered the phone and Aileen barely let me say hello. "There's a book . . . about Mom and Dad," she said between sobs. "You have to do something."

I'd heard of people who said their skin crawled in reaction to a sudden fear. At that moment, I knew what they meant. My skin crawled; my gut Gordian knotted; I could barely breathe.

Why now, after all these years?

Written by Ann Rule, the book *But I Trusted You and Other True Cases* comprised a collection of stories about Pacific Northwest murders. The second story—"Death in Paradise: The Haunting Voyage of the Spellbound" —featured our parents. No one in our family had been interviewed or forewarned of the book by the Seattle-based author. It had come out of the blue, from left field, fallen from the sky. Pick your cliché. We'd been blindsided.

"Does it have anything new?" I asked. "Or just the same old shit?"

"I haven't read all of it," Aileen said, her voice fractured by a sob, "but she says Mom shot herself in her bunk."

"Oh, Jesus. Read me what it says."

When she finished, I said, "Gary never said that; no credible person ever said that. It reads like a Keystone Cops routine."

"You have to do something," Aileen said again, a desperate plea straining her voice.

"I will. I'll get—"

"Can we sue?"

"I said I'll take care of it. But I need to read it first."

Not long after our parents died, the rumor mill posited that true-crime writer Ann Rule had a book in the pipeline, but we never heard any more about it. Until that night. Aileen had purchased the book after being alerted by a childhood friend.

"It's filled with mistakes, especially about Mom," she said. "From her car accident to how she met Dad to how she died."

"What else?"

I heard her flip through the pages. "It says no one had heard from them for almost ten days."

"That sounds more like *Gilligan's Island*."

"How can she do this . . . without our permission?"

I sighed, as much in response to her question as the book itself. "There's no law against it. But she does have an obligation to get the facts right."

Aileen read more passages to me, her words boozy and broken by frequent sobs. Some of the errors niggled but were inconsequential. However, the descriptions of how and why our parents died perpetuated the inaccuracies published in news accounts thirty-one years earlier.

Ann Rule said Dad had been struck on the head by the boat's out-of-control boom and died almost instantly. Never mind that Gary had changed his story when talking to the FBI, and I never heard Gary or Kerry say that Dad had died instantly. Rule described the wound over Kerry's right eye, omitting the more serious of the two wounds—the wound doctors said could not have been caused by an accident.

"That's not journalism, it's a joke," I said.

We signed off and I went to the kitchen. I plunked ice into a glass and poured a double shot of gin, followed by diet grapefruit soda. I slurped a long draught and savored it for a moment before swallowing.

Janis walked in, eyed the glass, then me. "I heard bits and pieces," she said. "Your parents?"

I nodded and tried to speak, but my words logjammed my throat and my reply sounded more like one of the crows that hung out in our yard. She laced her arms around me. I set my drink on the counter and crushed her in a return embrace.

That compartment, the one where I'd stuffed the images of my parents' deaths, had been flung open. After a moment, I gulped more gin and told her about the book.

She hugged me again and whispered, "I'm sorry. You've been doing so well."

Back in my office, I stared out the window. Nothing to see other than a few lights from the neighbor's house up the hill. A long night ahead, the darkness deepened by lowering clouds. Rain in the forecast.

I turned to my computer and logged on to Amazon. A quick search and the book's cover popped up on the screen. At least it didn't depict my parents or their boat.

The book had been released only days before to capitalize on the Christmas buying binge. The "Add to Cart" button tempted me, but I didn't want to wait for delivery. Surely a local bookstore had a copy I could get in the morning.

I worked from home as a senior writer for a small but respected public relations firm, having been lured away from freelance journalism by the steady work and higher pay. The next day, a Friday thankfully, I had a meeting at the office. As predicted, rain had begun to fall. I welcomed it. I didn't want any damned sun shining on my dismal parade. On the way in, I stopped by Barnes & Noble to buy a copy of the book, but the store didn't open until ten.

"Son of a bitch!"

I gunned the engine and squealed out of the parking lot, then lurched to a stop at the traffic light. I gulped deep breaths to calm myself and switched on the radio for distraction. At the sound of talking heads chatting about Christmas shopping, I stabbed the OFF button. "Fuck you and whether I've been naughty or nice!"

In the meeting, I tried to focus on our client's needs, but my thoughts slid sideways, like those cars spinning off the rain-slick roads. I glanced at my cell phone to check the time. Surely more than two minutes had elapsed since I last looked.

When I returned to the store, I threaded my way through the lunch crowd to the true-crime section and found just a single copy of the book.

Good, I'm taking the last one.

I glanced at the table of contents, found the page number and turned to the story about my parents. As I stared at the title, my thoughts drifted back to those dark days in 1978. I snapped the book shut and checked out.

At home, I went straight to my office and began reading. Although Rule had some things right, there were so many errors and misleading statements that blood pulsed at my temples and my hands shook. I thwacked the desk with the book.

Janis appeared at the doorway, shot me a worried look, then closed the door.

I eyed the book for a moment, then picked it up and began reading again. At thirty-five pages, it didn't take long. My notes filled the margins of every page. As Aileen had told me the previous night, Rule stated that no one had heard from the Edwards family for "almost ten days."

"More like ten hours, not ten days," I muttered.

She also wrote that the Spellbound was sixty miles from Rangiroa when found by search and rescue. Where had Ann Rule gotten her "facts"?

Her portrayal set up a tragic, lost-at-sea scenario, as if the Edwards family had fallen off the face of the Earth, then the survivors were dramatically rescued after a faint cry for help came via radio operator in faraway California on February 25. In fact, the correct date and time of the Mayday call was twenty-four hours earlier, on February 24, as had been reported in newspapers worldwide.

How could she have gotten that wrong?

I grabbed the FBI report, which had sat next to my desk for the past six years, and went over the radio transcripts again. And scoffed in disgust. Ann Rule had relied on a thirty-year-old newspaper account that was contradicted by earlier articles in the same newspaper. Her references to "pirates" and "sharks" heightened the melodrama but had nothing to do with my parents' story and how—or why—they died. She failed to mention that I was aboard the boat during the sail down the coast to San Diego, saying there were "four on board," including Lori. There were five on board, and Lori, like Gary, did not join the crew until after the boat reached San Diego. Rule also suggested that Aileen, Bobbie, and I opposed Gary in probate court because we wanted to cover up the truth of what happened aboard the Spellbound.

I huffed a derisive laugh. If anyone wanted to cover things up, it was Gary. He and his attorney asked for the out-of-court settlement, not us.

Rule claimed that she tried to find Gary, Kerry, and Lori, but "they slipped into obscurity." That was her excuse for relying so heavily on Elouise Schumacher's and Peyton Whitely's three-decades-old stories.

But Ann Rule had three decades to write the story, and Gary, Kerry, and Lori were easily located during most of that time. What's more, she could have tracked me down with almost no effort. At the time she was writing her story, my website—LarryEdwards.com— ranked number two on Google, just below the African-American female impersonator, also named Larry Edwards, who performed a Tina Turner routine in Las Vegas. I doubt she would have confused us.

Rule could have asked for my assistance in contacting the others, but she did not. I could have provided her with accurate information about my parents and the FBI investigation.

There's no fucking excuse!

I threw the book across the room and it smacked against the wall, dislodging one of the many award plaques I'd won for outstanding journalism. I went to the kitchen to make coffee. As I waited for the water to boil, I joined Janis in the living room, where she was working on scrapbook pages for Christmas presents.

"If I'd written that piece of crap, my editors would have told me to start over."

"Come here," Janis said. She stood and took me in her arms. I savored the moment, taking one of her hands in mine and stroking its fingers. Fingers that had always seemed fragile and vulnerable, like a child's. Her strength lay within. A strength that had carried me through rough times and held our marriage intact.

I stepped over to the French doors that opened on the patio and peered out. Still raining. The wind whipped the drooping branches of eucalyptus trees that arched over our backyard; a branch snapped and floated to the ground. A black phoebe huddled on the back of a patio chair, chirping a plaintive cry.

Coffee brewed, I filled a mug and carried it to my office, where I made a few work-related calls. Anything else could wait until Monday.

I phoned Bobbie, who had Fridays off. Aileen had told her about the book, but she hadn't seen it yet. "When you go to the core of her story," I said, "it's based almost entirely on what Gary said."

"And we can't believe a thing that came out of his mouth."

"I'll contact the publisher. We'll need to get a lawyer."

"That'll cost—"

"I'll pay for it. The important thing is that you, Aileen, and I present a united front."

"I'll go along with whatever you two decide."

I then spoke to Aileen, who'd been laid off and also was at home. We agreed that I would deal with the matter, given my expertise in public relations and crisis communications, as well as my years working as a journalist. Meanwhile, we'd do nothing individually that might undermine our mutual goals.

"I trust you," Aileen said. "But we have to *do* something."

"I'm working on it," I said, "but we can't go off half-cocked." I hung up and filled the room with the sound of tapping keys as I began listing the errors in the book. At one point I dashed off an email to Aileen, saying, in part: "Had you been within earshot, you would have heard frequent shouts of 'Bullshit!' "

To which she responded: "I am very tempted to send Ann Rule an email. Every time I try I get so mad I have to stop. I promise not to do anything."

I contacted friends of my parents to warn them of Ann Rule's book. I also sent an email to Kerry but never received a reply.

THE NEXT DAY, I attended the Survivors holiday memorial. As in the previous year, mothers and fathers, husbands and wives, sisters and brothers of murder victims told the stories of their loved ones and paid tribute by hanging ornaments on a Christmas tree. Boxes of Kleenex sat within reach of everyone in the room. Plenty of chocolate was on hand as well.

Having been through the program, I thought I'd have an easier time talking about my parents' deaths. But when I mentioned Ann Rule's book, my emotions bubbled to the surface like before. I snatched a tissue from a box on the floor and sucked a lungful of air, then went on, still stammering but with greater confidence.

"It might have been OK had she gotten the story right, but . . ."

I choked up again. I swallowed hard. Around the room, eyes pinpointed me, some new faces among the familiar. I wanted to curl up in a small, dark space, away from their probing eyes. I thought of my mountains, where I retreated when I needed to be alone. I looked at those who had spoken before me; they had been so articulate.

How the hell do they do it?

They offered me encouraging nods. Then I looked at those who had yet to speak for the first time.

I'm probably scaring the shit out of them.

Janis offered an encouraging smile and handed me a fresh tissue to replace the one I'd shredded. Then I continued. "But the book leaves my brother looking like the victim . . . the victim of single-minded law enforcement officials and money-grubbing siblings."

I welcomed the disapproving gasps of the others in the room. After thanking them for listening, I hung my pathetic ornament—the one I'd vowed to replace—on the tree.

Back in my seat, I looked at Janis and shook my head. She took one of my hands in hers and squeezed it. "You did fine."

A few others spoke, then people began drifting out the door amid wishes for a merry Christmas. Before I left, a deputy district attorney promised to send me the name of a lawyer, and Connie Saindon told me to call her, anytime, if I needed to talk. I said I would but didn't foresee the need.

At home, I went back to work on the letter to Ann Rule and her publisher. What I wanted to do was rip out the pages of the book and strike a match.

Unable to concentrate, I switched off the computer and mixed a drink. After dinner Janis and I watched a British mystery—the irrepressible Inspector Morse nabbed the killer and saw him off to the nick. Justice served.

The following day, I finished a draft of the letter, which would be signed by Aileen, Bobbie, and me. Too long, but I needed to pour it out. I cut it to five pages and sent it to Aileen and her daughter, Ruth, who was an attorney, requesting feedback. But I also had a job, and year-end deadlines loomed. A couple of days passed before I had a chance to discuss the letter with the others. Afterward, I cut it down to two pages. It read, in part:

> *Trust. It's the foundation of any enduring relationship between authors and their loyal readers. Ann Rule has violated that trust.*
>
> *Larry Edwards is particularly disappointed because, as an award-winning investigative reporter, he has a deep regard for getting the facts right.*
>
> *Unfortunately, Ms. Rule's portrayal of our parents' deaths is more fiction than fact. From people's names to critical dates to the details of the deaths.*
>
> *Sadly, Ms. Rule, as a highly respected and admired author of true-crime books and a recognized advocate of victims and victims' rights, could have written a substantive account of our parents' deaths, honoring them and their lives. Ultimately, however, her story portrays our brother as the victim.*

We ended the letter by demanding that all copies of the book be withdrawn from the marketplace immediately and that the story be expunged from future editions of the book. Unlikely to happen just days before Christmas, but we had to start somewhere. I hoped for a quick response, but the pragmatist in me said nothing would happen until the holidays were over.

After talking to Aileen and Bobbie, I phoned Ruth and updated her. Her next words, however, flashed a warning like caution lights on a mountain road: "Maybe we can blackmail them into publishing our books." Her tone sounded eager, not sardonic. I knew she hadn't meant it literally, but I could tell she was serious in a figurative sense, in effect suggesting that we won't make a stink about Ann Rule's book if she agrees to help us publish our books.

I said nothing while I calculated my response. My niece had been working on a book about my parents, but I knew little about it other than she had compared it to *Griffin and Sabine*, an epistolary novel. I never liked the idea, although in the interest of family harmony I never said so. I had ignored it as much as possible, figuring that, like many of her schemes, it would never reach fruition.

"We need to sit tight until we hear from Ann Rule and her publisher," I said. "Until then, as your mother and I discussed, we don't do anything that might jeopardize our position."

To which she agreed. Or so she said.

I trusted her.

I tried to focus on my PR clients, but that afternoon Aileen phoned. "You have to call Bobbie. Her daughter is going to post something on Ann Rule's website, saying how she got it all wrong."

"I don't need this shit."

I reached Bobbie at work. "What?" she said, her tone a reprimand. "I'm not supposed to take personal calls unless it's an emergency."

I told her what Aileen had said.

"That bitch! My daughter is doing nothing of the kind. You'd better talk to Aileen. She told me *her* daughter is going to contact Ann Rule, if she hasn't already."

Ruth's "blackmail" comment echoed, but I said nothing while Bobbie continued. "Aileen makes me sick, talking about Ruth's 'cute little book' and Mom and Dad's letters in envelopes that people can take out and read, and the 'tiny little wrench' and 'the tiny little gun.'" She paused. "And there's a game that readers can play online."

"A game?"

"Yes, a game! People can vote on how they think Mom and Dad died. Ruth thinks her book is going to make her rich and will solve all her financial problems."

"She's in fantasy land."

"I have to go."

I put down the handset thinking I needed a drink. But I couldn't indulge. Not yet. I still had to make nice with PR clients. I kept one eye on the clock as the minutes ticked by. At 5:01, I called it a day and gave some thought to what I'd say to Aileen. Up to that point, I had purposely used a soothing voice whenever we spoke. I wanted to be the rational one, the voice of reason. But I began to think I'd left her with the wrong impression. That she didn't fully comprehend the depth of my anger toward Ann Rule's book. I didn't need any additional heartache, especially from her or her daughter.

I uncorked a bottle of Two-Buck Chuck and downed the first glass while telling Janis what Bobbie had said. I poured another and carried it to my office as I felt the warming effect in my limbs. At my desk, I jotted a few notes, then called Aileen.

And began shouting. "A game? A fucking game?"

When she didn't respond, I continued. "These are our parents! Her grandparents! And she wants people playing a goddamned game about them?"

"She has just as much right to publish a book as you do," Aileen said.

I paused to gulp more wine, then resumed my rant. "This isn't about publishing books. It's about dealing with Ann Rule and her publisher, and getting that book off the shelves. Ruth should not be contacting Ann Rule."

When Aileen said nothing, I continued. "You called me a week ago begging me to do something and I am. Now your daughter is threatening to screw things up. We can't, on one hand, demand that they pull Rule's book, and on the other, say, 'Oh, um, could you please help me publish my cute little book?' Otherwise, we're going to appear duplicitous and lose all credibility. As an attorney, she should know that."

Aileen still didn't respond, and I wondered how she—my sister, one of my closest friends and confidants, my chief ally in our quest to know the truth of how our parents died—could condone Ruth's actions.

I'd been betrayed. By her. By her daughter.

"Talk to you later," I said and slammed the handset into its cradle. It bounced out. I slammed it a second time and polished off the wine.

33

Friday, December 18, 2009

The phone rang and I expected Aileen's tit for tat. Instead, I had to deal with a difficult client who, from my perspective, had an unreasonable request, considering how disruptive the pending holidays would be. Nursing a hangover and distracted by the fight with my sister, I snapped at him. I immediately apologized. But the damage had been done.

I contacted my employer, explained what had happened, and requested an emergency medical leave. He wasn't happy about it but said yes.

I leaned back in my chair, eyes shut, and listened to the birds in the yard. The high-pitched chirp of a hummer, the rattle of crows, the piercing cry of a red-shouldered hawk riding the updraft along the ridge behind the house. The tension eased a fraction. I had two weeks where I could forget about work and focus on Ann Rule's book.

Still, I couldn't shake the specter of my sister and her daughter plotting behind my back. I had to restore communications with Aileen. We couldn't let that story further divide our already splintered family.

I picked up the phone and started to punch in her number, but I doubted she'd answer. I phoned Ruth instead, got a recording, left a message.

In the yard, the ash trees spread leafless branches, the only indication of winter's onset. The temperature had already ratcheted past sixty degrees, destined for the high-seventies. Beach weather. In December.

I checked out Ann Rule's blog. She didn't mention me or my letter specifically, but she asked her substantial fan base if they thought she had portrayed Gary as a victim, so I knew she'd seen my letter.

I read book reviews posted on Amazon.com, and they ranged from five stars—her rabid fans—to a single star, the lowest rating possible. One especially harsh critic asked, "Where's the crime?" He questioned whether Ann Rule even believed my brother was guilty.

I thought she probably did believe it, but I figured her publisher's legal department deleted any indication of it in fear of being sued for libel. Which left the account so wishy-washy that several of the reviewers questioned why it was in the book at all.

I wrote a damning review and felt better but didn't post it, not wanting to do anything that might jeopardize the discussion with her publisher. Nor did I want to contribute to the book's publicity. In a fit of pique, however, I checked the boxes next to the most scathing reviews, indicating that I found them the most helpful.

I stared at the book, torn between the need to get started on the inevitable and the desire to play ostrich. *Screw it.* I took a shower.

The fogged-in hideaway had become my sanctuary, my womb, with an umbilical cord of pulsing, scalding water that massaged scalp, neck, and shoulders, along with my fragile mental state. The cascade drowned out all other sounds, my cares washed away, if only for the moment.

When I returned to my desk, I saw that my niece had responded with an email and the dread returned. I clicked on the message, read a few lines, then closed it, not wanting to deal with any more anguish that day.

The next morning, I read the message in its entirety. She hadn't returned my call because she's "not as thick-skinned and forgiving" as her mother. She went on to rationalize her actions regarding her book and contacting Ann Rule:

> *I saw an opportunity. I thought I could ask Ann Rule to help me publish my book. While the goal of my book is to get my grandparent's [sic] story told and spread as much as possible, there will be financial gain for me.*

Yeah, right. Ann Rule is going to welcome you with open arms so you can tell her how crappy her book is.

I showed the message to Janis, who said, "There will be financial gain? That self-serving little . . ."

I arched my brow.

"She has no respect for you or what you went through in Tahiti or what you're going through now," Janis said. "These are *your* parents and she herself says she has no memory of her grandparents. What she should do is get a job so she can pay back the money we lent her."

I called Bobbie to catch her up on the family drama and read her portions of the missive from our niece.

"Ruth and Aileen think they're going to be on Oprah and make tons of money," she said.

"I'm trying to deal with Ann Rule, but no," I said, "I have to spend my time on the phone or answering emails about Ruth's 'cute little book.'"

"And Aileen screamed about my daughter—"

"She called me, begging me to do something."

"They don't give a shit about anyone but themselves."

"Merry Christmas," I said.

"Yeah, right. Call me next week."

I refilled my coffee mug and set to work on a response to Ruth, spending nearly an hour massaging the language and tone. I asked her to remain at arm's length and not do anything that might jeopardize negotiations with Ann Rule and her publisher, saying, in part:

> *My primary goal is to set the record straight, not a book deal, not financial gain. Your "blackmail" comment offends me.*
>
> *If you have contacted Ann Rule, or if you intend to do so before we have exhausted our options, then you not only are likely to ruin any chance of a reasonable agreement with the publisher, but create a rift in this family. I'll call this afternoon.*

I clicked the Send button and went to the kitchen. I needed comfort food. I pulled peanut butter and mayonnaise from the fridge, then dill pickles, and began to make a sandwich. One of my favorites, introduced by my new mom when I was six or seven. I smiled inwardly, picturing the kitchen of our home in Juanita. Then my thoughts returned to Ruth, and I slammed the knife on the countertop. It bounced to the floor, leaving a smear of mayo on the brick-red tile. I reached for a paper towel and tried snapping it off the roll with one hand, but half the roll came with it, piling up on the countertop like fresh pasta from a Cuisinart. I cocked my leg, ready to field-goal the knife, caught myself, and leaned my arms against the cupboard, head down, gasping for air.

I'm coming unglued.

I breathed deeply several times, then straightened up. A shrill call from the yard caught my ear and I looked out the window. Then huffed a laugh. Mockingbird.

I tossed out a "fuck you" and returned to the business at hand: rolled up the paper towels, retrieved the knife, wiped the floor, finished making the sandwich and took a seat at the kitchen table. As I ate, I glanced at the morning newspaper, but the words blurred to indistinct black lines and I tossed it aside.

I hated to bother Connie Saindon on a Saturday, but she had extended the offer, and who better to talk to? Surely she had dealt with situations more volatile than mine.

I updated her on the events of the week, and she offered me phrases I could use in dealing with my family, particularly my niece. "Ask her to try to understand that the emergence of Ann Rule's book has triggered dormant emotions," she said. "Those emotions are as powerful now as they were at the time of the deaths."

She went on to say that my grief was genuine, the post-traumatic stress real. "Even more so for you. You were on the boat with the man you believe killed your parents, and you're replaying those death scenes in your mind."

She also said that true-crime books often increase the anguish of survivors of violent loss. "Those stories reopen the wounds." Connie's reasoned tone took the edge off my anger. "One more thing," she said.

"Yes?"

"I want you to get into individual therapy. Immediately. Claire will be there the week after Christmas. Call the office on Monday."

Connie's generous demeanor and her program notwithstanding, I had a knee-jerk distrust of the psychiatric profession. The thought of being "in therapy," of having to admit that maybe something was wrong with me, well, that scared the shit out of me.

That afternoon, I phoned Ruth. Unlike my off-the-rails rant at her mother two days earlier, I chose my words carefully and spoke in measured phrases, like a cop talking to a hostage taker. She promised not to contact Ann Rule or do anything that would jeopardize the situation until the matter was resolved.

So why did I no longer trust her? Maybe because, as an only child raised by a single mother, she'd rarely taken "no" for an answer.

I also had to broach the issue of legal representation. "I hope you, as an attorney, are not offended that I want to use someone else, someone with firsthand experience in such matters."

"I'm not offended. It's the smart thing to do," she said.

I doubted her sincerity but took her at her word, then told her about the realities of getting a book into print, that it could take two years or more. She acknowledged that she'd talked to an agent, but the woman wasn't interested in her work.

"That's why I'm taking this approach," I said. "I'll go through Ann Rule's story line by line, substantiate every objection, and present it to her publisher. If they don't respond to that, then we go to Plan B. I'll pay for the attorney, but this won't happen overnight. It's a safe bet that no one of any importance will be in the office for the next two weeks."

"I can't believe Christmas is less than a week away," she said.

"I wish it was behind us."

"If that's it, I have to pick up the boys at my mom's."

"I need to discuss the money you owe Janis and me."

"Don't worry, you'll get your money back."

Her glib tone didn't offer much comfort.

That evening, I collapsed in a chair in front of the TV, emotionally spent. Within arm's reach I had a bowl of popcorn, and my favorite cocktail—gin and diet grapefruit soda. Janis and I watched a week's worth of *The Daily Show with Jon Stewart*. It felt good to laugh.

The next morning, I wrote an email apology to Aileen and sent her a holiday greeting with a picture of Janis and me eating moose burgers in Jackson Hole, Wyoming, the tortured peaks of the Grand Tetons providing the backdrop. I wrote, in part:

> *I love you, and I love your daughter and her family, and what I want more than anything else is for us to come out of this stronger, not a family ripped farther apart.*
>
> *I took a two-week leave of absence from my job to get a handle on my emotions and deal with Ann Rule. That's where I want to focus my energy, not on battling you and your daughter.*

Later, I got together with the guitar player in the contra-dance band we both played in. As I bowed my fiddle, his clean, steady rhythm and melodic runs carried me to a more tranquil world.

Monday, December 21, 2009

I'd been leaving messages with an attorney the deputy DA had referred me to, but kept getting a machine. No response from Ann Rule or her publisher.

I looked at my DayMinder and the date finally registered—the winter solstice. I yearned to be in the mountains, alone, away from humanity, immersed in the fragrance of the pines. But I had obligations: to digitize voice recordings Janis had made of her parents and put them onto CDs—Christmas presents for her siblings. I made that appointment with Claire, the psychotherapist.

That night I built a fire under a Yule log and lit a candle. Spring, nature's rebirth, was on its way. *What will it hold for me? My family?*

Christmas Eve

I went for a late breakfast in Ocean Beach, a San Diego enclave that retained much of the flavor of Southern California beach communities. The server, sporting a holiday smile and a Santa hat, took my order.

While waiting for my scrambled eggs and home fries, I sipped coffee and wrote in my journal:

> *I understand why people go on killing sprees. I feel like it myself. I am Yellowstone incarnate. Geysers of tears, shouts. Will I blow like Old Faithful?*
>
> *Had to get out of the house. Hoping to hold it together to get through next 36 hours without doing something I may regret, or land me in prison—or in the morgue.*
>
> *Raging inside, no constructive outlet. Hate my job, Xmas bullshit, Aileen not speaking to me, but most of all it's Ann Rule. Her overwrought, melodramatic story is the shoddiest piece of journalism I've ever read.*
>
> *Janis supportive, exceeding expectations. But she's afraid I'll get drunk tomorrow and make a scene.*

After breakfast, I strolled to the pier, passing the usual coterie of panhandlers and social outcasts gathered on the seawall, where they sipped from brown bags and left a hint of ganja hanging in the sea air. On the pier, I leaned against the rail, mesmerized by the relentless, ruthless march of the waves rolling to the beach. At home, more holiday preparations awaited, but I dallied, in no rush to return to the Christmas countdown.

A seagull squawked from a lamppost overhead, and in the sound of the waves pounding the sand I heard the sardonic laughs of wizened souls. Below me, the rolling swells were pimpled with wetsuit-clad optimists—water dogs sniffing around for a fleeting board-gasm. But mostly the surfers aborted, flipped about, and tried again. Sisyphus in the surf.

I pushed away from the pier's rail. *Am I so different from them? Is anyone?*

That evening, Janis and I had dinner with Ian Law and his family. As a longtime friend, fellow musician, and best man at my wedding, he was among what I called my family of friends. The only baggage Ian and I brought to the table were twenty-something shenanigans we'd never shared with our wives.

He greeted me with a crooked grin and the offer of a drink. After I'd sampled the hors d'oeuvres and finished the Seven-and-Seven, he suggested another, but the whiskey had curdled my innards, a portent of things to come.

The holiday feasts came festooned with heartburn, beginning at Ian's and continuing through Christmas Day at my brother-in-law's home. The belly-stuffing spreads left my belly burning—a frequent companion that I figured I inherited; Grandpa Edwards had always had a roll of Tums handy.

The physical discomfort, however, paled in comparison to the fiery turmoil scorching my mind. Thoughts of my parents and Ann Rule's book had elbowed out any pretense of merrymaking. I wanted to Dancer-and-Prancer them from my cerebrum. Wine aplenty graced the tables, and I could justify—I yearned for—a proper holiday bash. But the booze burned my gullet, and I didn't drink much either day.

The model husband.

Janis's fears never materialized.

The day after Christmas, I fiddled for a contra dance and lost myself in the music and reverie of the dancers. For a dance fiddler, there's no greater joy than striking up a tune and seeing toes begin to tap, hips begin to sway. The dancers formed two lines that extended the length of the hall, men on one side, women facing them on the other. With the music, they wove a ballet of fluid motion as the caller choreographed their moves—forward and back, ladies chain, circle right, allemande left, do-si-do, promenade, balance and swing. Their synchronous steps created an ironic contrast to the discord in my life.

ON SUNDAY, I finally got a day I could call my own and escaped to Mount Laguna. An hour's drive from home, the weather-worn, 6,000-foot upthrust that passes for a mountain in the San Diego region had become my safe harbor when I craved solitude.

I crunched across patches of snow, the breeze in the pines a mother's cooing to her restless child; the cold air pricked my nostrils. I settled at a table in a vacant campground and unwrapped a Subway sandwich. Acorn woodpeckers chattered nearby and an optimistic Steller's jay scolded from a branch overhead. I poured coffee from a Thermos, warmed my hands on the cup.

I needed to be away from technology as well as people: emails and telephones, computers and complainers. I needed to be alone in my grief. For that's what I was doing—grieving. The Survivors program had helped me, but I needed to do more. I had never fully grieved for my parents. When they died, I became immersed in the criminal investigation and had to deal with familial dysfunction. I had suppressed the grief and the anger and the injustice, and had gone back to work. I got on with my life, as the saying goes.

But the underlying intensity never went away, surfacing periodically as tears, angry outbursts, or drinking binges, the upwelling triggered by a kind word, a perceived injustice, or a face in a crowd. Three decades later, Ann Rule's book triggered an avalanche of pent-up emotion, further exacerbated by the antics of my sister and niece. Sitting amid the pines and oaks, I tottered between fury and gloom. I careened from the desire to annihilate something—or someone—to wishing I could check out of the fleabag motel we call life. Two things kept me within the bounds of social acceptance—my music and my wife.

Were they enough?

I had reached the point of meltdown: white-hot rage transpiring to black-cold despair. My lights were going out.

Before leaving the arboreal retreat, I scavenged fallen oak branches for a fire at home, then headed down the mountain. Instead of driving directly to the freeway, I turned onto Pine Creek Road, a thin, rocky track that wound along the ridge above Noble Canyon. Through the truck's speakers, Aly Bain and Phil Cunningham played a Scottish air. The tune's melancholic strains fit my mood.

No guardrail secured the road, and the boulder-strewn slope fell almost vertically several hundred feet into the canyon. A momentary lapse of attention or heading into a sharp curve too quickly and it would be over.

There's a thought.

I stopped the truck and my gut quavered as I peered downward. Chaparral clung to a twisted, tangled life. Nothing would stop my pickup from plunging to the bottom. I could just flip the wheel and *wheeeee*, the final joy ride, like Slim Pickens riding the bomb to oblivion in *Dr. Strangelove*. No more death scenes or nightmares. No more sister and niece badgering me. No more Ann Rule. No more troubles, period. At least not for me. An ignoble ending in Noble Canyon.

Aly and Phil transitioned to an up-tempo reel, and my foot began tapping of its own accord. I thought of Janis and the horror her life would become if I didn't return. It could be days, if not weeks, before anyone discovered my body—and she got that surreal phone call. Like that surreal phone call I received nearly thirty-two years before.

And what if, by some fluke, I didn't die? But ended up as a quadriplegic confined to a wheelchair or a bed, unable to feed myself or even wipe my own ass?

A gust of wind rocked the truck. I had the heat on full blast, but my body shivered. I lifted my gaze from the canyon. Ahead, the roadbed disappeared as it rounded a sharp outcrop of jumbled granite, and the far side of the chasm faded into a misty blur. I eased out the clutch and urged the aging Toyota forward, a blood-red snail creeping along the edge of a ditch.

34

Monday, December 28, 2009

I awoke with less dread than I'd felt since that phone call from Aileen eighteen days earlier. Still, reality nipped at me like a neighbor's dog— another email from my niece.

"Son of a bitch!"

Janis appeared at the door, alarm creasing her face. "Larry, your anger . . ."

I waved a hand at the monitor. She came in and peered over my shoulder. "Ruth wants you to help her with her book? After the anguish she's been causing you?"

I shouldered a half shrug.

"You were the one in Tahiti after they died," Janis said. "The only reason that little hypocrite knows anything about your parents' deaths is thanks to you."

She went to the door, then turned to face me. "Please try to calm down."

"Dear, I'm just letting off steam."

"You're scaring me." She closed the door harder than necessary.

I rose, jerked the door open and followed her to the kitchen. "I'm sorry, but you know what this shit is doing to me."

"It's not just that." Her faced tightened. "I'm afraid that your brother . . ." Tears glistened as worry morphed into anguish. ". . . will try to kill you."

I'd lived with that thought for so many years I'd become numb to it. But Janis's twisted mouth and the fear in her eyes told me how real it was for her. I wrapped my arms around her. She tried to wriggle away, but I wouldn't let go. When she stopped struggling, I held her for a moment longer, then dropped my arms and stepped back.

Through gritted teeth, I said, "I . . . can . . . not . . . do . . . nothing. I did nothing for thirty years and look what it got me."

I replenished my coffee, returned to my office and reread Ruth's message. She'd offered to send me a draft of her work, so I replied, ignoring her request for assistance but telling her I'd like to see the draft.

THE NEXT DAY, I had my first meeting with Claire. At the door to the Survivors office, I hesitated before going in.

Do I really want to do this? See a shrink?

I toyed with driving home, going back to the mountains, to that canyon. And what of Claire? Young enough to be my daughter. How could this "girl," her PhD notwithstanding, possibly help me? Or was I making her the scapegoat when it was my fears, my own feelings of inadequacy, that fed my doubts about the value of counseling?

Yes, I'd been in the group sessions with her, but there'd been safety in numbers. Individual counseling meant being under the scrutiny of a penetrating gaze. I recalled the compassion in her face and her comforting smile, yet I also knew she could see through the bullshit, cut through the bulwark we all throw up to mask our demons.

With my hand on the doorknob, I thought of those private moments when I screamed until I gasped for breath, of those times that I put on a smiling public face when inside I felt more like Anthony Perkins in *Psycho*.

I opened the door and Claire greeted me with a comforting smile. She had been at the memorial and already knew about the Ann Rule book. I slumped into an armchair and updated her on the developments since then, including the situation with my sister and her daughter.

"It's sad. Aileen and I have—" I choked up.

Claire jotted on the pad of paper in her lap, then waited for me to continue.

"Ann Rule, them . . . I'm so angry it scares me. I'm afraid of what I might do."

"Anger can motivate you, which it obviously has, but it must be channeled appropriately. Have you done something that . . .?"

I shook my head. "I'm taking it out, metaphorically speaking, on Ann Rule by pointing out my objections to her story."

"That channels your anger. But you're also reliving your loss, and that revives the trauma you felt at the time."

I pictured Dad, then Mom, lying on the deck of the Spellbound in pools of blood. Emotion welled up. I tried to blink away the tears. Failing, I snatched a tissue from a box of Kleenex, the ubiquitous symbol of loss that sat within arm's reach throughout the office.

Claire marked her pad, then looked up. "We want you to create images of loved ones as still living, enjoying life, and laughing, so that becomes the focus. Positive images, not the death scene."

"But I don't have much choice. To respond to the book, I have to revisit every detail."

"I know, and that's why it's so traumatic for you. I can help you get through that. Then we can go back to the life images, like the ones you brought to the group session."

I stared into the far corner of the room and tried to recall those pictures. Then, like an ominous thundercloud, an image of the headstone sitting atop empty graves overshadowed the others.

AT HOME, JANIS and I sat at the kitchen table. "I should have done this years ago, but I never trusted those people."

"You said this is different."

"It is. They . . ."

"Do I need to get the Kleenex?"

I nodded and gazed out the window until she returned. The winter sun warmed the dormant garden. A California towhee scratched the ground around the Cleveland sage; a crow floated by.

Janis plopped the box in front of me and returned to her seat. I snatched a tissue and dried my eyes. She took my hand in hers. "I'm really glad you're doing this."

We talked for nearly an hour, then I checked the day's mail. Still no response from Ann Rule's publisher. I phoned Aileen, relieved that she took my call. I apologized for shouting at her the previous week, then we chatted about Christmas. I told her about my session with Claire. But the old familiarity had not returned. *Will it ever?*

My niece sent another e-mail, again badgering me to help her. I worried that because she never really knew my parents—they left Seattle when she was three years old—her work might be as lame as Ann Rule's. And I still had no idea what she intended to do with it. I closed the email without responding and returned to the task at hand.

I ended the day by sending a letter of resignation to my employer. I'd need more than two weeks to finish cataloging my objections to Ann Rule's story and providing the backup material a lawyer would require. I hadn't accomplished as much as I'd hoped, and with the prospect hanging over my head like a mid-ocean squall, I could not return to the pressures of my job. In my state of mind I had no business playing kiss-ass with PR clients. Besides, I needed to finish a job I'd left undone: telling my parents' untold story.

Wednesday, December 30, 2009

Identifying my complaints about Ann Rule's story turned out to be the easy part—they leaped from the pages. Identifying the corroborating material, however, required tedious, time-consuming research—not to mention the emotional toll it took on me. It meant poring over the Spell-bound's logbook and the FBI report, rereading my parents' journals and letters, and analyzing the news articles published in the wake of my parents' deaths, then fashioning that material into a coherent document.

I stared at the piles of books and newspapers on my desk and soughed a weary sigh. It could take weeks.

I opened the FBI report, which I'd organized in a three-ring binder, and lost myself in a fog of minutiae, as if I were back in college, writing a research paper for a history assignment, footnotes and all.

The house creaking and windows rattling jarred me out of my dream state. I glanced around the office as things settled down, realizing that a small earthquake had just rolled under foot. Like my life, the world ripping apart at its seams.

DURING MY NEXT session with Claire, she, like Connie Saindon, said I suffered from PTSD. "It's common in cases like yours. Events in one's environment trigger episodes in which you relive the trauma and the injustice, even after all this time. These things manifest themselves in anger and rage."

On the drive home, I wound down the hill toward Mission Bay, its gray reflection having enticed only the bravest vacationers to test its chilly waters. I pounded a fist on the steering wheel. "Gary did it! There is no other explanation."

Or is there?

When I returned to my journals, the news clips, and the letters, that niggling scrap of doubt crept back into my consciousness. *What if I'm wrong? What if Gary didn't do it?* While preparing the document for Ann Rule and her publisher, I'd reexamine the evidence against him.

With the holidays mercifully over, I made significant progress. And after another round of phone tag, I tracked down an attorney who had worked as legal counsel for book publishers before going into private practice.

I updated Bobbie and Aileen, and on Friday I returned to the back-country, this time for a mountain-man rendezvous. A decade earlier I'd gotten involved in living history, reenacting the era of the Rocky Mountain fur trappers. As a school kid I'd read about John Colter, Jim Bridger, Kit Carson, and other bigger-than-life figures who'd gone to the mountains to seek their fortune trapping beaver.

Dressing in buckskins appealed to me, and because I played fiddle tunes of that era, the reenactors welcomed me at their nightly campfires. I also enjoyed the serenity of the primitive camping—no modern gear allowed. No diesel-powered RVs, generators, boom boxes, TVs, radios, gas lanterns, or even flashlights to pollute the Arcadian atmosphere. I sparked my fires with flint and steel; candle lanterns provided the only light after dark. From a distance, the camp appeared as though it had fireflies flitting through it. The music had to be live, and it had to be acoustic.

Some folks set up tepees, but most had a canvas tent or a simple lean-to fashioned from a canvas tarp. The campers participated in competitions for muzzle-loading guns as well as primitive bows and arrows. Other sources of amusement included tomahawk and knife throwing, dominoes, dice games, and telling tall tales. Campfire smoke hung in the air as the explosive sound of flintlocks reverberated across the meadow. And, in a salute to the rendezvous of old, alcohol flowed freely.

I considered not going, but after nearly a month of dealing with the Ann Rule matter and family issues, I needed the break. I'd time-travel back to the 1830s. I also wanted to get shit-faced. However, I couldn't stomach the whiskey, tequila, rum, or a popular concoction known as "pie," a mixture of fruit juice and high-proof spirits. I drank water instead and sawed on my period-correct 1820 fiddle, trying to forget, for two days, the heartburn that awaited me at home. But as I looked into the flicker of the campfire, demonic faces tormented me.

AT HOME, MY welcome back to the twenty-first century came in the form of two emails. The first from my niece, who whined because I hadn't answered her questions. The second was the long-awaited response from Ann Rule's attorney, who wrote, in part:

> *We regret that you are unhappy with the account of your parents'*
> *tragedy in the story* Death in Paradise: The Haunting Voyage of the
> Spellbound. *However, with all due respect, we see no legal basis for your*
> *request that the publisher remove the story from the book.*

The response was about what I expected. Yet, I had hoped for more, at least a glimmer of acknowledgment that our anger was justified. I noted the phrase "no legal basis." Principles, apparently, had nothing to do with it. They had flicked us like fleas.

The first volley's been exchanged. Now I load for bear.

35

Wednesday, January 13, 2010

I picked up the Ann Rule book and cocked my arm to fling it at the wall. I had met with an attorney, and I had to choose the path we'd take in response to the dismissive email from the author's corporate counsel.

I let the book fall to the desk and crossed the room, where I opened the commemorative display I'd made for the group session nearly a year earlier. Mom and Dad smiled back at me. *I can't abandon you now.*

I returned to my desk. I would document every objection to Ann Rule's story. She would no doubt argue that many of the errors were not hers. She merely culled the information from news articles. No excuse. She should have done her due diligence and corroborated those details. As a former newspaper reporter and a respected writer of true crime, she would know that newspapers make mistakes when reporting breaking news. In the case of my parents, some of the news stories contradicted one another, which should have been an immediate red flag. Rule also embellished the details with imagined portrayals, in particular her depiction of Mom dying in her bunk.

But those errors, regardless of where they originated, became the cornerstone of Ann Rule's melodrama. The rest of her fanciful account played out from that sensational but inaccurate setup.

Why the big deal? Timing is the central issue underlying the truth of what happened aboard the Spellbound. Ann Rule missed that proverbial boat.

The next morning, I sent Aileen an email, telling her the back-and-forth could take a couple of months and cost more than I had originally thought. Meanwhile, I had to round up some freelance writing and editing jobs—the mortgage, utility bills, and groceries wouldn't pay for themselves.

That afternoon, I received yet another email from my interfering niece. Even before I opened it, a tingle of premonition swept over me. When I did open it, my fears were confirmed:

> *I will publish my book online. I think an online version will get the facts out there now so there is more than just what Ann Rule wrote available to the public.*

I began to reply, then picked up the keyboard and would have tossed it through the window had it not been for the cord. A phone call being out of the question, I waited before crafting a response, hoping I'd calm down. But, after having spent nearly a month of being reasonable and gotten nowhere with my niece, I had trouble reining in my anger. I said, in part:

> *I asked you twice and now I am asking you a third time: Please take no further action until Aileen, Bobbie and I have developed and acted upon our response to Ann Rule.*
>
> *The response to our letter is what I expected and have planned for, providing the opportunity to set the record straight. But, as you should know, it must be done in a thoughtful, methodical manner under the guidance of expert legal counsel.*
>
> *The course of action must be determined by the consensus of Aileen, Bobbie and me. While we value your input, the decision ultimately, and rightly, rests with the three of us, not you acting on your own.*
>
> *I am disheartened by your callous disregard for the emotional turmoil you are causing and the potential for creating an irreparable rift within what remains of our small family.*
>
> *For you to decide unilaterally, without consulting us, to publish your work online is disrespectful, it shows poor judgment, it will undermine our*

credibility, and I believe it is unethical. Particularly in light of the "blackmail" comment you made earlier.

The damage by Ann Rule has been done. Acting rashly is likely to make matters worse. Taking a little more time to do this in a thoughtful, well-planned manner is the best course of action.

After sending the email, I phoned Bobbie and brought her up-to-date.

"Aileen and Ruth are pissed off because you hired an attorney instead of using Ruth," she said.

"But Ruth acknowledged that she doesn't have the experience."

"Doesn't matter. After all, Aileen has the perfect daughter."

"What do they think I've been doing for a living for the past four years, just sittin' on my ass? I've handled crisis communications for corporate CEOs, for chrissake."

"There's something else."

I groaned. "What now?"

"They asked me not to tell you this, but I don't think it's right," she said, then paused and took a deep breath. "Ruth is sending me a copy of her book, but she told me not to show it to you."

"Son of a bitch."

"I'll send you a copy as soon as I get it."

Monday, January 18, 2010

I waited two days before calling Aileen, hoping I'd calm down. But it turned into a replay of my call a month earlier. No booze this time, but I still hit her with both barrels of R & R—as in rant 'n' rave.

"No one should be doing anything until we've drafted a response to Ann Rule's publisher, and that will take time. I have to go through all the material—the news clips, my journals, Mom and Dad's journals, everything. I have to corroborate every objection. If I thought publishing something online right away would be useful, I'd put my book online. We don't need Ruth's. I don't even know what's in it. For all I know, it has as many errors as Ann Rule's. She promised to send me a copy weeks ago, but I have yet to see it."

Aileen didn't reply, and I paraphrased a comment I'd made earlier to Ruth: "She doesn't even have all the facts. Otherwise she wouldn't be begging me to respond to her questions, saying she can't finish it unless I provide her with the answers. Well, too fucking bad. What concerns me more, however, are the questions she's not asking, which tells me she doesn't know enough about this matter to even ask those questions. She thinks she knows, but she doesn't. She wasn't there. I was."

"She's heard us talk about it over the years . . . and she's read what you wrote—" Aileen cut herself short, as if her last comment had slipped out, not meant for my ears. The snake coiled in my gut again.

That conniving little bitch! She's not only going behind my back, she's using my material.

I renewed my rant, gasping for air. "She's going to fuck . . . this . . . up. I retained an attorney for *us*, at my expense, and *we* should be following his—"

I heard a click and the line went dead.

Rain drummed the roof and ran in torrents from the eaves. Wind battered the trees in the yard. But Mother Nature's storm did not rise to the level of the tempest raging within me.

Aileen sent an email that evening. She apologized for hanging up, saying, "my heart was racing so fast I thought I might have a heart attack." She rationalized her behavior and that of her daughter with the same tired argument: Ruth has a right to do this.

Which missed the point entirely.

She ended her message with:

> *Larry, although I am angry at you right now (and yes, I know you're angry at me too) I want you to know that I love you and I respect you. I really hope we don't lose each other over Ann Rule, the bitch.*

I huffed a sardonic laugh. *Tell that to your daughter.* I replied, saying:

> *The best thing you can do at this point is to have a heart-to-heart discussion with Ruth and ask her to please stop her effort to publish her rushed and incomplete book, online or otherwise.*

I also wrote to Ruth:

I am attempting to negotiate a settlement that would be satisfactory to all concerned parties. If you, as a member of our family, publish your book online before these negotiations are completed, it could be viewed as a hostile move, as acting in bad faith, and jeopardize a successful outcome.

I shut down the computer, mixed a drink, and collapsed in a chair in the family room. Janis shot me a look of concern. "I heard you swearing . . ."

"I don't know how much longer I can take this shit," I said.

The typhoon swirling within manifested itself in a 101-degree fever. I battled pharyngitis for several days, accomplishing little, lying abed, alone with my thoughts.

Knifed in the back by a self-serving, dispassionate niece who has placed her own ambitions ahead of the best interests of our family; another opportunist trying to capitalize on my parents' tragedy. Causing me to lose focus of the bigger picture: who killed my parents, and why. The rain has passed. Now comes the sun. Go away, sun! The world should be crying with me.

Once the antibiotics kicked in, I returned to listing my objections to Ann Rule's story, submerged again in the horror of my parents' deaths.

36

Sunday, January 31, 2010

"I'm so mad I could spit," Bobbie said.

"Mom used to say that."

"I know. That's funny, huh?"

"What's got you so riled up?" I asked, having phoned her to see if she had any news of "those other people," as Janis had been referring to Aileen and Ruth.

"I finally got Ruth's manuscript in the mail," Bobbie said, then paused.

"And?"

"It's just as bad as Ann Rule. Except it's worse because it's by a family member."

In a cracking voice, accompanied by sniffling, Bobbie read me the passages that upset her the most—not Mom's and Dad's deaths, but their lives. "Aileen knows there are mistakes," she said, "but she doesn't want to hurt Ruth's feelings by telling her there's anything wrong with her 'cute little book.'"

"So Aileen's outraged at Ann Rule, but her own daughter can do no wrong," I said.

"At the front, Ruth says these are her memories. These aren't her memories, these are Aileen's memories. Aileen and I disagree about it. She only remembers being unhappy. I remember a happy childhood. Yes, I got into trouble, but I blame myself. Aileen blames Mom and Dad. It wasn't their fault she started taking drugs and having sex in junior high school. But this makes Mom and Dad look horrible. They weren't bad parents."

"Under the circumstances, I think they did the best—"

"Ruth showed it to her friends months ago, but she couldn't show it to her own family before she publishes it?"

I sniggered. "That should tell you something."

Bobbie promised to send me a copy, then added, "Ruth also called me. She told me I had to choose between you and her."

I closed my eyes and sighed, then asked in a weary tone, "What'd you tell her?"

"What I've always said, that I'll go along with whatever you decide."

MONDAY MORNING, I tracked down Peyton Whitely, The Seattle Times reporter who'd written the most about my parents and their deaths. He lived in Kirkland, near the marina where my parents had moored the Spellbound. He said Ann Rule had phoned him "several months ago," but he hadn't seen the book. I read him what she had written about the current whereabouts of the Spellbound, which she had attributed to him.

"That's not accurate," he said. "I told her that the last time I saw the boat was a few years ago, at Moss Bay Days in Kirkland. The name had not been changed. I walked out on the pier to see the boat, but no one was aboard. If someone told her the boat had a new owner and the name had changed, it wasn't me."

Ironic, I thought, that Ann Rule had relied so heavily on Whitely's news coverage, and now he had confirmed that, as I suspected, she had misquoted him. He also acknowledged that there probably were errors in his coverage of my parents' deaths because breaking news often has mistakes due to scant details and short deadlines. He said it can take days, weeks—even years—before the truth of a matter is known.

Whitely had been acquainted with my parents. He'd kept a boat in the same marina, and he talked to them a few times about their plans for cruising to the South Pacific.

"Do you know where the boat is now?" he asked.

"Olympia," I said. "It's still owned by the family of the man who bought it from my parents' estate. The man died last year. Now his son has it for sale."

I told him about my book and promised to send him a copy when I finished it, then thanked him for taking time to chat. I regretted not having been more cooperative with him at the time of my parents' deaths. Back then, I viewed him as the enemy.

He could have been an ally.

Wednesday, February 3, 2010

I cringed at the sight of another email from Ruth, which she'd sent the night before. She informed me that, for her birthday, her husband had designed a website and they had uploaded her "book." She hadn't even given Bobbie a chance to comment, let alone me.

She hadn't bothered to provide the Web address either, and when I searched for it, the results listed nothing. I concluded that the URL had not propagated throughout the Web yet. Sometimes, it takes a week or more.

She also tried to turn our dispute into a disagreement about her book versus mine. It wasn't. It was about honoring *my* parents. She suggested that my parents would be "saddened to see the state of their family now." On that we were in agreement.

I replied, saying that she still had not answered my questions about the money she owed me and Janis, and that she should have cooperated with me, not become an adversary. I closed by saying:

> *As for my parents, people you know only through your mother's perspective of her childhood, I will tell you exactly what I think their reaction to your book would be: This is not how we want to be remembered.*

She fired back, claiming that because I hadn't read her work, I had no right to criticize it. Never mind that Bobbie had read significant portions of it to me over the phone.

As for the money she owed Janis and me, she wrote: "I wanted to keep these issues separate. When the house sells, I will pay you as I have said in the past. The money owed is not related to this issue."

In her closing remarks, she added: "I am gaining weight, and this is solely due to you and your actions."

I showed the last comment to Janis. We both laughed. But I found no humor in the way she'd portrayed my parents, or me, in her "cute little book."

Practice sessions with two bands, a couple of jam sessions, and a contra dance took up the remaining evenings of the week, a welcome respite from the family soap opera. During the day, however, I could not ignore the task at hand. With the end in sight, I returned to cataloging my objections to Ann Rule's book, along with documenting the evidence the FBI had compiled against my brother.

Friday, February 5, 2010

Done. Twenty-three pages, single-spaced.

I pulled the pages from the printer and whooshed a sigh of relief as I rapped them on the desk, straightening them into a neat stack. It had taken longer than anticipated, but it had to be meticulous. I set the document on my desk, figuring to give it one more read before sending it to my attorney on Monday.

37

Thursday, February 11, 2010

Oh, the irony. The day my attorney FedEx'd my document to Ann Rule's publisher I received a copy of my niece's "cute little book" from Bobbie.

My mood flopped from relieved to ugly.

As I began reading, I thought, she's stolen *my* story. The first page was about me, and later she included a section portrayed as if I'd written it myself. I also found material she could have gotten only from an early draft of my book.

I damned her to hell yet again.

Bobbie had read parts of it over the phone, but there, on paper, I had it in my hands, which clenched as I read. Didn't take long. Barely one hundred pages. Like Bobbie had said, worse than Ann Rule's. And as I'd done with Ann Rule's book, I filled the margins with notes and expletives.

In the opening paragraph alone, I counted eleven factual errors and a typo. On the first page, I found a total of twenty-eight factual errors, at which point I stopped counting.

Not only was it riddled with mistakes, it demeaned my parents—people she never knew. She described them as people who "did like to party," and she attributed to me a comment I did not say, nor would I: "parties my family is famous for," as if Mom and Dad were a couple of pie-eyed drunks.

I scoffed, recalling a day, not long after I'd turned twenty-one, I returned home to a houseful of people gathered for a birthday or anniversary of some kind. Dad offered me, for the first time, a cocktail. I thought, hey, things are beginning to look up around here. But that was it. One drink. No wine or beer with dinner. No after-dinner drinks.

My parents, especially Mom, were sociable, but I always thought a little more drinking might have livened them up. If anything, Dad was a workaholic. He frequently took side jobs to bring in extra cash, working evenings and weekends. When he got home, he was too tired to do much of anything other than fall asleep in front of the TV.

Ruth also wrote that my father blamed the "monotony" of raising children for delaying his dream of sailing the Seven Seas, as if the reason for the voyage was to escape from his children.

It wasn't monotony, it was money—and the lack thereof.

The point of the trip was to unify our blended family by taking everyone on an adventure we'd never forget. Child rearing for my parents, especially when Ruth's mother began using drugs and running away from home, had been anything but monotonous. At that point, they would have yearned for monotony.

My niece described Mom's parents as "boring" farmers, and in the chapter presented as if written by Mom, Ruth lavished praise on her own mother while dismissing Bobbie as being "small and often sick," and who hid in the bathroom "to avoid her share of the work."

No wonder Bobbie's pissed off.

When describing how Gary took Mom's underwear from the laundry hamper, she put these words in Mom's mouth: "It became an odd routine, but I didn't think there was much harm in it."

How can she write this shit? How can Aileen condone it?

Ruth also revealed confidential medical information about me.

That's not just unethical, it's breaking the law.

I called Bobbie and thanked her for sending me the "ugly little book," even as infuriating as it was. Bobbie picked up where we'd left off the week before.

"She says Mom referred to her children as 'accidents,' " Bobbie said, her voice cracking. "She might as well have said Mom didn't love us."

"Inexcusable," I said. "And she has Lori comparing Mom and Dad's deaths to Romeo and Juliet, saying that Mom's death was 'almost romantic.' "

"There's nothing romantic about having your head blown off."

"Considering that Ruth made most of this stuff up, I doubt Lori actually said that. But even if she did, Ruth should not have let it pass without comment. When I read it, I wanted to puke."

I paused for a beat. When Bobbie didn't say anything, I went on. "She also got the date of my biological mother's death wrong. She says Phyllis died in May 1979. It's the date I use to open that chapter in my book, but that's not when Phyllis died. She lived several years after that. The only place Ruth could have gotten that date is from a draft of my book—which she claims never to have seen."

"Like I said, Aileen knows that but doesn't want to hurt Ruth's feelings."

"What about our feelings?"

"She doesn't give a shit about us."

"What really gets me," I said, my voice rising, "is the way she ends it, saying that Gary didn't contest our petition in probate court because he didn't want a 'ghoulish court battle.' She bought into Gary's bullshit without offering any critical analysis or counter argument. That comment was from a statement Gary's attorney spoon-fed to the news media. Pure spin."

"She's a fool," Bobbie said. "It's like Ann Rule saying we wanted to cover up what actually happened on the boat. Gary wanted to cover things up, not us."

I huffed a sardonic laugh. "Ruth didn't even quote Gary's statement accurately, even though it was printed in the newspapers and all she had to do was copy it."

I heard tears in Bobbie's voice as she said, "I can't talk about this anymore."

I hung up and stared at the pages before me. With much of it presented as if written by each individual—including Gary—it was largely a work of fantasy, not fact. Worthless as a response to Ann Rule. It even repeated some of the errors I found in Rule's story, in particular the distance of the Spellbound from Rangiroa, the linchpin of the FBI's case against Gary.

I hurled the packet through my office doorway. Unbound pages peeled off and fluttered to the floor as the bulk of it thumped against the wall in the hallway. I dropped my head into my hands. *When will this shit ever stop?*

I went to the kitchen, mixed a drink and gulped the curative. Janis eyed me warily, asked me if I wanted to talk.

"No, not right now."

I returned to my office and picked up the papers scattered on the floor. Reorganizing them was a challenge. There weren't any page numbers. I sent letters of caution to Mom's sister Verney and some of my parents' friends, along with copies of Ruth's work. I wanted them to hear about it from me, rather than from someone outside the family or by stumbling across it accidentally.

A week later, I spent an entire morning on the phone and answering emails. Verney, Laura Watson*, and others wanted to talk about the not-so-cute little book.

Verney said, "That's not who your parents were." Nor did she care for the way her own "boring" parents, Ruth's great-grandparents, were depicted.

Laura Watson had a stronger reaction. "When Ruth asked to talk to me about her grandparents, she misrepresented herself. There was no mention of writing a book like this." Laura threatened to take legal action and report Ruth to the state bar association for questionable ethics. Only then did my niece agree to give Laura a pseudonym and correct what had been said about her.

"Talking to Ruth was like talking to Gary," Laura said. "She can't see how she's done anything wrong."

Verney and Laura both labeled my niece's action as "unforgivable," and wondered how Aileen could have approved of it.

That evening, I attended a music jam session, which took me to a happy world, far removed from my parents' deaths and the family feud.

～

A couple of days later I finally located Ruth's website and monitored it for the corrections she'd promised Laura Watson. Ruth also made changes in the section pertaining to me.

I drafted a letter to her, advising her that she did not have permission to use any material from my book—highlighting specific passages—and if she did, it would be considered copyright infringement.

Fucking waste of time and expense. Her work will die online.

But I wanted my position on the record. The letter would come from my attorney.

That afternoon I met with Claire and put quite a dent in the Kleenex box. She, too, characterized what Ruth had done as "unforgivable."

"What you're feeling is betrayal," she said. "It's an ancient emotion that lies deep in the oldest part of the brain, the amygdala. It leads to intense anger and hurt."

Afterward, I walked along the shore of Mission Bay. An osprey hovered, then dove, emerging with a fish that struggled to free itself from the raptor's taloned grasp. Gulls squawked in pursuit. A Little Blue Heron, oblivious to the commotion overhead, craned its neck at the water's edge. Palm fronds rustled in the onshore breeze, and a rainbow of hues sprouted from a hotel's garden.

Lo, it's Sprang again. Flowers boom, exploding in Crayon colors, and doors bloom, opening on pistil-lined paths to that New Life of greater compassion, for others as well as Self—yet ever wary of a hint of betrayal.

Back home, I sent Aileen an email—no way I could have a conversation over the phone. I wrote, in part:

> *When you called me in December, hysterical about Ann Rule's book, I assured you I would take care of it and I am. The publisher's attorneys are currently reviewing the 23-pages of documentation I sent them, and I expect a response in the next few weeks. Had you and Ruth not been so hell bent on publishing her "cute little book" online, you would already know this.*
>
> *Ruth's actions have impeded the process and ultimately may jeopardize the negotiations. She acted selfishly, with utter disregard for me, Bobbie and our extended family. Her so-called book is pitiful. It has many factual errors. You know this, yet apparently you don't have the spine to correct her.*

In addition, because of the structure she has chosen, it is a work of fiction. As such, it has no credibility as a response to Ann Rule's book and, in effect, undermines any effort to set the record straight.

I'm sorry it's come to this. I have enjoyed our close relationship over the years, but you and Ruth have no one to blame but yourselves. Maybe someday we can reconcile our differences and become a family again, but not as long as you and Ruth continue to put your interests ahead of the best interests of our family.

Aileen responded with:

I want to reiterate you do not speak for me and cannot negotiate anything for me. I am sending a letter to Ann Rule's publisher to inform them of this.

Blood pulsed at my temples. I called Bobbie and filled her in. "They are pond scum," she said.

38

Thursday, April 1, 2010

If there is a god, she has a demented sense of humor.

The response from Ann Rule's publisher was no joke: Yes, there are mistakes in her story, but they are "de minimis."

What's that, Latin for fuck you?

When I told Janis, she frowned.

"I looked it up," I said. "*De minimis* is a legal term that means 'of no consequence.' "

"So, they're admitting there are errors in Ann Rule's story?"

"Yes, but they say the errors are insubstantial."

"Ann Rule created a fantasy. How is that insubstantial?"

"According to the law, you can't defame dead people."

"So, they're doing nothing?"

I nodded.

"It's so unfair," she said.

"There's more," I replied, then paused, waiting for the upwelling emotion to subside. "Members of my family contacted the publisher to say they were not party to my complaint."

"Aileen and Ruth."

"Who else?"

"Bobbie's still on your side," Janis said.

"Yes, but the publisher is under the impression that I'm the only one in the family with a complaint. They see me as a lone wolf, crazy Uncle Larry, who's acting on his own. It's harder to make a case against them."

I laid out my options, none of them palatable. If I proceeded, it meant hiring a New York attorney to the tune of five hundred bucks an hour and filing a lawsuit. The publisher had deep pockets and could drag it out for years. If it went to court, it could end up costing me $30,000 to $50,000. Even if I won, it would be a Pyrrhic victory. The odds of any damages being awarded were effectively zero.

"If there aren't any damages, what's the point?" I said.

"So much for principles."

"Principles don't pay attorney's fees."

Janis hugged me again, but it didn't lessen the ache in my belly.

"You know what's really sad," she said.

I shook my head.

"You may never see Ruth's boys again. The fallout from your mom and dad's deaths is now affecting not just three generations of your family, but five. At least you still have Bobbie. You two have gotten closer."

"I regret not having given her enough credit previously, not fully appreciating her wit and no-nonsense observations."

I went to my office to phone Bobbie and tell her what had happened. "Aileen obviously contacted—"

"She's a cunt," Bobbie said. "I'm sorry for my language, but that's how I feel."

"At times of crisis, people fly their true colors," I said. "Aileen and Ruth have shown theirs."

We chatted a few minutes more before signing off. I went to the kitchen to mix a drink, then thought, if I get drunk every time Aileen and Ruth piss me off, they win. I put the bottle back in the cupboard.

A FEW DAYS later, I had a session with Claire and filled her in. "I feel as if I let my parents down," I said, fighting the inevitable wellspring.

"It's not your fault," she replied. "You've spent a lifetime blaming yourself, first for your birth mother leaving, then your parents' deaths, and now this. You need to be kind to yourself." I shrugged. "You did everything you could," she said. "Leave the regrets for your sister and her daughter."

"I'm not going to abandon my book."

"Do you think your father would approve of what you're doing?"

"I'm not sure. Parents tend to forgive their children, no matter what they've done. Dad might blame himself for what happened."

Claire did not disagree. "Do you think your dad saw your brother the way you do, the way others see him?"

"He had blinders on when it came to Gary. I was always the good kid and what did it get me? Gary misbehaved and he was rewarded for it by not being punished. So, yeah, Dad might disapprove of what I'm doing—my book, Ann Rule, my sister, my niece. But I believe I'm doing the right thing, trying to set the record straight, to see that some sense of justice is achieved."

I dried my eyes and continued. "And maybe my father deserves some of that blame . . . and Birth Woman . . . for the choices they made even before my birth, for setting in motion a series of events that led to their tragic ends and the disintegration of our family. Not that that excuses my brother."

"Do you think you can forgive your father?"

"I'm working on it."

She nodded, marked her notepad and said, "You're remarkably well-adjusted for what you've been through."

I snorted and looked at her in disbelief.

"Many people in similar circumstances have broken marriages and substance abuse problems."

"It's a testament to Janis, not me," I said. "And these past months her support has been unconditional."

"It also has to do with your willingness to let her comfort you, to let your emotions show, rather than keeping her at arm's length."

"Like I did for years, you mean."

Claire continued. "It makes a big difference. Studies of soldiers with PTSD show they do better when they have a comforting spouse or partner. It's hard for them when they've been told they have to be tough, that they can't show their emotions over loss and separation."

"Boys don't cry."

She nodded.

I reached for another Kleenex.

HAVING HEARD NOTHING from my niece regarding the status of her house, I wrote a demand letter for payment of the money she and her husband owed Janis and me. Then I sat on it for twenty-four hours, debating whether to send it or not.

Janis reminded me of Ruth's lack of cooperation over the past four months. "Don't ever forget, she and Aileen betrayed you. Knifed you in the back. She has not earned our sympathy."

I sent the letter.

In reply, Ruth emailed me the name of her bankruptcy attorney. So much for her repeated assurances that it and the Ann Rule matter were separate, that we'd get our money back.

Sunday, April 18, 2010

I attended the SVLP's River of Remembrance ceremony, organized by Connie Saindon at the San Diego Crime Victims Oak Garden. Sam Knott had created the garden as a memorial to his twenty-year-old daughter, Cara, who was murdered in 1986 by a California Highway Patrol officer. He'd grown dozens of oaks from acorns and planted them on the site, located near where his daughter's body was found. Each oak stood as a living memorial to a victim of violent crime.

Because all the oaks had been assigned, attendees were invited to paint the names of their loved ones on rocks and place the rocks in the "river," which wended through the garden. I painted Mom's and Dad's names on rocks and joined the others in telling our stories.

Saturday, July 24, 2010

Bobbie phoned to say she'd gotten a call from Aileen. "I picked up before I realized it was her," she said. "Did you call her on her birthday?"

"I thought about it but couldn't," I said. "She say anything new?"

"Ruth finally filed for bankruptcy."

"I know. The same day as my colonoscopy. I got butt-holed twice."

Bobbie laughed, then apologized.

"That's OK," I said. "Imagine preferring a camera up your ass to opening the mail."

"Does that mean you and Janis never get your money back?"

"Looks that way. I think you'll be interested in who else got reamed."

"Not Aileen."

"No, she got her money," I said. "But Ruth's mother-in-law lost twenty-six grand."

"Like I said, those two are pond scum." Bobbie paused, then added, "Verney called to remind me of the Howatson family picnic."

"You going?"

"I doubt it," Bobbie said. "I don't want to see Aileen or Ruth."

"I hear ya."

"That's what's really sad about this."

"Oh?"

"You and Aileen were so close."

"Yeah. Were."

We disconnected and I stared at the DayMinder splayed on my desk, the date mocking me. The telephone dared me to pick up the handset and punch the requisite keys—keys whose numbers had faded from wear, in part from the hundreds of times I'd called Aileen before.

Epilogue

Thursday, February 24, 2011

The anniversary of my parents' deaths. Always a tough day. A trigger day, as they say in traumatic bereavement circles.

The beach at the bayside golf course looks the same. A mix of sand and riprap frame the cropped grass carpeting the former Coronado marshland. Golfers rattle by in garish uniforms—fruit-colored Popsicles melting into palm-lined fairways.

I gaze out over the small inlet that angles off of San Diego Bay. My home thirty-three years ago and my parents' final U.S. anchorage before sailing into a whirlwind of horror.

I stop and imagine the boats still anchored there, among them the Puffin, the Browers' Fair Winds, my little sloop—and the Spellbound. At my feet, a rock the size of an egg lies half buried in the sand. I bend down and work it free, then hurl it toward the spot where the Spellbound once anchored. A faint splash marks its entry, and the ripples spread out in ever-widening yet weakening arcs, like my family, rolling across Life's sea in opposite directions.

Mom and Dad may be gone, but their memories, the pleasant memories, live on, rippling through my mind. Mom standing at the head of the kitchen table in our Juanita home, reading one of her poems while framed by her prized baskets of fuchsias hanging outside the window, adding a splash of color to an otherwise dreary day. Dad at the helm of his beloved Spellbound, wearing a grin as broad as the ocean: The boat lifts to the crest of a swell, then dives headlong into the trough, a thrill like no other.

I had yearned to discuss with Dad the pursuit of life and love and happiness. Was he reticent by nature, or design? Then one day . . . gone. We never got to sit down with that six-pack of Lucky Lager and have our little chat.

And what of Mom? What had fueled the undaunted spirit of that farm girl sailing to her end on Earth? We never got to have that little chat, either.

The senselessness of the deaths had amplified the loss, magnified the anger. Loren and Jody Edwards got no justice. I had drained the six-pack without them.

Yet there is some solace in believing I know what happened. And why.

In responding to Ann Rule's story, I reviewed all the evidence: the contradictory accounts of how Dad died; Kerry's fractured skull being no accident; the conflicting statements about Mom's death; Gary's refusing assistance offered by other boaters; FBI witness statements that contradicted Gary's claims as to the Spellbound's location and distance from land; Lori's meteorite comment and claim of being "asleep" while chaos reigned around her; Gary's secret signing of the contract for the movie deal even before I left Tahiti; Kerry's sworn affidavit stating that Gary had assaulted and raped her, as well as her statements over the years that shed more light on what happened aboard the Spellbound; Gary's declining to contest in court my allegation that he slayed our parents; the FBI's assertion that Kerry admitted to a sexual tryst with Gary, the termination of which ignited the violence.

Dare I call it murder?

Based on the evidence lying before me, I believe I can reasonably conclude that Dad did not die by accident, that Mom did not take her own life.

What *actually* happened aboard the Spellbound? Both Gary and Kerry said to me, "You *don't* want to know."

Well, I *do* want to know. I have a right to know. Our family has a right to know. Society has a right to know.

A NOXIOUS WEIGHT has lifted. The nightmares have stopped. But learning to be resilient and live with the memories goes on, demanding daily attention to wounds that never truly heal.

I gaze across the bay. The ripples, like my parents, have vanished. I toss another rock and new ripples contour the water.

What the hell happened to my family?

What forces had converged for my family to end up the way it did?

Dad dreamt of building a boat and sailing around the world with his family. A modern-day Magellan. His oceanic tour ended like that of the explorer—in early death. I understand his motivations, his good intentions. He wanted to unify a family that was drifting apart. Regrettably, his fantasy only made matters worse.

Meanwhile, people talk of "closure."

What a crock.

When a parent, sibling, or child dies a violent, unnatural death, there is no closure. That person has been stolen from you; your life is changed forever. There is no going back. Before I encountered the Survivors of Violent Loss Program, I thought maybe I alone had reached that conclusion. But it is a common thread among the members of this unique club, a club no one wants to join.

Yet, I do have clarity. Even so, clarity comes with anguish. My parents' deaths broke up my family, not once but twice, leaving in me a sadness as deep as the Mariana Trench.

As unbearable as our parents' deaths were, it had drawn me closer to Aileen. We had become the best of friends; Ruth had been like a daughter to me. Which makes their betrayal that much harder to bear. I still yearn for the laughs and outrage Aileen and I shared for so many years.

The loss alone causes unimaginable trauma; the loss of family compounds the anguish exponentially. Do other families—survivors of violent loss—endure a similar fate? Are their families ripped apart?

Besides my sister Bobbie, friends now fill that gap, a family of friends found in various strata of life—writers, musicians, reenactors. The ordeal has strengthened my relationship with Janis, my safe harbor in the tumultuous sea of emotional upheaval. With these people I experience sparks of joy.

I am comforted in knowing there is no statute of limitations for murder. If Edgar Ray Killen could be brought to justice forty-one years after conspiring to murder three civil rights workers in Mississippi, there's a chance that my parents' killer will, too, cold comfort though it may be.

I launch another rock over the water, tracing its flight and splashdown, watching the ripples roll toward shore, tiny tsunamis lifting the debris floating on the bay. A seagull squawks in reprimand. The odor of souring sea life hangs low in the air. As the ripples lap at the shoreline, I turn and walk away.

Above: Jody Edwards christens the Spellbound.

Left: Loren and Joanne "Jody" Edwards and their blended family: Aileen, age 22 months (top center), Bobbie, age 10 months (top right), Larry, age 6 (lower left), and Gary, age 5 (lower right), June 16, 1956.

Above: Loren and Jody Edwards at their bon voyage party, July 1977.

Left: Spellbound sailing on Puget Sound, circa 1976.

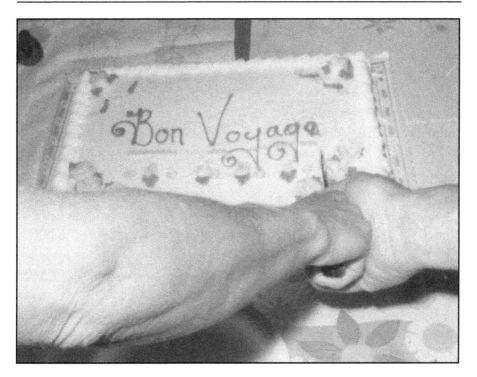

Above: Loren and Jody Edwards cutting the bon voyage cake, July 1977.

Left: Larry Edwards at the helm of the Spellbound, 1977.

About the Author

Larry M. Edwards is an award-winning author and investigative journalist; he has written three books. He won first place in the 2012 San Diego Book Awards, unpublished memoir category, for the original manuscript of this work.

Previously, he won Best of Show honors from the San Diego Press Club in 1994, 1997, 2004, and 2005, in addition to numerous other awards from the Society of Professional Journalists and San Diego Press Club.

Edwards served as business editor, investigative reporter, and feature writer for *San Diego Magazine*. He also served as editor of *The T Sector* magazine, *Maritime Quarterly*, and *San Diego Log*, as well as a staff writer for the *San Diego Business Journal* and *San Diego Log*; he worked as a stringer for the Associated Press while covering the America's Cup.

His articles have appeared in dozens of publications worldwide, including *48° North, Alaska Airlines, Grand Prix Sailor Weekly, Los Angeles Times, New Zealand Herald, Puget Sound Business Journal, Sailing, Sailing World, San Diego Metropolitan, San Diego Reader, San Diego Union, The Yacht* (Germany), *Yachting,* and *Yachting World* (UK).

He currently works as a freelance writer, book editor, and publishing consultant. Outside of writing and editing, Edwards plays the fiddle in old-time music and bluegrass bands. He also does historical reenactment, depicting the fur-trade era of the American frontier.

He lives in San Diego, California, with his birding-enthusiast wife, Janis Cadwallader.

For more information about the author, please visit:
LarryEdwards.com

For more photos and information related to this book, please visit:
DareICallItMurder.com

Acknowledgments

A work of this nature and scope would not have been possible without the assistance, contributions, and comments of relatives, colleagues, and my family of friends, whom I thank with all my heart:

My sister Bobbie for her ongoing support and encouragement to tell our parents' story and achieve a semblance of justice.

Verney Dickson, my mother's sister, for her kind thoughts, support, and encouragement for an effort that revived equally painful memories for her.

My cousin Linda Caruso, who stood by me from day one, and her brother, Joe Parks, who wanted to know the truth.

Margaret Marshall for her unwavering support, contributions, and insight—and for catching those gerunds crying out for a possessive pronoun.

Chris Peters, who encouraged me to write this book and contributed to it.

Tom Horsley and Cheri Brennan, who have remained friends since high school.

Fiddler and raconteur Kenneth Brank, who filled a void when my father died and offered his backwoods wisdom (and moonshine recipes).

Ian Law, fellow musician, life-long friend, and host of the Cape May Cultural Center who lent me his ear, and who opened his home for many a Thanksgiving and Christmas dinner.

Fiddler Judy Lipnick for offering keen insight during our lengthy birthday lunches.

Rich Hazelton, publisher of *48° North* sailing magazine, friend, colleague, and my first editor, for his biting wit and acerbic observations of people and life, and who offered me the lesson he brought home after surviving the rice paddies of Vietnam: "If you've got a dry place to sleep and something to eat, everything else is gravy."

Arthur Raybold, for his wit, poems, and thoughts during our mountain hikes and birthday breakfasts.

Fellow scribbler Rick Dower, for his comments and feedback on the book, and his sardonic take on life over our "O.B. brekkies" and during walks on the Ocean Beach Pier.

My team of brutally honest critiquers and editors at the La Jolla writers' group, who scoured every word and without whom this book could not have been completed: Jean Forsythe, Mike Irby, Penelope James, Melody Kincade, Cathy Lubenski, Laurie Richards, Jenny Russell, and Walter Warshat. (And to Connie Nation for allowing us to take over her dining room most Tuesday evenings.)

Members of the Escondido writers' circle, who got me on track and kept me focused: Ellen Holzman, Bill Fark, Jo Rubin, and Shelly Schmaltz.

Graphics guru Tim Brittain, who put up with my ceaseless fiddling with the cover design, and editor Jackie Logue, whose eagle eyes caught those niggling errors I could no longer see.

Historical reenactors Strummer, Hat Man, and Broken Hand for quiet nights sitting at a campfire, telling our tales and making joyful music.

Connie Saindon, founder of the Survivors of Violent Loss Program, who helped me get my life back, and the SVLP counselors for their attentive ears and astute observations.

Fellow Survivors, who give their support freely, with nothing asked in return.

Attorney Mark Reichenthal of the Branfman Law Group for his sound counsel.

All the good folks, too numerous to name individually, who gave me feedback on prospective titles for the book.

My in-laws for their patience with me over the years.

I especially thank my wife, Janis Cadwallader, for her unconditional love and unequivocal support, without which I could not have completed this book.

CPSIA information can be obtained
at www.ICGtesting.com
Printed in the USA
LVHW111515130120
643454LV00007B/66/P